COMPUTER SCIENCE

GEORGE ROUSE
SEAN O'BYRNE

The Publishers would like to thank the following for permission to reproduce copyright material:

Photo credits see back of book

Every effort has been made to trace all copyright holders, but if any have been inadvertently overlooked the Publishers will be pleased to make the necessary arrangements at the first opportunity.

Orders: please contact Bookpoint Ltd, 130 Milton Park, Abingdon, Oxon OX14 4SB. Telephone: (44) 01235 827720. Fax: (44) 01235 400454. Lines are open 9.00–17.00, Monday to Saturday, with a 24-hour message answering service. Visit our website at www.hoddereducation.co.uk.

First published in 2016 by

Hodder Education
An Hachette UK Company,
Carmelite House
50 Victoria Embankment
London EC4Y 0DZ

Impression number 5 4 3

Year 2020 2019 2018 2017

Illustrations by Aptara Inc.

Typeset in India by Aptara Inc.

Printed in India

A catalogue record for this title is available from the British Library.

ISBN 978 1 471 86614 2

Contents

Clear Examples show students computational approaches to problem-solving

Example

A simple function to calculate the area of a circle given the radius:

- function name 'area'
- parameters to be passed 'radius'
- the code area= 3.14159*radius*radius
- the output returned to the main program 'area'.

```
# the function definition
def area(radius):
    area=3.14159*radius*radius
    return area

# the main body of the program
value=int(input("Enter the radius for the circle"))
print("Area of circle is")
print(area(value))
```

Figure 14.11 *The code for this in the Python programming language*

Procedures

Procedures like functions are also subprograms defined outside the main body of the program. The only real difference between a procedure and a function is that a function should return a value. Procedures do not have to do this. They are subprograms that act independently of the main program.

Regular Notes contextualise content so students can understand and further explore topics and features of computer science

Note

While functions should return values to the main program, several languages do not have the concept of a procedure and allow for functions that do not return values.

Questions

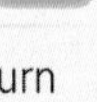

6 What is a *function*?

7 What is the difference between a procedure and a function?

8 What are the advantages of using procedures and functions in a program?

Example

A procedure to print out some text a number of times:

- The procedure 'multiprint' is passed two parameters, 'text' and 'times'.
- It prints the text as many times as it is told to, then returns control to the main program, but no values are returned.

```
# the sub program to print out text several times
def multiprint(text,times):
                for i in range(0,times):
                    print(text)



# Main program
sampletext=input("input text to be printed")
value=int(input("number of times to be printed"))
multiprint(sampletext,value)
print("Now control is back with the main program")
```

Figure 14.12 *A procedure in the Python programming language to print text several times*

Figure 18.1 The early computer ENIAC (Electronic Numerical Integrator And Computer)

Key Points clarify significant information for students to be able to process and recall easily

Key Points

- Computers run programs given to them as a set of instructions.
- These instructions must be in binary-coded format.
- Binary-coded instructions are called machine code.

Giving instructions in this way is obviously very tedious and it was very easy to make errors. Humans are not conditioned to think in terms of 0s and 1s.

There had to be better ways to give instructions to the over the years more and more convenient ways were c process continues to this day, where ever more easy way produced to pass instructions to a computer.

Practice Questions help build students' coding, programming and problem-solving skills

Questions

1 Describe two ways that you have given program instructions to a computer.

Key Terms help students develop computing language skills to facilitate greater subject understanding

Key Terms

Translation The conversion of human-friendly program writing back to pure machine code.

Translator A program to convert high-level or assembly-level commands into machine code.

Assembly language and translators

The evolution of programming techniques beyond pure machine code has led to writing programs in a more human-friendly way and then converting what is written back to pure machine code. This conversion is called **translation**. The translation is achieved using special software, unsurprisingly called a **translator**.

We have seen that it is possible, although not sensible, to write a computer program in pure machine code. There is one advantage of

Introduction

What is computer science?

We are all affected by computer systems, in every aspect of our lives. They are used in communications, entertainment, manufacture and finance as well as many other human activities. They are also built into a huge range of devices and other objects that we use every day.

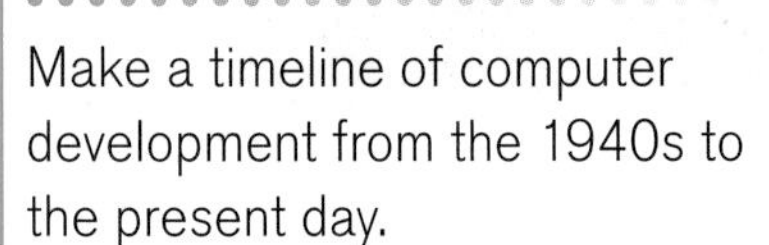

Extension Activity

Make a timeline of computer development from the 1940s to the present day.

Include on your timeline at least five of the breakthroughs that you think are the most important.

Look up the five generations of computers and add them to your timeline.

Computer systems are immensely variable. They include laptops, desktop machines and tablets. Sometimes they are less obvious, such as smartphones, which originated as communication devices but are now fully functional computer systems like any other.

Computer systems have been around for only about 60 years. The first breakthroughs took place in the lifetimes of many people who are alive today. The development from the first electronic computers to the powerful devices we all have in our pockets has been incredibly fast.

It was not all that long ago that the nature of information was only vaguely understood, but in 1948 Claude Shannon, working at Bell Labs in the US, pointed out that all information can be reduced to bits: text, numbers, images, music, instructions – anything.

Figure 1 *Claude Shannon*

It was realised over the succeeding years that because information can be represented by bits, with each bit being either 0 or 1, this could lead to information being stored in many simple ways, for example a pulse of electricity versus no pulse; a switch set to on or off; a patch of material magnetised this way ↑ or that →.

This incredible simplicity has led to very reliable computers and now, of course, very reliable communications.

These breakthroughs, together with developments in hardware, have led to a revolution in all our lives, with computer systems involved in most human activities.

Studying these systems is the business of computer science. To put it another way, computer science is the theoretical and practical study of computation and how it may be put into effect.

Key Term

Algorithm A series of steps designed to solve a mathematical or other problem.

Central to computer science is the study and development of **algorithms** and, importantly, how to automate them and make machines carry them out.

Why study computer science?

There are some compelling reasons to study computer science and there has never been a better time to get involved.

First, it is inherently fascinating and fun to study. Its wide application provides something for everyone. Whether your interests are in business, gaming, music, art or just solving puzzles, computer science provides endless opportunities for fun and learning.

Secondly, computer science is different from many other subjects because it touches on them all. Everyone needs to access and process information, no matter what their main occupation is.

Thirdly, computing provides instant feedback. If you are learning how to program, you can make your mistakes without any risk of embarrassment and the computer feeds back on your errors, immediately offering help to fix them.

In addition, computer science teaches you to think better. When you analyse problems carefully in order to produce some software, you learn to think clearly about what the problem involves and it becomes easier to plan a solution. This develops your skills for solving and understanding other problems too.

Finally, computer science provides an opportunity to make things that have not been made before. You can be really creative when you invent computer programs and systems.

Careers

A practical reason to study computer science is that it can lead to any of a wide variety of jobs and careers in the computer industry and beyond. Most companies now need staff who are computer savvy; if they also understand the industry that the business is involved in, they can become valuable employees and consequently well-paid assets.

There is every indication that the skills shortage in computer-related fields will continue for quite some time so studying computer science remains a good investment.

The new OCR specification

Philosophy

There is one underlying philosophy behind the new specification that needs to be understood; that is, the central role of computational thinking. This places a lot of emphasis on algorithms; how to develop them, understand them and how to turn them into reality by writing programs.

There is also much emphasis on the hardware and software that make up all computer systems. Notably, because of the importance of computer communications, there is a lot of attention given to networks, how they work and the threats they face.

The NEA

The Non-Examined Assessment (NEA) is the new term for coursework, also formerly known as *controlled assessment*. There have been changes to this component. It is now worth a smaller proportion of the marks than in the previous specification. Also, it is completely based on planning, writing and testing programs.

Chapter 20 covers the principles of the NEA and how students can make the best of its opportunities.

Questions

1. Make a list of computer skills that are in demand at the moment.
2. Explain how you found this out.
3. In what ways did computers help you find this out?
4. Name some of the types of software that were used overtly, or maybe behind the scenes, in letting you find out these facts.
5. Describe alternative ways you could have found this out.

1 The importance of computational thinking

Computational thinking

Key Term

Computational thinking Applying the methods of computer scientists to problem solving.

As was stated in the introduction, this GCSE course, along with those from the other examination organisations, is very much centred on **computational thinking**. Indeed, there is a whole chapter developing that idea later (Chapter 13).

You will see that computational thinking is making use of the tools of computer scientists to solve problems in a methodical way – a way that is more likely to result in success than less disciplined ways.

Computational thinking is an idea that has recently been given much prominence. It was first suggested as an algorithmic approach to problem solving by Seymour Papert in 1980. In more recent years, the idea has been championed again, notably by Jeannette Wing and her former colleagues at Carnegie Mellon University.

Figure 1.1 *Seymour Papert*

Figure 1.2 *Jeannette Wing*

Computational thinking involves the application of thought processes to open-ended problems. This is a relatively new direction for computer science because, in the early days of computing, most problems that were tackled by computers were closed problems; in other words, fairly clear cut and well defined, such as how to schedule deliveries to cafés or how to process a monthly payroll. The inputs and outputs were well defined, which made the production of solutions fairly understandable, even if they often turned out to be complex.

What computer scientists learned from all these fairly closed problems was that the methods they used could be extended to apply to more 'human' problems, more 'messy' problems, problems that did not always suggest neat solutions – in other words, most of 'normal' human existence.

Heuristics

Note

When good enough is good enough

An important principle that needs to be remembered when devising solutions to problems is that, as Turing proved, it is not always possible to devise a computable solution. This does not mean that it is a waste of time to seek one though.

Many problems can benefit from having at least a part of their solution being computed.

Sometimes you have to make decisions where knowledge of inputs and outputs is incomplete. In these situations, past experience can help you to make quick decisions that are at least likely to produce a usable result.

When you cross a road, you do not have time to gather data about the speed and volume of traffic, how long it will take to cross the road or if the gap is big enough. You make a fast assessment of the situation that, most of the time, will get you across the road unharmed. We call this sort of analysis the use of *heuristics*.

Heuristics are sometimes called 'rule of thumb' solutions. They incorporate experience and judgement but do not guarantee a reliable solution. They aim to produce a solution that is 'good enough'. Often there are not the time or resources to be certain of an outcome. Life is too short, as they say. If we can produce a solution, or even a piece of software, that generally brings benefits, it might be sensible to go with that rather than devote thousands of hours of programming effort to find a perfect solution.

However, some situations are more critical. You would not want to use a heuristic approach in producing avionics software that guides an aircraft through the skies at a safe height and distance from other planes. Most people would rather not rely on software that is just 'good enough' for this.

Sometimes, though, the heuristic approach works. New computer viruses and malware appear all the time. Often examples are totally different in construction from previous examples, so detecting new viruses based on how they are coded might miss an innovative virus. But if you look for software according to its behaviour, then you might pick up some new variants, despite the fact that they are coded differently, because they behave like viruses.

Note

The duck test

If it looks like a duck, swims like a duck and quacks like a duck, then it probably is a duck.

You are then applying the 'duck test', a form of inductive reasoning that has its place in computational thinking.

Computational thinking does not always have to involve precision. Often it can include heuristics or human experience as an added extra.

Example

Take the case of choosing which course to study at university.

This can be a difficult problem. There are so many courses. They all involve the commitment of time and expense. You need to look at the whole situation and weigh up the costs and benefits.

You might apply algorithms to known data such as:

- Which course am I likely to qualify for?
- Which course has placed most of its graduates into suitable jobs?
- How long will it take to repay my student debts?

All these points can be found out, at least fairly accurately, using statistics and calculations.

What you cannot be so sure of is:

- Which university is in the nicest city?
- Which course is taught the best?
- Which university has the best social life?

A combination of computed solutions and human judgement is often the most sensible approach to some problems.

Extension Activity

Find out about facial recognition software.

To what extent does it rely on the duck test?

Little by little, the turning of computing methodology towards all manner of human conditions has been spectacularly successful and has led to the wide variety of gadgets and services that we all take for granted today. Notice in particular that a lot of these benefits were not produced by attacking a specific problem; they have developed piecemeal from the collected actions of very many creative people.

Figure 1.3 *Alan Turing*

Figure 1.4 *Tommy Flowers*

Figure 1.5 *Tim Berners-Lee*

Once we had the benefits of miniaturised circuits, we soon had faster and faster processors, cheaper memory and cheaper production costs, and this provided a fertile soil for new ideas to grow.

How new ideas happened

Along the way, we have seen how certain individuals have been responsible for the great steps forward. Most people have heard of Alan Turing, who laid the foundations for computation in his 1936 paper 'On computable numbers with an application to the *Entscheidungsproblem*', which means the 'decision problem'. This problem was a challenge to find whether there is an algorithm that can take a statement of logic and output whether or not it is always true. Turing demonstrated that it is not possible, by imagining a computing machine that could test the algorithm.

This imagined 'Turing machine' formed the basis upon which Tommy Flowers was able to build the first actual programmable electronic computer, Colossus.

Many other milestones have been passed since the early days, notably the invention of the internet and the development of ever easier-to-use programming languages. We are currently seeing a huge growth in the development of mobile devices and some say that this is where the future of computing lies – but we do not know. There are bound to be further developments that we have not anticipated yet that will again change the computing landscape completely.

It is easy to spot some of the key players along the way, such as Tim Berners-Lee who devised the worldwide web and Steve Jobs who promoted a range of 'must-have devices' that people bought in huge numbers even before they knew they needed them.

However, this onward progress towards faster, cheaper, more powerful, more capable, more desirable, more useful would have happened anyway. If Tim Berners-Lee or Steve Jobs had not devised their products, someone else would have developed something similar. And that is how most advances are made, in computing and elsewhere; little by little, many people make changes and refinements that lead to an evolution of ideas and devices in the same way that, little by little, the environment leads to an evolution of living things.

The more people understand the basic principles of computing, and notably the importance and application of algorithms, the more progress will be made both in the development of devices and in the applications of computing.

Playing a part in this ongoing revolution is something in which many people can get involved, making their own contributions and sometimes satisfying careers as well.

Crowdsourcing

In recent years, it has become recognised how powerful it can be to harness the efforts of many to produce some desirable resource. If you are studying computer science, you will know about how online communities have co-operated to develop some of the most important computing tools used both individually and on the web. The development of Linux® and Linux-based derivatives is a particular example (see page 86). Many enthusiasts the world over have co-operated to produce this and other examples of open-source software that have transformed the way we work.

Extension Activity

Nowadays it is possible to profile someone's DNA very quickly and this has had a huge impact on solving crimes.

Look up the technique of shotgun sequencing and find out how computational methods have made this possible.

Find two other ways in which computational methods have led to progress in scientific understanding.

Key Points

- Studies in computer science now place great emphasis on computational thinking.
- Computational thinking means applying the tools of computer scientists to problems.
- This particularly involves the study and production of algorithms.
- Computational thinking can produce powerful and reliable solutions.
- Sometimes these are partial rather than complete solutions.
- Often the best way forward is to combine the creativity of humans with the concise abilities of machines.

Questions

1. Search for examples of software that have been developed or maintained by online communities.
2. List two or three examples of situations where Linux has been used or adapted to run innovative products.
3. Discuss how computational thinking can be helpful in making an everyday decision such as planning the choosing and cooking of a meal.
4. Describe a situation that is best solved in part by computers and in part by human creativity.

2 Systems architecture

Computer hardware

Hardware is the term that describes the physical components of a computer system, anything that can be seen or touched. This includes the input, output, storage and processing devices. The range of devices available today is quite staggering but this was not always the case. Colossus, the first electronic digital programmable computer, built in 1943, was never able to store programs and the operators had to enter the program afresh each time, using switches and patch cables.

Figure 2.1 *Manchester University's Small Scale Experimental Machine, nicknamed 'Baby'*

But work on computers like Colossus led to the development of modern computer systems. The first computer able to store a program was Manchester University's Small Scale Experimental Machine, nicknamed 'Baby'. In 1948, Baby ran its first program, to find the highest proper divisor (that is not 1 or itself) of the number 262 144. It took 52 minutes to find the correct answer, 131 072. This computer was originally able to store 1024 bits (that is just 128 bytes) and had just seven instructions available to the programmer.

Figure 2.2 *John von Neumann*

Von Neumann architecture

In 1945, John von Neumann, who had been working on the Electronic Discrete Variable Automatic Computer (EDVAC) for the American military, published a document that would provide the way forward for the development of the modern digital computer.

Note

John von Neumann was a gifted mathematician. He was born in Hungary in 1903 but moved to America in his 20s. He became an American citizen and, because of his skills, was recruited to work on the Manhattan Project, designing the first atomic bomb. He made many contributions to computer science including working on the EDVAC. His work on this project defined the computer architecture that became known as the Von Neumann architecture.

Key Term

Computer architecture The internal, logical structure and organisation of the computer hardware.

Von Neumann architecture describes a **computer architecture** in which:

- the data and the program are both stored in the computer's memory in the same place
- all instructions and data will be stored as binary digits in the same place. (Binary is a system of numbers using only 0 and 1 based on powers of 2. For more about binary see Chapter 16.)

This is the fundamental design concept behind all modern computer systems.

The CPU

Key Terms

Central processing unit (CPU) Contains the control unit, ALU and cache memory.

Clock chip The electronic device in a computer that controls the timing of signals.

Fetch–decode–execute cycle The process of fetching the instructions from memory, decoding them and then executing them that the CPU performs continuously.

The **central processing unit (CPU)** carries out all the processing for the computer system by following all the instructions given to it. A CPU is made from billions of transistors (effectively electronic switches) that combine to build the logic gates to process the data and instructions. (For more about logic gates see Chapter 17.)

Processors work at incredible speeds determined by an electronic clock. The **clock chip** is a chip that uses a vibrating crystal that maintains a constant speed. Typically, modern processors will operate at speeds around 4 GHz (Giga Hertz) or 4 000 000 000 instructions per second. The processor is continually fetching new instructions from memory, decoding them, then executing them. This is called the **fetch–decode–execute cycle**.

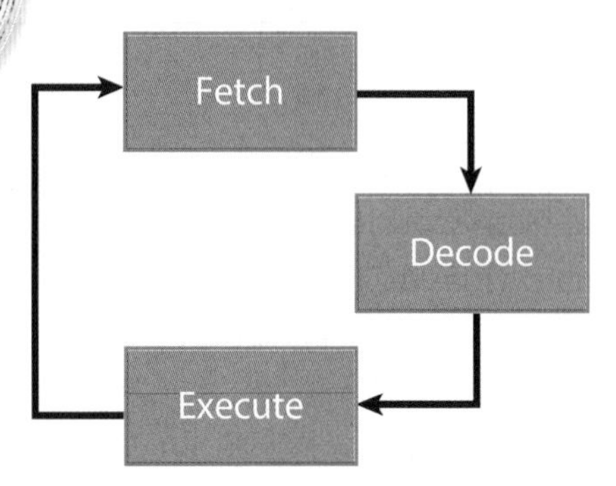

Figure 2.3 *Fetch–decode–execute cycle*

Questions

1. Describe the purpose of the CPU in a computer.
2. What is meant by *2.3 GHz* when describing a CPU?

Extension Activity

Little Man Computer (LMC) is a simple representation of a computer using a nine-command assembly language. There are various versions of LMC available on the internet, for example the Peter Higginson LMC simulator (http://peterhigginson.co.uk/LMC/), which shows each step of the fetch–decode–execute cycle and the data and instructions being moved along the buses.

Type in a simple program, for example:

```
INP
STA 7
INP
ADD 7
STA 8
HLT
```

Run the simulator in step mode to see the data and instructions being moved around the CPU and memory to fetch, decode and execute the program. Can you see what the program does?

Initially, after the computer is switched on, the CPU will look at a specific place in read-only memory (ROM) for the first program to load and execute. This is the boot sequence; it is always stored on ROM in a specific place so that the CPU knows where to find it. The CPU then begins the process of executing the program commands to get the computer up and running and the operating system started. After this initial boot process is completed, control is handed to the operating system to provide the programs for the CPU to run.

Inside the processor

The processor is a very complex item but we can explore a simplified model of the CPU to understand how it works.

There are two vital components in the processor:

1. **Arithmetic and logic unit:** The ALU carries out the calculations and logical decisions required by the program instruction (for example addition, subtraction and comparisons such as equal to, greater than or less than).
2. **Control unit:** The CU is responsible for decoding the instructions and it sends out signals to control how data moves around the parts of the CPU and memory to execute these instructions.

To enable data and control signals to move around the CPU and memory there are a number of buses. A **bus** is a communication channel through which data can be moved. There are many buses in

Key Terms

Arithmetic and logic unit (ALU) Performs all the arithmetic and logical operations within the CPU.

Control unit Works with the CPU to control the flow of data within the system and to decode instructions.

Bus A part of the computer architecture that transfers data and signals between the components of the computer.

a computer; one example is the universal serial bus (USB), which can transfer data between the computer and external devices.

There are three main buses inside the computer we need to consider with the CPU:

1 **Data bus:** Carries data between the CPU and memory.
2 **Control bus:** Carries control signals around the CPU and memory.
3 **Address bus:** Carries memory addresses for locations to be read from or written to.

Key Terms 

Accumulator (ACC) Stores the results of any arithmetic or logical operations carried out by the ALU.

Current instruction register (CIR) Stores the next instruction ready to be decoded.

Memory address register (MAR) Stores the location for data to be fetched from or sent to memory.

Memory data register (MDR) Stores data that has been fetched from, or is waiting to be sent to, memory.

Program counter (PC) Stores the location of the next instruction in a program to be executed.

Registers are memory locations within the CPU and can be accessed very quickly. Some of the main registers in a computer are:

- **Accumulator (ACC):** Register that stores the results of any calculations made by the **ALU**.
- **Current instruction register (CIR):** Register that stores the most recently fetched instruction while it is waiting to be decoded and executed.
- **Memory address register (MAR):** Register that stores the location in memory to be used by the MDR, that is where to locate data it needs to fetch or where to send data it needs to store.
- **Memory data register (MDR):** Register that is used to store any data fetched from memory or any data that is to be transferred to, and stored in, memory.
- **Program counter (PC):** Keeps track of the memory location for the next instruction to be dealt with. In many cases it is simply incremented to the next memory location at the fetch stage of the fetch–execute cycle to allow the program to be executed line by line. There are, however, program instructions that can modify the value in the PC to alter the flow of the program to continue from a new location.

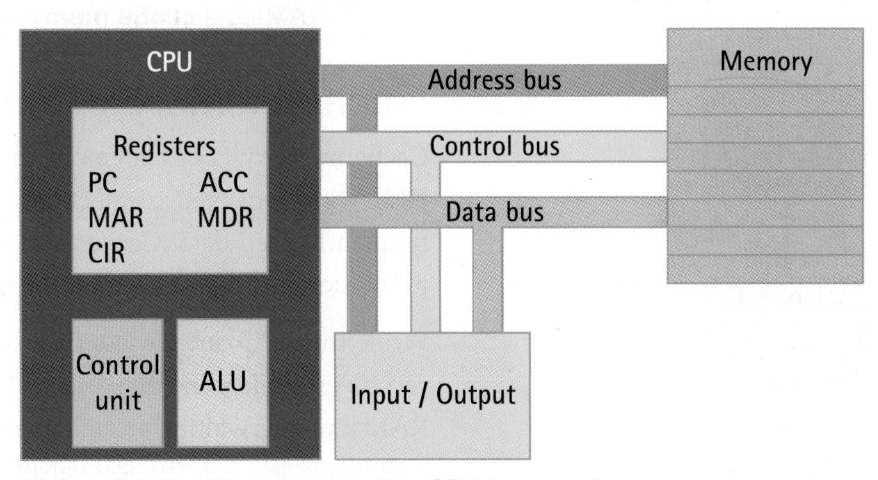

Figure 2.4 *Simplified diagram of the CPU, buses and memory*

The fetch–decode–execute cycle:

1 The PC has the address of the next instruction to fetch.
2 The value in the program counter is copied to the MAR.

3 The control unit locates and fetches the data.
4 If it is an instruction, it is placed in the CIR.
   (a) The PC is incremented by 1.
   (b) The instruction in the CIR is decoded by the control unit.
   (c) Finally, the instruction is executed by placing any request for data into the MAR for the data to be collected and copied to the MDR.
5 If it is data, it is placed in the MDR.

Task 

Use the diagram of the CPU to follow data and control signals through this process.

Questions 

3 Describe the purpose of the MDR.
4 What is the purpose of the ALU?
5 What is the purpose of the ACC?
6 What is stored in the MAR at the end of the fetch–execute cycle if the instruction decodes to 'go to the instruction in location 15'?

Key Terms

Random access memory (RAM) The main memory of a computer that stores data, applications and the operating system while in use. When the power is turned off, RAM loses its data.

Cache memory Special high-speed memory used by a computer.

Factors affecting the performance of the CPU

We have noted that the processor operates at very high speeds, billions of cycles per second and the clock speed of the processor is one factor affecting the overall performance of the CPU, but it is not the only one.

In order to process data the CPU needs access to memory. There are two kinds of memory it needs to access, main memory (we normally call this **RAM**) and **cache memory**.

Cache memory

Cache memory is fast memory that is located very close to the main CPU with dedicated connections so that the CPU has fast access to frequently used data. Cache memory is relatively expensive compared to the standard RAM used for the main memory of a computer.

While the CPU can process data very quickly, getting data from RAM can be quite slow in comparison. If the CPU has to wait for data from RAM it will be waiting around for much of the time and will be running well below its capacity. To overcome this when the first instruction in a program is requested by the CPU, the remaining instructions are automatically copied into the cache memory.

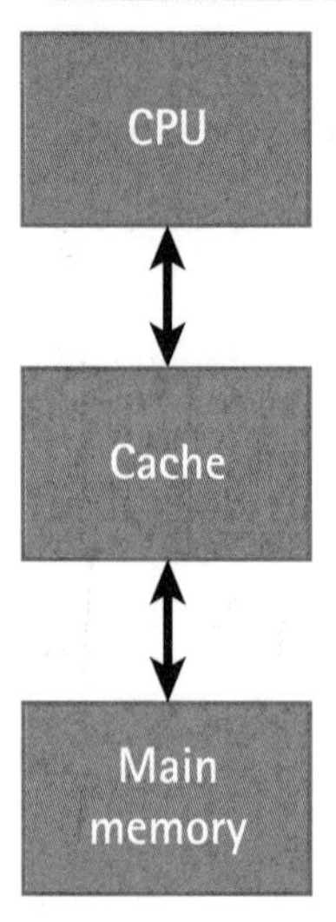

Figure 2.5 *Cache memory*

Cache memory has access times similar to the CPU, which means it is a lot faster than main memory. To improve performance, the CPU's control unit will automatically look first in the cache for the next instruction to see if it has already been copied. If it is not there it will go to main memory to locate and fetch the data.

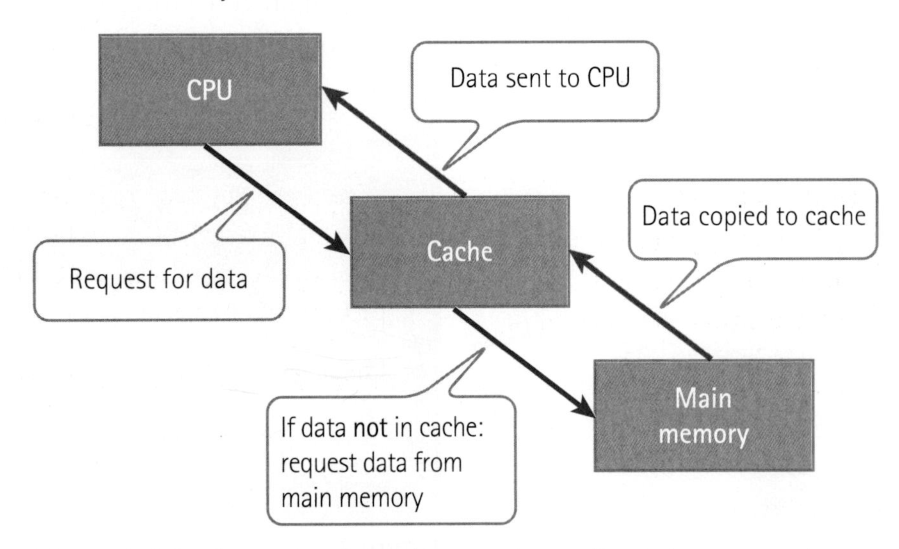

Figure 2.6 *Cache memory is used to store data waiting to be processed*

By checking first if the required data is in the cache it reduces the time taken to access the data, making the process much more efficient. The more cache memory there is, the more likely the required data has already been requested and copied to the cache memory and does not have to be fetched from main memory.

Cache memory is very fast, but also relatively expensive. Where main memory will normally be provided in gigabytes, cache will be provided in megabytes. 1 GB is 1000 megabytes so there is a big difference in size between the amounts of cache and main memory provided with a typical computer. A mid-range laptop may have 8 GB of RAM but only 2–4 MB of Level 3 cache.

There are three levels of cache memory in modern computer systems, Level 1, Level 2 and Level 3 (L1, L2 and L3). The numbers refer to how close each of these is to the CPU.

- L1 cache is often located on the CPU itself, it has a very low capacity and typically runs at the same speed as the CPU.
- L2 cache is often part of the CPU module, runs at CPU speeds (or close to them) and is usually a bit larger and slower than L1 cache.
- As might be expected L3 cache is further away from the CPU, on the motherboard, and it is larger and slower than both L1 and L2 cache.

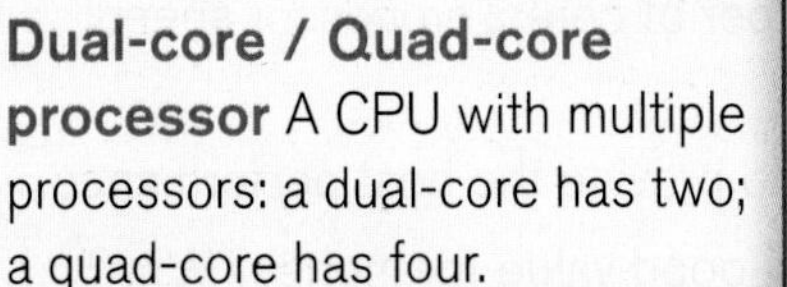

Key Term

Dual-core / Quad-core processor A CPU with multiple processors: a dual-core has two; a quad-core has four.

Cores

Another factor that can affect the performance of the CPU is the number of cores in the processor. A **dual-core processor** has two

cores working together, a **quad-core** processor has four. Since all the cores can fetch, decode and execute instructions at the same time a multi-core processor can handle more instructions simultaneously, for example running multiple programs at the same time.

A typical multi-core processor will have L1 cache and L2 cache attached to each core and will share L3 cache.

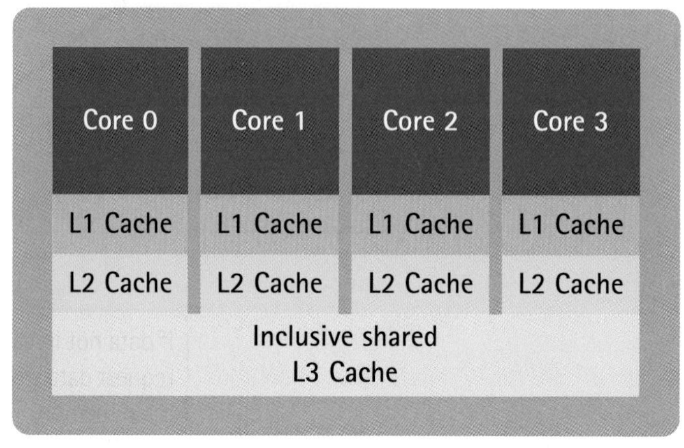

Figure 2.7 *A typical multi-core processor arrangement with L1, L2 and L3 cache*

Key Points

- The purpose of the CPU is to:
  - control the movement of data and instructions
  - fetch data and instructions from memory
  - decode and execute instructions
  - perform arithmetic operations such as add and subtract and logical operations such as AND, NOT, OR.
- The performance of the CPU depends upon the:
  - processor speed
  - bus speed
  - amount of cache available
  - number of processor cores.

Questions

7 Describe how cache memory is used by the CPU.

8 What are the key factors that govern the performance of the CPU in a computer?

Extension Activity

Many people choose a laptop by the size of the hard drive and amount of main memory advertised, but do not explore the detail for the processor.

1. Find some computers advertised on the internet.
2. Identify the processor each one uses and look up the processor specification.
3. Compile a table of all the facts about the computers: main memory; L1, L2 and L3 cache memory; number of cores; processor speed; and main memory.
4. Identify the computer that is likely to provide the best performance.
5. Is one of the computers particularly good value for money? Why?

Types of computer system

We often think of a computer system as the keyboard, monitor and metal box on the desk, or as a laptop or even a tablet, but computer systems come in all shapes and sizes.

There are large supercomputers used to predict the weather and the large rooms full of storage and processors that provide cloud services. There are also computer systems embedded into many electrical and mechanical devices and systems.

Figure 2.8 *Supercomputer used by Chinook*

- **General-purpose computers:** The term 'general-purpose computers' describes those systems that can be programmed to perform a wide range of tasks. The typical desktop system, laptop or tablet device can be programmed to perform multiple tasks. Various applications can be loaded so that these devices can be used for a wide range of applications.
- **Dedicated systems:** These are produced to perform a single function or set of functions. One example would be a ticket vending machine typically found in a railway station – it is not capable of performing any other task.
- **Control systems:** Designed simply to control machinery and probably only provide limited output for humans to respond to. Control systems are important in the manufacturing process and are frequently found in common domestic appliances or personal gadgets such as fitness monitors, hand-held gaming devices and smart watches. Industrial robots are an important application of control systems.

Embedded systems

Key Term

Embedded system A computer system that forms part of an electronic device.

An **embedded system** is a computer system that has a dedicated function as part of a larger device. All the main components of the computer are manufactured either as a single chip (micro-controller) or by combining the separate integrated circuits for processing, memory and interfacing within a larger device.

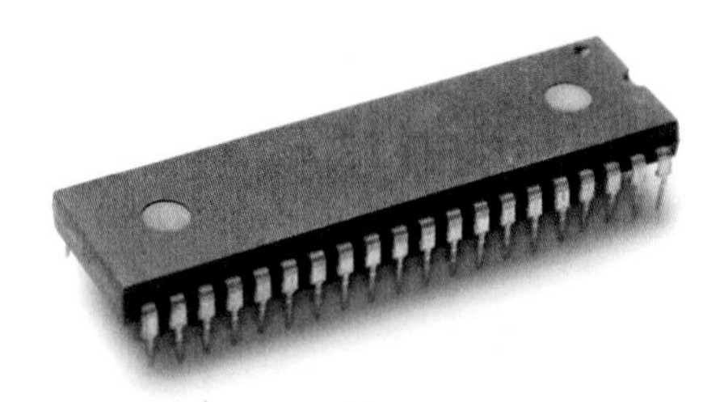

Figure 2.9 *A microcontroller*

Embedded systems are found in consumer products and a large number of household devices such as watches, telephones, televisions, washing machines, set top boxes, and so on. Any device with a digital interface will have an embedded computer system. They are also found in much larger and more complex systems such as car engine management systems, aeroplane avionics, traffic lights, computer controlled manufacturing systems, military applications, and so on.

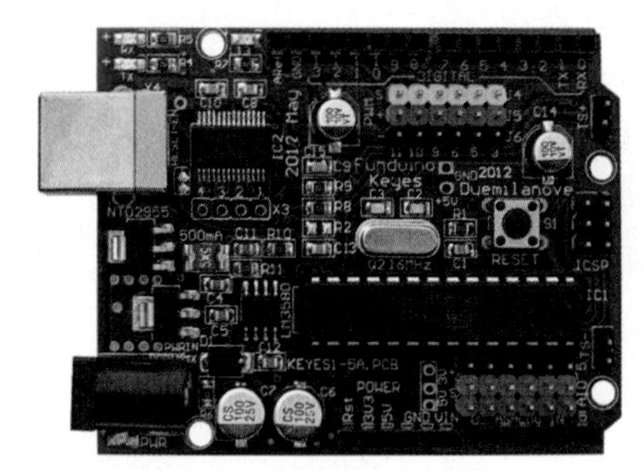

Figure 2.10 *An Arduino programmable controller unit*

Figure 2.11 *Engine management system*

Embedded systems have many advantages over general-purpose computers for this sort of application. Since the embedded system is created for a single task it can be engineered to reduce its size and cost and improve performance.

Embedded systems have software that is programmed into the device at the manufacturing stage or uploaded directly into the device. The software will be designed for a specific purpose and will either have no options to program it or very limited programming options through buttons or a simple interface.

The dedicated hardware and software make the systems significantly more reliable and robust than they would be if general-purpose computer systems were used.

Embedded systems can be:

- low-power devices so they can operate effectively from a small power source, for example in a mobile phone
- small in size to fit inside a wrist-worn device such as a fitness bracelet
- rugged so they can be used in wide range of applications such as car engine management or avionics
- low cost, making them suitable for use in mass produced items, such as the controller in a washing machine or set-top box
- dedicated to just one task with dedicated interfaces and software, for example in a computer-aided manufacturing system.

Task

Think about how many devices incorporate embedded systems.

Consider the many different interfaces these devices use.

Consider the advantages of embedded systems over general-purpose systems in those of applications.

Questions

9 Why would you use an embedded system rather than a general-purpose computer to control a microwave oven or a washing machine?

10 How might the use of embedded computers improve daily life for those with a physical disability?

11 Embedded systems for a domestic appliance will often have both ROM and RAM; why might they need RAM?

3 Primary storage

Key Terms

Byte Eight bits; symbol *B*.

Bit Binary digit 0 or 1; symbol *b*.

In the 1940s, when work on the modern computer started to take shape, memory was very limited – often just a few **bytes** – and quite unreliable. Originally data was stored using vacuum tubes with each vacuum tube able to store a single **bit** (0 or 1).

Figure 3.1 *Vacuum-tube memory*

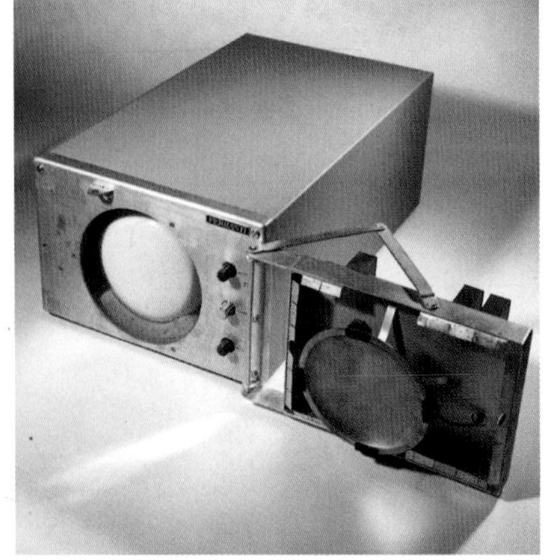

Figure 3.2 *A Williams–Kilburn tube*

In 1947 Freddie Williams, working at Manchester University, devised a method for storing data as charged spots on the surface of a cathode-ray tube. This was the first workable RAM and was known as the Williams tube. This device was able to store 512–1024 bits or just 64–128 bytes.

The search for cheaper and more reliable technology led to the development of magnetic core memory in the 1950s. This type of memory was used for nearly 20 years until the mid-1970s. It used circular iron magnetic cores with wires passing in both directions through the centre of the magnet. The data stored was set by passing

Key Terms

Kilobyte 1024 bytes.

Volatile memory Loses data when there is no power.

Figure 3.3 *Magnetic core memory*

a current through the wires to set the direction of the magnetic field to clockwise or anti-clockwise in the iron core. It was possible to combine several of these into a single memory unit able to store around two **kilobytes** of data.

The invention of the transistor by William Shockley in 1947, led to the development of the integrated circuit or silicon chip. The first working, solid-state RAM was developed for IBM by Robert Dennard in 1968. These devices store data as a small charge in tiny transistors etched into a circuit in the device. The charge has to be refreshed every few milliseconds, otherwise it leaks away. This type of memory referred to as **volatile** because it needs power to maintain the contents.

Random access memory (RAM)

RAM is volatile memory and needs power to maintain it; if the power is turned off then RAM loses its contents.

When a program is loaded, it is loaded from secondary storage such as a hard drive into RAM so that the CPU can access the program instructions and associated data.

RAM is the main memory in a computer and it is required for the operating systems, applications that are loaded and any data currently in use. The CPU can access any part of RAM at the same speed and at a speed much greater than it can access data on a storage device.

Clearly the more RAM in a computer, the more data and programs it can keep available in main memory for the processor. Consequently, the more RAM available to a computer system the faster the programs will run.

We have seen that the CPU transfers data that is required immediately into cache memory to improve access speeds to data. The diagram in Figure 3.4 illustrates how access to data and programs is improved by using RAM and cache memory together.

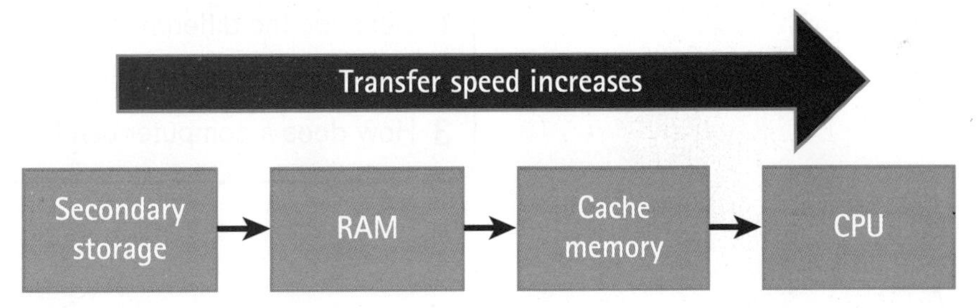

Figure 3.4 *Data transfer speeds for storage, memory and CPU*

There are two main types of RAM: dynamic and static.

1 **Dynamic RAM** has a single transistor and capacitor that can hold a charge for a few milliseconds to represent one bit. In order to maintain the charge in the capacitor, this type of RAM must be refreshed every few milliseconds, hence the name, dynamic.

2 **Static RAM** is more complex with four or five transistors wired together for each bit. This means it can maintain data without the need to be refreshed every few milliseconds, provided there is a power source. Static RAM uses a much more complex design, with more transistors and additional wiring required to store each bit, leading to a much smaller capacity than Dynamic RAM. While this design is significantly more complex and consequently more expensive, access to the data is much faster. Static RAM is ideally suited for use as cache memory.

Figure 3.5 *RAM chips*

Read only memory (ROM)

Key Term

Non-volatile memory Retains data even when the power is turned off.

Computer systems would not be as useful if we had to keep them connected to the power all the time or had to perform an initial set up every time we started them. Computers need some form of memory that can retain its contents even when the computer is switched off. By connecting several transistors together in a specific way, a memory chip can be created that remembers what is being stored. This type of memory is called *read only memory (ROM)*. ROM is **non-volatile** and can retain information programmed into it by the manufacturer. ROM is also read-only, meaning it cannot be overwritten by the computer, making it ideal for storing the instructions required to get the computer system up and running. The set of instructions required to make the computer start is called the *boot process*. The boot program will initialise the computer hardware and load the operating system so that the system is ready to be used shortly after the power is switched on.

Questions

1 Describe the difference between ROM and RAM.

2 When a computer is working, what is stored in RAM?

3 How does a computer use ROM?

Extension Activity

We have talked about RAM, but there are several different types of RAM in use in a desktop or laptop computer.

1 Research these different types of RAM and their performance and typical cost per GB.
2 Create a table of the different types of RAM module and the speed at which each one works.
3 Identify how much and what type of RAM is in the computers you use regularly at school/college and at home. Could these systems have their RAMs upgraded to improve performance?

Flash memory

In the 1980s, Toshiba developed a new type of ROM chip. In this type of ROM what is stored could be programmed by applying a relatively large electric current to force an electron through a barrier. Once forced into the 'storage' layer, the presence of the electrons can be detected without changing them, making this useful as a secondary storage device. The flash of charge used to force the electron through the barrier gives this type of memory its name, flash memory.

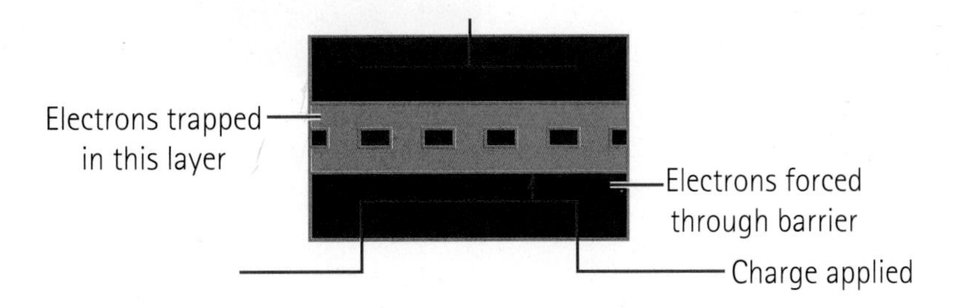

Figure 3.6 *The principles of flash memory*

Virtual memory

Running more complex programs or several programs at once can mean that the computer does not have enough space in RAM to store all program instructions. When there is not enough RAM to deal with all the demands on the computer, it will use a section of the hard disc as a temporary store for some of the data in main memory.

Key Term

Virtual memory A section of the hard disc used as if it were RAM to supplement the amount of main memory available to the computer.

Data in RAM not currently being used will be moved to the hard disc while data that is needed will be moved from the hard disc into RAM. This switching of data between the hard disc and RAM is a slow process and will have a significant effect on the performance of the computer system. The area used for the temporary storage of data being switched in and out of RAM is called **virtual memory**.

If a computer does not have sufficient RAM to run all the programs it is required to, it will use virtual memory. Access to the hard disc is significantly slower than access to RAM. If the computer is using virtual memory a lot of the time, adding more RAM will improve the performance of the system significantly because the CPU will not have to access data on the hard drive as frequently.

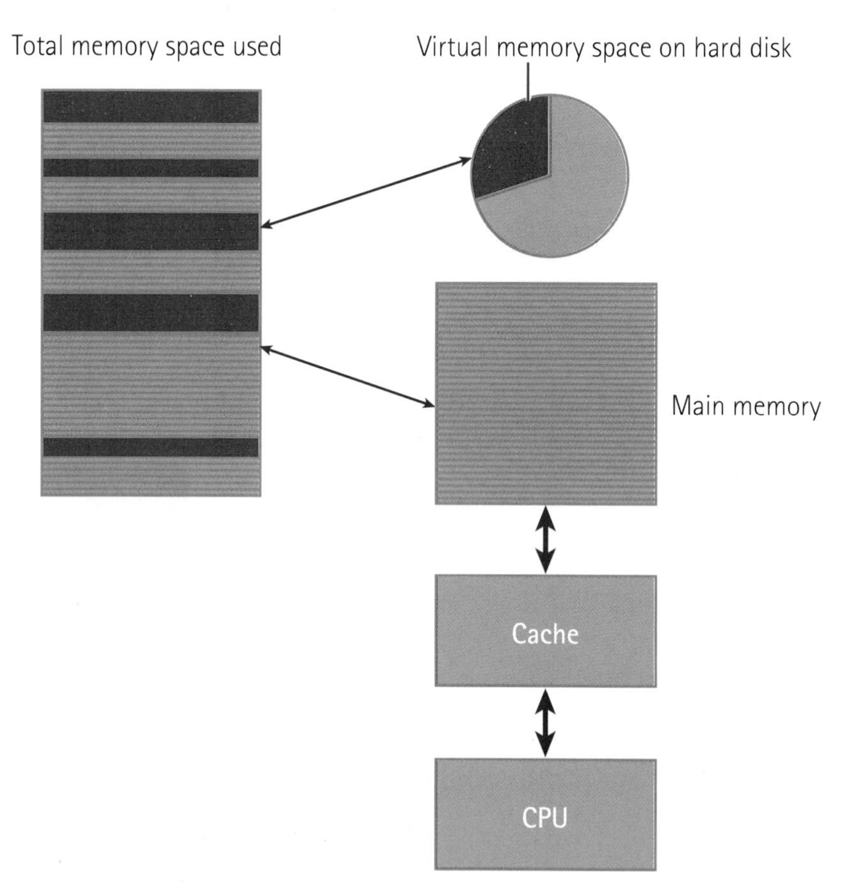

Figure 3.7 *Virtual memory*

Questions

4 What is *virtual memory* and why is it needed?

5 How does installing more RAM affect the use of virtual memory and how does this affect the performance of the computer?

Key Points

- A computer uses two types of main memory:
  - RAM (random access memory): This type of memory is volatile memory and data is lost when the power is turned off. RAM is used to store the operating system, programs and any data currently in use.
    Cache is a fast type of RAM used by the CPU for fast access to data.
  - ROM (read only memory) is non-volatile memory so data is retained even when the power is turned off. ROM stores settings and sequences required during the boot process when the computer is started up.
- A computer also uses:
  - Virtual memory. Part of the hard disc is used to supplement the available main memory, moving data and instructions from the hard disc to main memory as it is required, and back to the hard drive when it is no longer required.
  - Flash memory. Solid-state memory that can also be used in portable or removable devices to store data. It has access times, which are faster than hard discs but slower than RAM.

Secondary storage

While computers are able to process data to solve problems, they would certainly not be as useful and in such widespread use as they are, if every time we needed to process something the programs had to be typed in. Colossus only ever ran one program and had no secondary storage. It was left switched on at all times with the program in memory unless something had to be fixed.

An embedded system that only performs one role, for example a control system in a consumer device, probably does not need secondary storage. In this case the ROM in the system can be pre-programmed to hold the set of instructions necessary for it to perform its task.

Note

It is worth noting that the data is stored on the media and the device is the hardware that can read from and write to that media.

Most of our computing needs, however, require a general-purpose computer able to deal with a range of tasks. Since RAM is volatile and ROM can only store pre-programmed sets of instructions we need some form of non-volatile secondary storage to keep programs and data when the power is turned off.

There is a range of devices able to store data on appropriate media available for use on modern computer systems.

Magnetic devices

The use of magnetic media goes back to 1898 when audio was first stored on a magnetised wire wrapped around a drum, but magnetic data storage on hard disk drives is still the most widespread approach to data storage on computer systems.

The magnetic hard disk uses a stack of magnetised rigid plates that rotate. The heads hover over the surface and can move in and out across the platters to read the data. The magnetic disk drive was first invented by IBM in 1956. It had a stack of 50 platters, was the size of fridge, was able to store around 5 Mb of data and cost $50 000.

Figure 4.1 *A wire recorder*

Modern internal magnetic disk drive sizes are now typically measured in terabytes (1 million megabytes). A 6 TB hard disk drive can be bought today for under £200 (about $300).

Figure 4.2 *The Met Office computer*

Note

The Met Office computer has 17 petabytes of data storage (17 000 terabytes). It also has 48 000 CPU cores and weighs 140 tonnes.

The magnetic disk drive is a reliable and cost-effective storage solution, providing high capacity at low cost. It is used in most personal desktop and laptop computers as well as in large commercial systems, where several large disks are combined to provide large data storage facilities. The magnetic disk drive (or hard disk drive) will store the computer's operating system(s), installed applications or programs and users' data.

Figure 4.3 *A hard disk drive showing the platters and heads*

There are also portable versions of the magnetic disk drive that can be used as external devices to transfer large amounts of data or to act as a backup for important data.

Figure 4.4 *An external hard drive connected to a laptop*

Optical disks

The optical disk, the CD, was invented in the mid-1980s and the DVD in the late 1990s. This type of storage is read using laser light. A sensor detects the reflections from the surface when a laser light is shone onto them. There are rewriteable optical storage media that can be modified using laser light. In these media the surface has a dye layer that changes colour when a laser light is shone onto it. It is this change in colour that is detected when the media is being read.

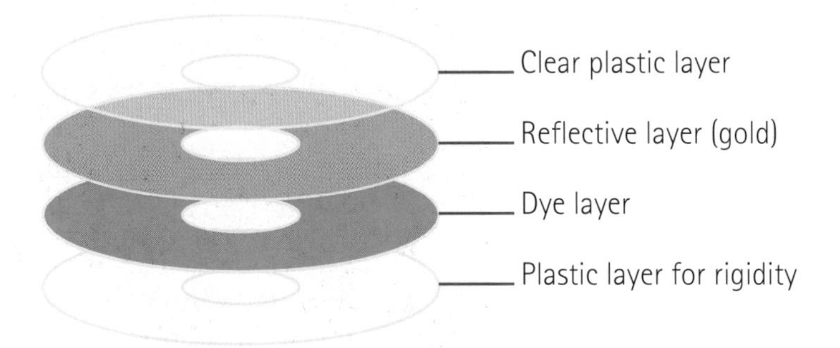

Figure 4.5 *An exploded view of a CD-RW showing the layers*

Optical disks are supplied in two basic forms: read only and read/write. The read-only media (CD-ROM, DVD-ROM) are written to once at the manufacturing stage and are used to distribute programs, video or data that is read-only. The read/write variety (CD-RW and DVD-RW) can be used as secondary storage to back up data or to safely transfer data between computers. A CD can hold around 700 MB of data, a DVD around 4.7 GB. The transfer times for data are quite slow compared to other portable media but the low cost and robust nature of these make them ideal for transferring large files, making one-off backups or distributing copies of programs or data.

Initially, DVD was the chosen medium for distributing video and film, but higher resolution films meant that the storage capacity of the DVD was not sufficient. In October 2000, Sony introduced the Blu-ray Disc™, so-called because it used a blue laser light capable of reading data stored at much higher densities than the red laser used on CD and DVD drives. The Blu-ray Disc is capable of storing 25 GB per layer and is available in dual layer (50 GB), triple layer (100 GB) and quad layer (128 GB) formats. It is available as a read-only or read/write device. The Blu-ray Disc is also used as a medium for distributing video games for a number of video consoles.

Flash memory

Flash memory (or solid-state memory) was described in Chapter 3. It is a very common form of personal portable file storage and is often used as a USB device to transfer data between computers, in cameras to store images and in tablet computers and other portable devices as the main form of storage. Many laptop computers are now using large solid-state drives (SSD) as an alternative to magnetic disk drives. Very large solid-state drives are increasingly available for large-scale data storage.

Figure 4.6 *Various solid-state drives*

The solid-state drive uses faster flash memory than that found in a typical personal USB device and is consequently relatively expensive. Solid-state drives use interconnected flash memory chips that can be permanently installed into the device, as in tablet computers or plug-in drives similar in shape and size to a typical magnetic disk drive.

Solid-state drives have many advantages over magnetic hard disks:

- SSD have lower latency times since there is no read/write head to move, so faster read and write operations
- there are no moving parts and there are no spinning platters, so they are low power devices that do not generate heat or noise
- magnetic disk performance can be affected by data being fragmented across the surface of the platters; this does not apply to SSDs
- SSDs are significantly lighter than magnetic disk drives so are better suited to lightweight, portable devices
- since there are no moving parts SSDs are not susceptible to problems caused by sudden movements, making them ideally suited to portable devices.

Figure 4.7 *Hybrid drive or SSHD*

Solid-state drives are, however, expensive compared to magnetic disk drives and current devices for home computers do not have the same capacity as magnetic disk drives. For just under £200 you can buy a magnetic hard disk with 6 TB capacity, the same amount of money buys just 512 GB of SSD storage.

One solution to the conflict between SSD fast access times but high costs and magnetic disk capacity at lower cost is a hybrid drive combining an amount of SSD with a typical magnetic disk drive. The most frequently accessed data, for example boot data, is stored in the SSD drive to improve performance, while less frequently accessed data is stored on the magnetic disk drive.

Capacity

The choice of media is often determined by the number and type(s) of files to be stored. The required capacity can be estimated by adding together the file sizes for all the files that need to be stored.

A typical text file will often only require a few kilobytes of space; a high-resolution video will require many gigabytes.

A simple text document with 256 characters if saved in different formats can vary in size considerably:

- as a text file (.txt): 257 bytes
- as a rich text file (.rtf): 601 bytes
- as a Microsoft Word document: 36 kilobytes.

textfile	13:46	36 KB	Microsoft Word document
textfile	13:44	601 bytes	Rich Text Document
textfile	13:51	257 bytes	Plain Text Document

We can estimate the size of a file from its contents but, as you can see, the formatting can add considerably to the size. We will discuss how to estimate the size of a data file in Chapter 14 ('Programming techniques'), and the size of various other types of file in Chapter 16 ('Data representation, conversion and arithmetic').

Table 4.1 *Some examples of file sizes (approximate sizes)*

File type	Approximate size
1-page word-processed file with no images	100 KB
postcard-size photograph	6 MB
3-minute MP3 music track	6 MB
3-minute music track on a music CD	50 MB
1-minute MPEG video	50 MB
DVD film	4 GB
high-definition film	8–15 GB
Blu-ray film	20–25 GB
4k high-resolution film	100 GB or more

Example

If we need to store five minutes of video, twelve minutes of music and ten photographs, we can estimate the total size as:

5 minutes of video @ 50 MB/minute	250 MB
12 minutes of video @ 50 MB/minute	600 MB
10 photographs @ 6 MB/photograph	60 MB
Total space required	**910 MB**
Plus approximately 10% to allow for overheads	90 MB
This brings the total to around	**1 GB**

This will not fit onto a standard CD, and so we would need either a DVD-RW or a small flash drive.

If you want to store a collection of high-definition films, then a 500 GB drive with 300 GB of free space will be able to store 300 ÷ 15, or 20, such films.

Choice of secondary storage

When choosing the secondary storage for a particular situation, there are a number of things to consider:

- **Capacity:** How much data does it need to hold?
- **Speed:** How quickly can the data be transferred and read?
- **Portability:** Does the data storage device need to be transported?
  - If so, the size, shape and weight are also important.
  - If the device is to be used to distribute data and the media cannot be reused, the cost is also important.

- **Durability:** How robust is the medium?
  - Will it be damaged if the device is moved around?
  - Will it be used in an environment where it is subject to significant external shocks or extreme conditions?
- **Reliability:** Does it need to be able to be used over and over again without failing?

Researching a range of typical devices shows how these data transfer rates vary by device:

Table 4.2 *Storage type and transfer rates comparison table*

Storage type	Transfer rate (typical)
RAM	12–20 GB/s
SSD	200–550 MB/s
Magnetic hard disk	50–120 MB/s
Blu-ray Disc	72 MB/s
USB flash drive	45–90 MB/s
DVD	1.32 MB/s
CD	0.146 MB/s

Key Points

- Secondary storage is needed to store programs, data and other files that would otherwise be lost when the power is turned off.
- Magnetic hard disks are relatively slow to access, but have a large capacity for a relatively low cost and are commonly used within commercial and personal computer systems.
- Optical disks (CDs and DVDs) are often used to distribute programs and data because they can be read only, are low cost, robust and light so can easily be sent through the postal system. They have capacities of: CD 700 MB, DVD 4.7 GB. Rewriteable optical media can be used to backup data at low cost. Access times for optical media are relatively slow.
- Flash (solid-state) memory is very flexible and can be used as a portable storage device using relatively low-cost flash memory or as a high performance, relatively high-cost solid-state drive in a computer system. It is used in a range of portable devices such as cameras, mobile phones and tablet computers. Flash memory is small, fast and robust.

Questions

1. Explain why computers need secondary storage.
2. Describe the characteristics of magnetic and solid-state storage and the advantages and disadvantages of these when used in a laptop computer.
3. A student uses several computers at home and at school. Describe how a flash memory drive will help this student to manage work.
4. State which is the most suitable secondary storage:
   (a) for transferring work from office to home
   (b) for distributing a video of a performance
   (c) as the main storage for a school computer network
   (d) for use in a camera to store digital images.

Extension Activity

The cost of data storage has steadily decreased.

Research the cost per GB of storage since 1980 and record this in a table or graph.

Compare the cost of magnetic hard disk storage with solid state and hybrid storage per GB.

Compare the costs with the access speeds to decide which is the best value for money.

Networks – introduction

A network is a collection of computer systems linked together. This means more or less all computers these days.

Networks consist of two types of components, nodes and links.

Each device on a network is referred to as a *node*. Nodes are connected by some means such as cabling or wireless.

Inside every computer system, digital signals are moved about between components. Signals are passed as a stream of 0s and 1s between the peripherals and the computer, and between the internal components of the computer. It is no great extension of that mechanism to connect computers together so that they can share data and 'talk' to each other.

Networks are successful because digital signals can be transmitted reliably. On the whole, a 1 is always going to be a 1 and a 0 will be a 0. Data can and does get corrupted, but with such a simple basis, it is easily possible to detect and correct errors.

Most computers are connected, if not to a local network, then probably to the internet. Even embedded systems are often connected. Car engine management systems can signal problems online to central systems. Burglar alarm systems can contact controllers. Large installations such as aircraft avionics contain multiple processors all connected to each other.

Benefits of networks

Networks have become important because they allow:

- work to be shared out between nodes (distributed systems)
- easy communication between users
- sharing of files
- sharing of peripheral devices
- monitoring of user activity
- control of access and other security-related features
- centralised administration and updates.

Types of network

Networks can be classified in various ways such as by their extent, the nature of their components or the nature of their connections.

Classification by extent

LAN

A LAN is a local area network. This means that the computers and connections are located on one site. This network might be in a single building or a group of buildings such as a university campus.

The owner of the LAN usually owns all the infrastructure and normally will have a team of network engineers and technicians to look after the installation.

Note

If you look up network types online, you will find a huge variety. The main thing to get from this is that networking computers is extremely useful and there will always be new ways to connect computers and new uses found for networks.

WAN

A WAN is a wide area network. This typically covers a large geographical area, taking in many cities, often worldwide. The connections are typically provided by a telecoms company. As with a LAN, the users will see a transparent resource, normally not needing to know about where individual computers are located.

Other forms of network

There are lots of other configurations nowadays that make use of connectivity for many reasons. A PAN is a personal area network where personal devices are connected, often in the home. A MAN is a metropolitan area network where devices are connected in a city. However, this, as in many other examples, is less common now than it used to be because of the widespread availability of internet connections.

Extension Activity

Look up controller area network (CAN [CAN-bus]) as it applies to a car.

Find out why the use of computer networks in cars has made them easier to drive and more reliable and easier to repair.

Find out the purpose of at least four electronic control units (ECUs) in a typical car. List the inputs and outputs for each one.

A SAN is a storage area network where multiple servers provide a transparent, large-scale file-storage facility in a data centre.

A VPN (virtual private network) is a part of the internet that is sealed off from the general public for the use of some organisation. It is not a real physical network but behaves as one, with enhanced encryption to keep it secure. A VPN removes the need for an organisation to maintain its own network infrastructure.

Key Term

UTP (unshielded twisted pair) A common connecting cable made from copper wiring; two wires are twisted around each other to minimise induction and cross-talk between the cables.

Transmission media

Most LANs have traditionally been connected by means of copper wire. This allows fast and reliable data transmission. The wire is usually **UTP (unshielded twisted pair)**, which provides fast data transmission and minimal interference. UTP cable is thin and flexible, which makes it relatively easy to install.

Coaxial cable is still used but this is bulkier than UTP and less convenient to install.

Figure 5.1 *UTP cable*

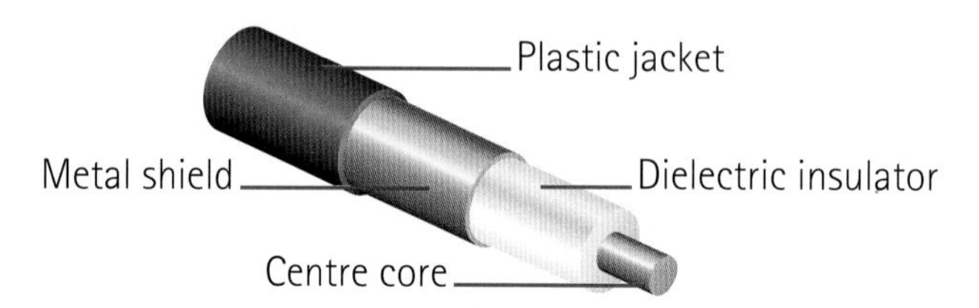

Figure 5.2 *Coaxial cable*

Fibre-optic cable is used for long distances. Light is transmitted along glass fibres. Total internal reflection keeps losses to a minimum. Fibre-optic cable is not subject to interference from neighbouring cables and does not deteriorate in exposed locations.

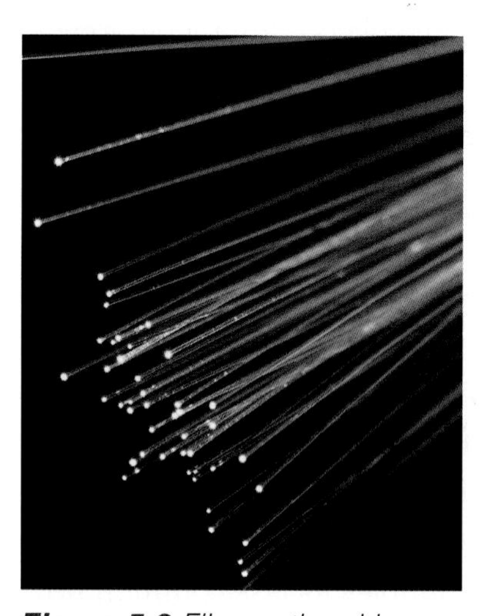

Figure 5.3 *Fibre-optic cable*

Wireless networks

Wireless connection is very common because it avoids the need to install cables and make alterations to buildings. It also allows easy connection of new devices. This is especially useful when visitors to an organisation need to connect their portable devices to the organisation's LAN or the internet.

There are some issues that have to be looked at when setting up and using wireless networks:

- Transmission speed is less than with wired connections. This can be a big problem if many users are sharing the same bandwidth.
- Security is a potential problem. The wireless signals can be intercepted very easily, so protective measures are needed such as:
  - Hiding the wireless service set identifier (SSID). This can make it less obvious that there is a wireless network in the area.
  - Restricting access to authorised MAC addresses only.
  - Using WiFi protected access (WPA) encryption so that the signals are meaningless to outsiders.

Classification by how a network is organised

There are two major ways in which networks are organised. They differ in the roles given to the connected computers.

Client–server

Client–server is the most common way to organise a LAN. One or more computers are designated as servers. A server is a high-end computer that provides services for the rest of the network. The server typically looks after:

- logins and security
- file handling
- printing
- internet access.

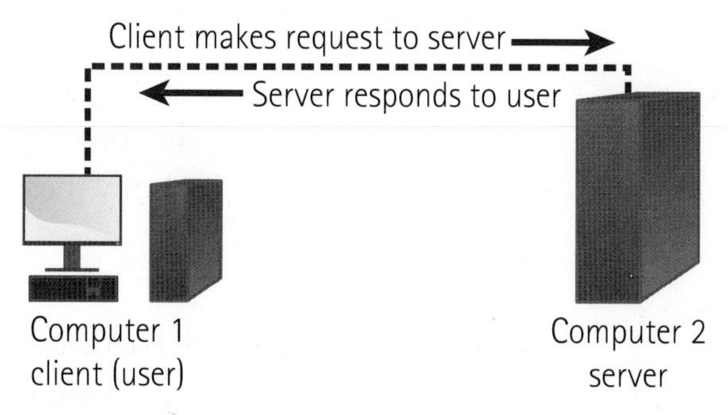

Figure 5.4 *A client–server relationship*

There are often many servers in a network, with some specialised to do particular functions, for example there may be an email server where the corporate emails are stored.

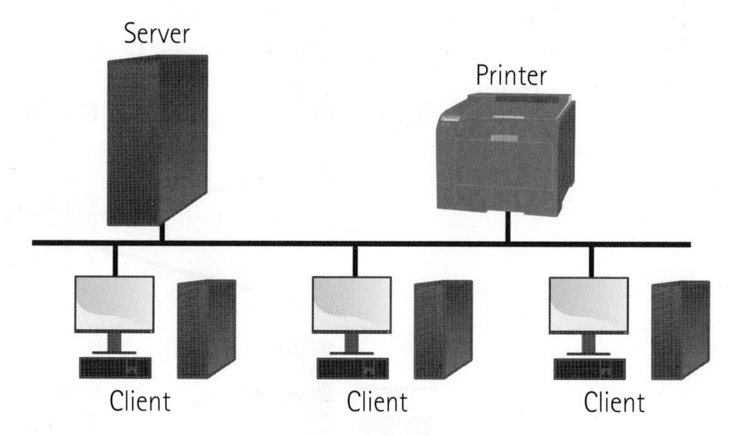

Figure 5.5 *A client–server network*

Large databases are often stored on and processed by dedicated servers, for example an online vendor may have a large database of customers, products and orders that interacts with remote customers using its DBMS (database management system), which will typically be manipulated by a query language such as SQL (structured query language) (see page 129). The transactions and security are carried out by the database server. The client machines (the ones used by the customers) will use their browsers in order to display information and interact with the online service.

Communication servers are sometimes used as a point of access to a network for remote users.

Web servers are computers that interact with remote users who access them via their browsers. They deliver HTML pages, CSS stylesheets and scripts to the users. The term 'web server' also applies to the software used to deliver these services. One of the most common examples of this is the Open Source Apache web server.

Client computers are the lower specification machines that access the services of a server. Typically these are where users log in and work.

Peer-to-peer

A peer-to-peer network is a distributed system, where functionality can be divided among the network nodes. In a peer-to-peer network, all computers have equal status. Each computer can potentially act as a server and supply services and/or data to the others. The administration of a peer-to-peer network is entirely up to the owner to decide.

Peers are both suppliers and users of network data and services.

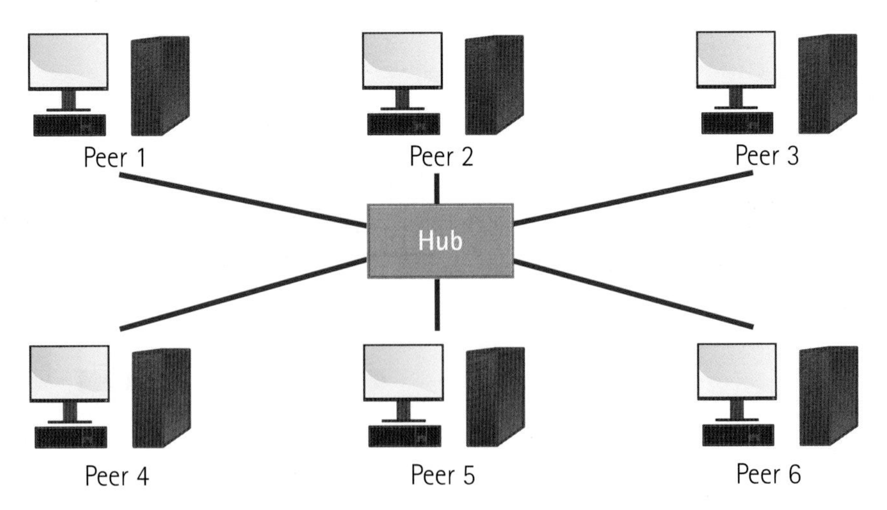

Figure 5.6 *A peer-to-peer network*

Peer-to-peer networks are easy to set up but their 'democratic' nature can lead to chaotic working. Security is hard to implement and network performance can become unpredictable and slow. Keeping track of data and its updates can become difficult and maintenance routines such as backup are also difficult to keep track of. Peer-to-peer is generally only suitable for small or domestic installations. The architecture is useful on the internet when sharing files without the need to route data through servers. Online communities can make good use of the architecture in such enterprises as software development and distribution, for example Linux and file sharing using such protocols as Bittorrent.

Peer-to-peer activity on the internet, because of the lack of server involvement, has led to much illegal file sharing and copyright infringements.

Network hardware

Key Terms

Ethernet A set of standards used to connect devices in a LAN. Nowadays, it tends to use mainly UTP and fibre-optic links or WiFi standards. Ethernet networks split messages into units called *frames* (see page 53). Ethernet is still very widely used and provides reliable and high-speed links.

WiFi A common standard for wireless connectivity based on a standard known as IEEE 802.11. This is a good example of how widely accepted standards have led to practical solutions for connecting devices.

We have already seen how various types of transmission medium (cable and wireless) are used to provide the links between nodes in a network. Various hardware devices connect the nodes to this transmission medium.

NICs

A NIC is a network interface controller, sometimes referred to as a network interface card. The term *card* is more or less obsolete now that the circuitry is normally part of the computer's motherboard rather than a specially added 'card' or circuit board.

The NIC is present on all devices connected to a network and provides the electrical signals for sending messages on the network and also for receiving incoming signals.

The NIC makes use of the correct protocol (see page 44) in order to communicate successfully on its particular network. Typical protocols will be **ethernet** or **WiFi**.

Note

IEEE: Institute of Electrical and Electronics Engineers

This is a professional standards body based in New York. It oversees standards for electronic communications in order to promote good practice and interoperability between computer and communication systems.

Wireless access points

The point at which a wireless-enabled device such as a laptop or a tablet connects with a network is a hardware device called a *wireless access point*. It normally connects to a router that is often integral to the device.

Figure 5.7 *A wireless access point*

Routers

Routers are devices that send data packets (see page 54) between networks. In a small home network, they connect individual computers to each other and also to the internet.

Routers are extensively used on the internet and provide the connections between nodes, making decisions about where to send data and by what route. For that reason, routers are the primary piece of equipment that allows the internet to exist at all. Routers collect data about available routes and use algorithms such as Dijkstra's shortest-path algorithm to determine the optimum route to send data.

Hubs and switches

Hubs and switches connect devices to a LAN. Hubs are less common these days on large enterprise networks. Home users sometimes get small hubs to connect a few devices because they are cheaper than switches or routers and require no setting up.

Hubs receive signals from a device and rebroadcast them indiscriminately to all connected nodes. They do not have any routing tables and they have no means of deciding where to send data. Hubs also switch the available bandwidth between any connected computers so they slow down network traffic.

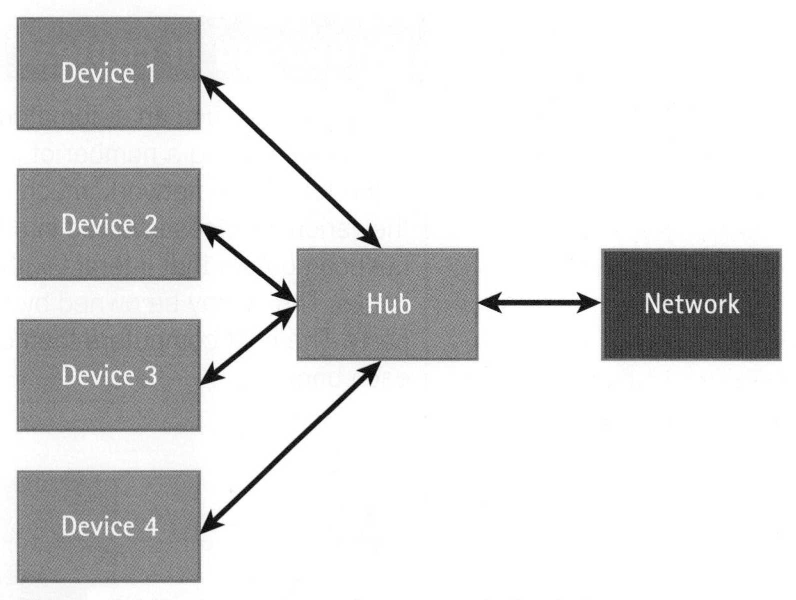

Figure 5.8 *Devices connected to a network via a hub*

Switches also connect computers together but a switch sends packets of data only to the intended destination, not to every connected node. Switches are usually self-learning so that they build up a table of connected devices and use this to route data packets to their correct destination. They do not send data uselessly to unintended nodes. Switches do not share bandwidth so they are more efficient than hubs and are preferred in most medium to large installations.

Switches are more expensive than hubs but they vary in cost according to their capabilities. The number of ports built into a switch can make a difference to its performance because the throughput of data may be divided between them. Most switches are capable of handling 14 480 pps (packets per second), which is enough for typical ethernet installations. They can usually also handle fast ethernet networks where 148 800 pps is necessary.

Switches usually work at a higher capacity than the ethernet transmission medium, which is traditionally 10 Mbps (megabits per second). Modern installations are more likely to be gigabit ethernet (GbE), which can transmit ethernet frames at a rate of a gigabit per second (1 000 000 000 bits per second).

Computing in context

Every time you use an automated teller machine (ATM) you are immediately using a number of networks. At the very least, there is the telephone network, much of which is digital. This connects the various devices involved in a transaction. The banks maintain host computers that interact with the cash machines from various banks. These may be owned by a number of banks or by a third party. The host computers then connect to the relevant servers of each bank.

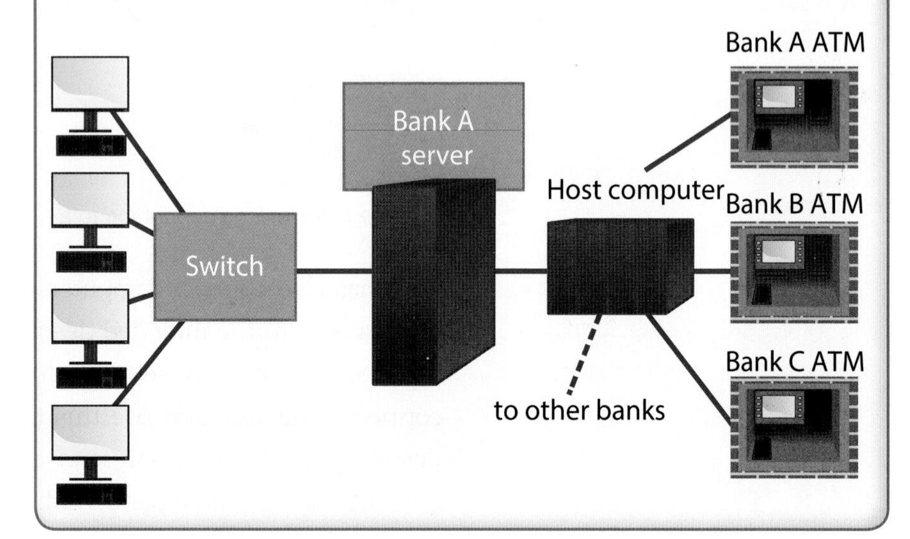

Questions

1. What term refers to a computer connected to a network?
2. Describe the essential features of a LAN.
3. Describe the essential features of a WAN.
4. Describe the difference between a hub and a switch.
5. Describe the purpose of a router.

Networks – topologies and protocols

Topologies

All networks work in essentially the same way. The computers on the network prepare a signal to send to another device, which is located by an address of some sort. The signal is then placed on a transmission medium that, as we have seen, is either a copper wire, a fibre-optic cable or some form of wireless medium.

However, networks can be laid out in different ways. The layout of a network is called its *topology* and this will affect the cost and performance of the network.

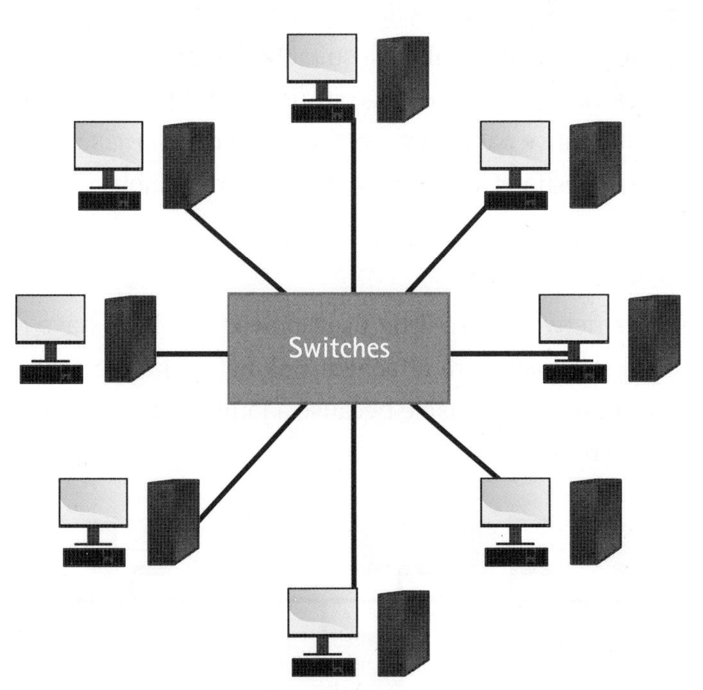

Figure 6.1 *A star network layout*

Star network

The star topology is the most common network layout. All the nodes are connected to a central device or a wiring cabinet, using switches (see page 36). It can be a lot of work to set up a star network, in order to lay the cables through walls and ceilings. Star networks tend to be fast and reliable because each node has its own connection to the centre and on to the servers, so if a fault occurs in one link, other links are not necessarily affected.

A further advantage of the star topology is that data collisions are less frequent when each node has its own connection to the servers. This also speeds up overall throughput.

Mesh network

In a mesh network, all the nodes are involved in the transmission of a message. There are multiple paths between the nodes and no central router is required. The nodes can talk directly to each other. A big advantage of a mesh network topology is that alternative routes are available and there is no single point of failure, where a problem could bring the whole network down.

In a full mesh network, each node is connected to every other node. In a partial mesh topology, one node will connect to all the others but some nodes will communicate directly with some of the others.

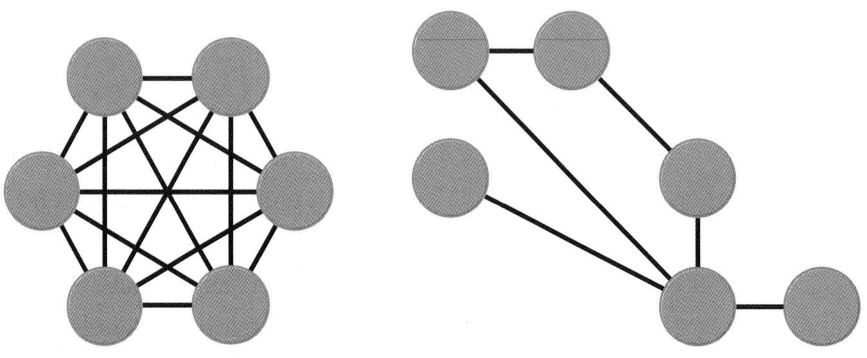

Figure 6.2 *A full mesh network layout*

Figure 6.3 *A partial mesh network layout*

Mesh networks can propagate messages either by sending them throughout the network where they will be picked up by the intended receiving nodes or by routing them along a suitably available pathway. If a particular route is blocked by a failure, algorithms are used that re-route the message along alternative pathways, a process called *self-healing*. This flexibility ensures that mesh networks are generally very reliable.

Other topologies

Cable-connected bus networks are little used nowadays. They have a 'backbone' to which the nodes are attached. Bus networks are prone to data collisions and can be unreliable because a fault in the backbone will disrupt the entire network.

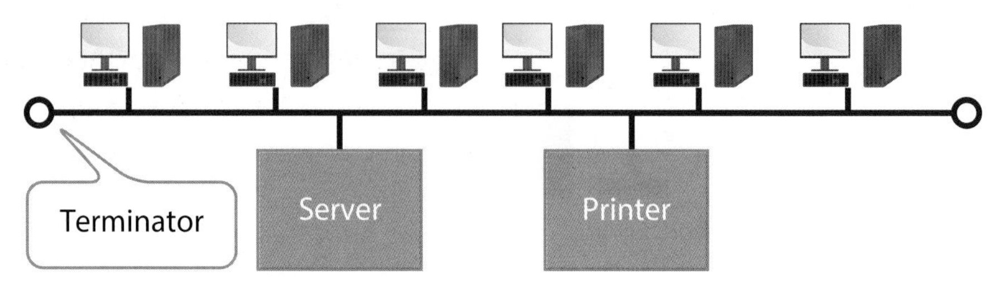

Figure 6.4 *A bus network layout*

Ring networks, as the name implies, are based on nodes arranged in a circle. Each node is connected to exactly two other nodes. Messages pass through each computer, which is then responsible for passing the message on. Data is sent in packets (see page 54) and if a computer has a message to send, it modifies packets as they pass through it. When a message is received, the receiving computer sends a message back to the originator to acknowledge delivery. As with bus networks, a fault in the ring connection will disrupt the entire network.

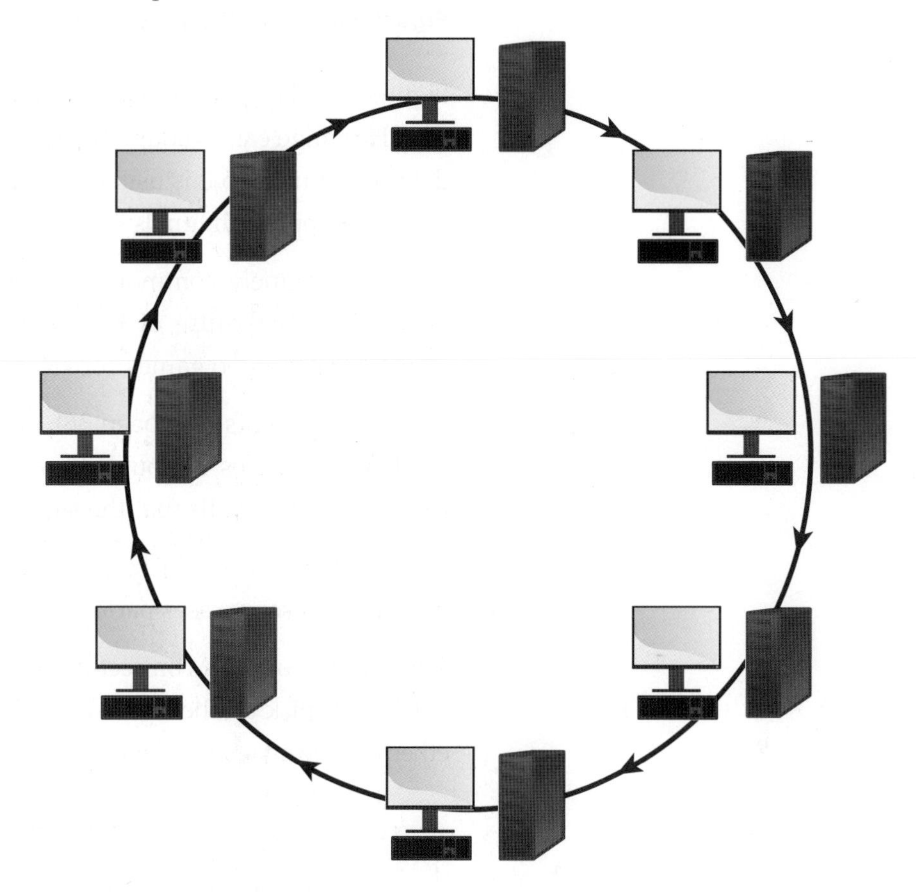

Figure 6.5 *A ring network layout*

Key Term

Channel A communication link carried on any suitable medium such as a wire conductor, fibre-optic cable or a wireless signal; for example a bit-stream can be sent between devices on a WLAN along a channel formed by a particular sub-frequency in a WiFi frequency band.

WiFi

WiFi is the technology that uses wireless frequencies, notably the 2.4 GHz and 5 GHz wavebands. They conform to the IEEE 802.11 standards (see page 35). These standards allow for the division of a waveband into a number of separate **channels**. Many channels can be set up in any given waveband but there are legal constraints on how many and how much power they use. This is because if the channels overlap they can interfere with each other.

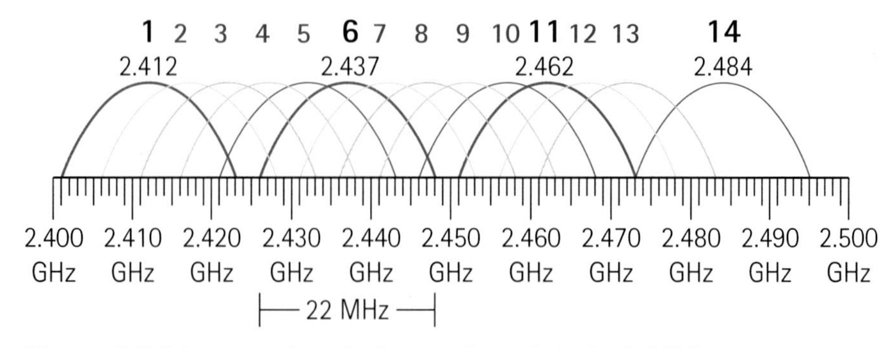

Figure 6.6 *A large number of adjacent channels in the 2.4 GHz range*

Figure 6.6 shows how a large number of adjacent channels in the 2.4 GHz range can overlap. Adjacent signals can cause interference and data corruption, so it is usual to limit a waveband to a small number of non-overlapping channels such as three or four.

WiFi is extremely common because it is so convenient. All sorts of devices can make use of WiFi connections, such as laptops, tablets, smartphones, video games consoles and e-readers.

WiFi access points (see page 36) can be connected to at a range of up to about 20 metres although this varies according to the nature and thickness of the walls that the signals need to pass through.

A single WiFi access point has to share its bandwidth among the connected devices so in some cases performance can be severely compromised.

The security of WiFi connections can be an issue because any enabled device can pick up the signals. This makes them more vulnerable than ethernet networks, so encryption is an important part of any WiFi installation.

Key Points

- Networks can be constructed using various layouts called *topologies*.
- Topologies have various advantages and disadvantages, notably regarding speed of operation and reliability.
- Star and mesh are the key topologies to learn for this specification.
- Wireless networks are common because of ease of implementation.

Encryption

Due to the vulnerability of wireless signals being picked up by unauthorised individuals, it is necessary to protect the data on a wireless network with some form of encryption. Encryption is the transformation of a message so that it can only be understood by its intended recipient. The transformation normally involves a data item called a *key*.

An old and simple method of encryption is called the *Caesar cipher*. Letters are displaced by a known amount; for example using the number 4 as the 'key'.

The process of encrypting a message is an algorithm.

Example

A displacement of 4 would produce the following look-up table:

plaintext letter	A	B	C	D	E	F	G	H	I	J	K	L	M	N	O	P	Q	R	S	T	U	V	W	X	Y	Z
cipher letter	E	F	G	H	I	J	K	L	M	N	O	P	Q	R	S	T	U	V	W	X	Y	Z	A	B	C	D

An encrypted message such as 'COMPUTING' would be transformed into:

GSQTYXMRK

The message would be sent along with the key '4' to allow decryption.

Question

1 Write an algorithm to encrypt a message using a Caesar cipher.

This method is too simple for serious encryption. It would be easy to try out different keys in order to construct a meaningful message, so it is more common to use elaborate algorithms with much bigger keys.

The bigger the key, the more secure the encryption. Also, the use of more than one key will make the encryption even more secure.

A common method is to use two keys such as the public/private key method. This is an example of asymmetric key encryption. This means that the two keys are different but complement each other. One key is used to encrypt a message but a different key is necessary to decrypt it.

One key is publicly available. It is used to encrypt a message. A secret private key is linked to this and is required to decrypt the message. Only the holder of the paired private key can decrypt the message. The way this works is like this:

1. Alice gets Bob's public key from a directory.
2. Alice sends a message to Bob encrypted with Bob's public key.
3. Bob can use his secret key to unscramble it.

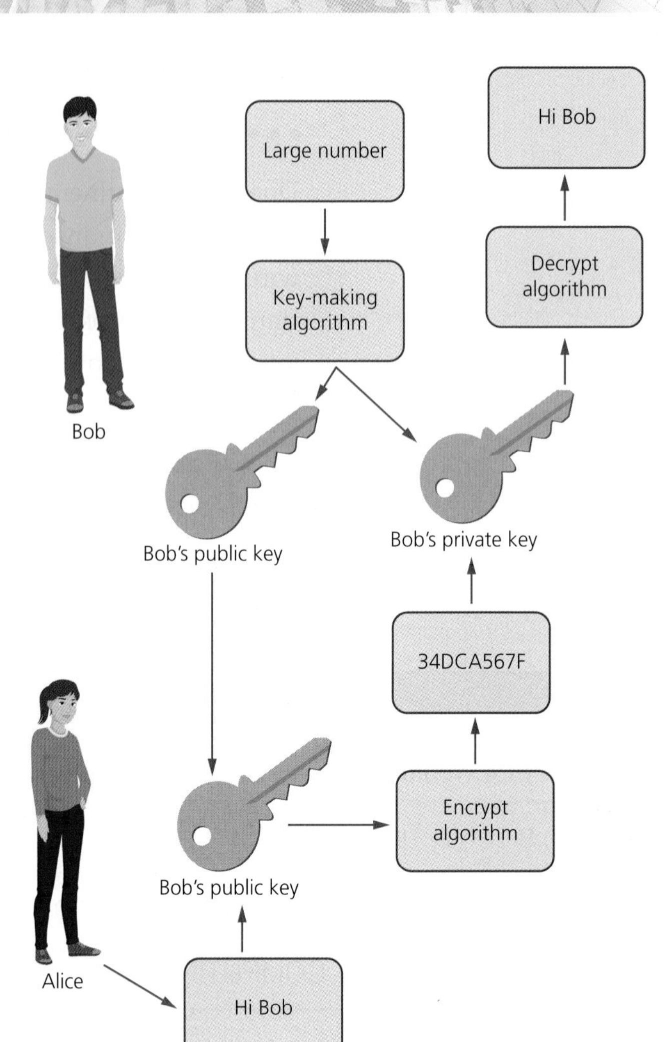

Figure 6.7

Key Points

- Encryption is the process of making messages secure from eavesdropping.
- Encryption is particularly important on wireless networks and when transmitting financial or other sensitive data.

Protocols

Network communications are governed by protocols. These are rules and standards that are agreed in order to make it possible for different devices to talk to each other.

Protocols exist for most aspects of large networks and of course for the internet. They cover the sending and receiving of messages, the technicalities of the hardware and also the file formats used by different types of message.

Network addressing

For a message to get from one node to another on any network, there must be an indication of where it is to go, just as a letter must have an address on the envelope.

There are various ways to address a message. The main ones involve IP (internet protocol) addressing and MAC (media access control) addressing.

With IP addressing, each node on a network is assigned a unique numerical IP address. An IP address is composed of a series of binary numbers, normally displayed in decimal or hex.

IP Version 4 (IPv4) uses four octets (that is, 32 bits), for example 194.83.249.5. This arrangement gives a possible 4 294 967 296 IP addresses.

Internet Protocol Version 6 (IPv6) uses 128 bits, allowing addresses such as:

2001:db8:0:1234:10:567:12:11

This provides about 340 trillion trillion trillion IP addresses.

IP addresses can be static, that is they are assigned permanently by an administrator but this ties up addresses even when the device is not in use.

To conserve IP addresses, they are often assigned dynamically, to allow reuse. This is called *DHCP* (*dynamic host configuration protocol*).

Networks often have their own subnet addresses, again to conserve addresses. The router connecting to the outside world has one address and the clients inside the LAN have their own.

MAC addresses are uniquely assigned to devices connected to a network. These are stored in the NIC of the device's hardware by the manufacturer. If a network node has multiple hardware items attached to it, each one will have its own MAC address.

Examples of protocols and other standards

Internet developers have adopted a set of protocols in order to ensure that devices from different manufacturers can communicate with each other.

This set is known under the general heading of TCP/IP (transmission control protocol/internet protocol). Details of how this operates are given in Chapter 7.

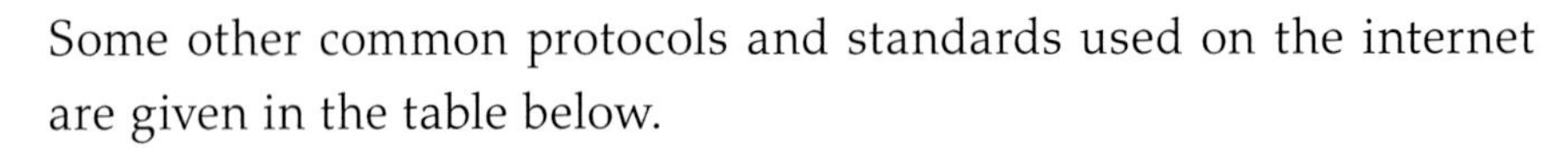

Some other common protocols and standards used on the internet are given in the table below.

Standard	Meaning	Use
HTML	Hypertext mark-up language	Writing web pages for display
XML	Extensible mark-up language	A text-based means of describing data. XML complements HTML by providing a way to store data for reuse. It separates data from HTML, thereby simplifying updates.
HTTP	Hypertext transfer protocol	Client–server protocol for requesting (client) and delivering (server) resources such as HTML files.
HTTPS	Alternately known as HTTP Secure or HTTP over SSL (secure sockets layer)	This is HTTP used over a secure encrypted connection. HTTPS provides authentication between the web server and the client so that there is confidence that one is actually communicating with the intended server. This is much used in internet banking and similar services to prevent interaction with spoof websites.
CSS	Cascading style sheets	Define how HTML elements are to be displayed. CSS files are stored separately from the HTML they affect.
POP	Post office protocol	This is a protocol used by email clients to retrieve email from a remote email server. It is simple to implement and generally removes email from the server and downloads it to store on the client's computer. POP is more or less obsolete nowadays. IMAP has largely replaced it. The last version was known as POP3.
IMAP	Internet message access protocol	This is an alternative protocol for accessing email messages from a server. It is more capable than POP and allows complete management of a remote mailbox.
SMTP	Simple mail transfer protocol	This is an old standard for the transmission of email. Most modern email services have their own protocols for sending and administering emails but they are able to use SMTP in order to communicate with other proprietary systems. SMTP is only used to push or deliver mail onto a mail server. Other protocols such as POP or IMAP are used to retrieve the mail.
FTP	File transfer protocol	This is used to send computer files from one host (node) to another over the internet or other TCP/IP network. FTP is commonly used for uploading web pages to web servers and is normally supplied as part of most web page editors.

Key Point

- Protocols are communication standards. They are needed so that devices can talk to each other.

Extension Activity

1. Find out some of the jobs that a web-authoring tool can do.
2. Make a list of two or three examples of such web-authoring tools.
3. Use one to create a simple web page that contains some text, at least one graphic and a link.
4. Use a CSS stylesheet to modify the appearance of your web page so that you can switch between different versions of the same page without altering the basic HTML code.

Questions

2. Describe two methods of keeping a network secure from online hackers.
3. Explain the purpose of a router in a network.
4. Explain what a *network protocol* is.
5. State two protocols used in the transmission of emails.
6. Describe the difference between an IP address and a MAC address.
7. Describe the steps taken to send a message from Bob to Alice using asymmetric key encryption.
8. Describe the characteristics of a mesh network.

7 Networks – layering

Layering

When we write an email to someone and send it we have no idea what they will retrieve it on. They could use a desktop computer or a mobile device. We also have no idea what operating system or which email software they will use. It is a complex problem and, like all complex problems, they become easier to deal with if broken down into several distinct processes, or layers.

Layering is not confined to computer science; many cars are built using interchangeable parts, with the same components being used on various makes and models of car. For example a Ford engine is used in various Mazda models.

There are several advantages to layering. Layering reduces the complexity of the problem because the problem is broken down into smaller, more manageable parts, which facilitates modular engineering. This modular approach means that different suppliers or developers can work to improve, add new facilities or fix problems with one layer without needing to modify the other parts of the system. This in turn means that several developers can provide solutions for specific layers of the system and be assured they will work when included within the whole system. It is important that these layers are **interoperable**. It is also important that these layers are able to pass data between them, i.e. the data from one layer is formatted so that the next layer is able to recognise and process it.

Key Terms

Layering Rules organised into a distinct order in which they need to be applied.

Interoperable The ability of different systems and software applications to communicate, exchange data, and use the information that has been exchanged.

Extension Activity

Layering is used in a range of situations. The example given here is motor-car manufacturing, where components are interchangeable. Another example is the range of electrical connectors used in computer hardware, for example those used in USB connectors to enable hardware from different manufacturers to interconnect.

Can you think of some more?

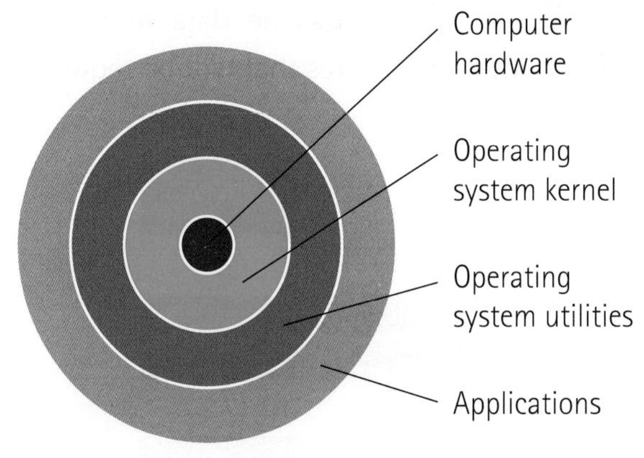

***Figure 7.1** A layered overview of a computer system*

In computer programming, layering is the organisation of a program into separate functional components that interact in some sequential and hierarchical way. Each layer will often have an interface only to the layer above it and the layer below it. This means the layers can be individually sourced and merged into a functional system. The Linux kernel is the basis for various distributions of Linux-based operating systems. The system libraries and utilities are developed and added to the kernel to create various versions of Linux-based operating system.

In Figure 7.1, a simple model of a computer system demonstrates the use of layering between the computer hardware and the applications.

Key Terms

Protocol Set of rules and standards governing how networks should function and communicate.

TCP/IP Transfer control protocol/internet protocol: A set of protocols that governs the transfer of data over a network.

Task

Consider the problems that might arise if the computer software or hardware developers decided to use different rules for communication.

Communication programs are examples of layered applications. One example of a layered **protocol** is **TCP/IP** (transfer control protocol / internet protocol). The TCP/IP protocol is used to define how data is transferred through a network, for example over the internet or over a private network.

The TCP/IP stack (shown in Figure 7.2) is a complete set of protocols covering the movement of data across a network. These rules include how data should be formatted, addressed, routed and received.

Layer 1: Application
This layer is concerned with making sure the data produced is in an acceptable format for the application that will make use of it.
The software application generating the data needs to supply the data in a format acceptable to the software that receives it.

Layer 2: Transport
This layer is concerned with establishing connections across the network. It communicates with the receiving device to agree on communication protocols, what size of packet, the speed data can be sent and received, whether receipt of data packets is to be acknowledged etc.

Layer 3: Internet
This layer is concerned with transmitting the data across different networks. It identifes the destination IP and establishes a path across the network, via routers, to the destination.

Layer 4: Network
This layer is concerned with passing data to the local physical network. It converts the data into electrical signals that can be understood by the network hardware making it hardware-independent and able to be transmitted over any transmission media such as copper wire, optical fibre and wireless.

***Figure 7.2** The TCP/IP stack*

Key Terms

Encapsulation Enclosing the data inside another data structure to form a single component.

De-encapsulation Removing the data from inside an encapsulated item.

When data is sent, each layer **encapsulates** the data and adds information around the data, to identify features that will be required to unpick the original data once received.

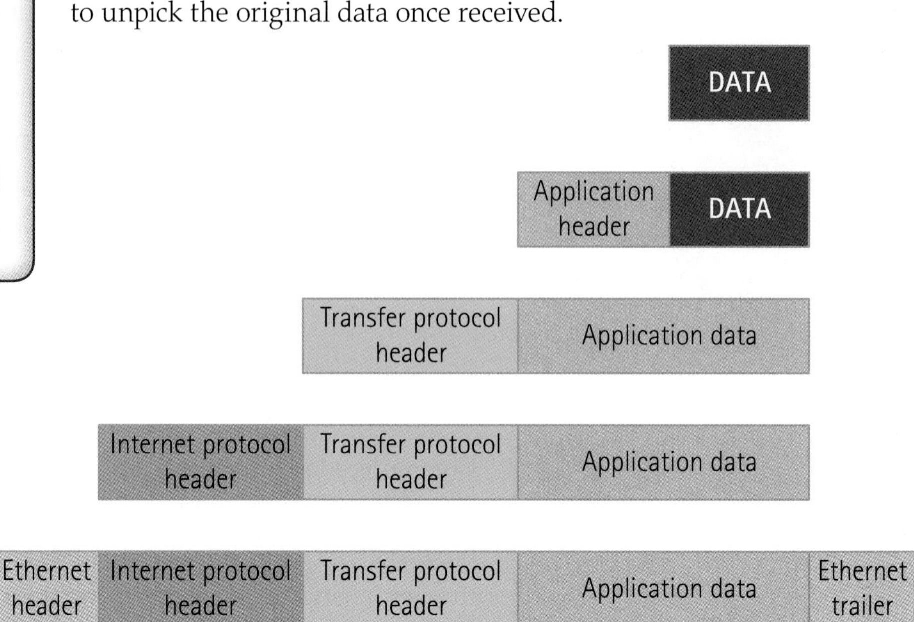

Figure 7.3 *Encapsulating data for transmission*

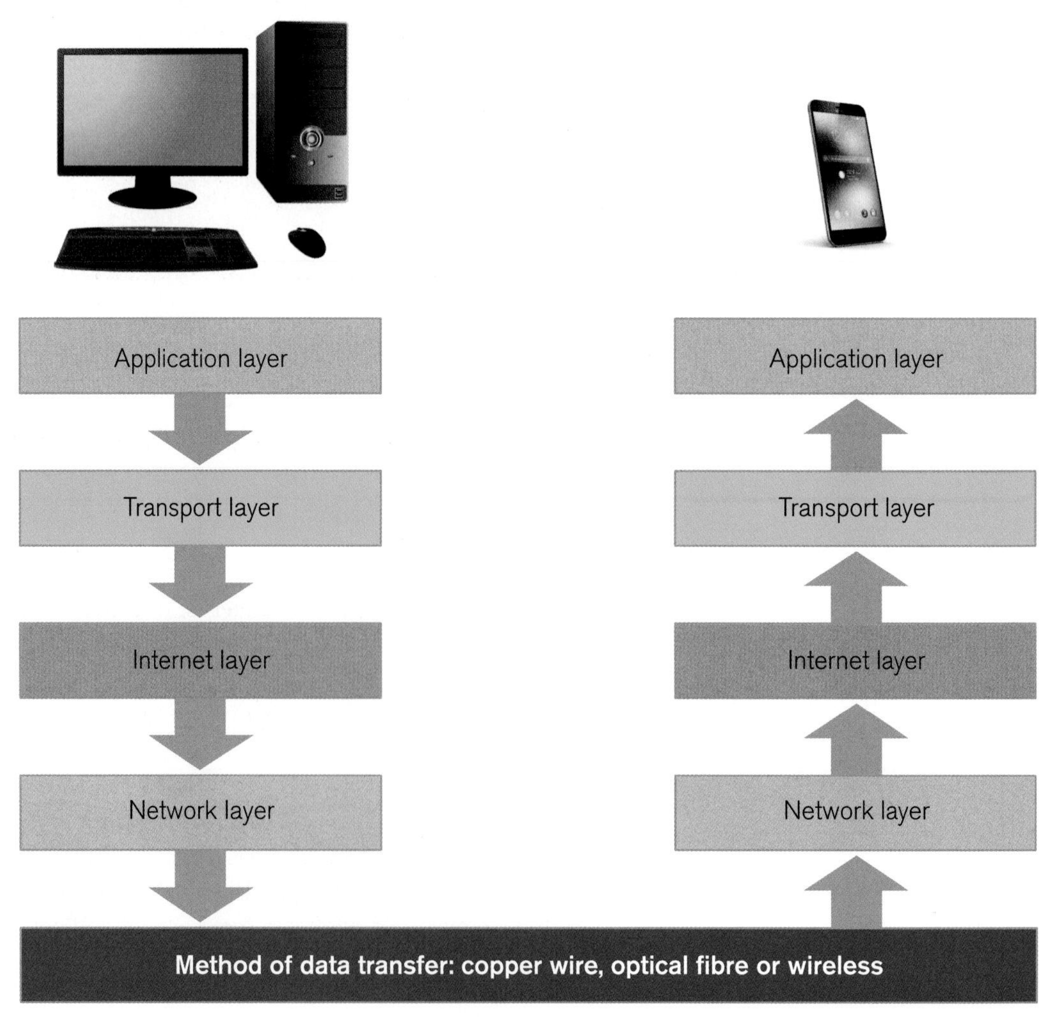

Figure 7.4 *Data being transferred between devices*

Extension Activity

Layering is a common computing strategy. It is basically a divide and conquer approach to problem solving that separates the various functional aspects of a problem. TCP/IP is just one network model, but there are others, including the OSI (Open System Interconnection) model. Look at the OSI model to see how the layers compare with those for the TCP/IP model.

Typically a protocol such as TCP/IP will determine

- how to establish and terminate communication between devices
- the format of any data to be exchanged
- how to detect and correct errors
- any compression to be used.

Key Points

- In order for different devices to communicate they need to establish common rules or protocols.
- Protocols are layered so that each can be developed independently.
- Layering has several advantages:
  - reduced complexity
  - standardised interfaces
  - facilitates modular development
  - a range of developers can contribute to the system
  - development is faster.
- Interoperability is the ability for the layers in a system to work together exchanging information.
- So that protocols developed independently work together, they are layered with strict rules about the format and the method by which data is transferred between these layers.

Questions

1. Why do we need protocols to establish communication between devices on a network?
2. What are the advantages of layering in computer program development?
3. Why do we need to layer protocols such as TCP/IP?
4. What is the key feature of a layer in a layered system?
5. What are the four layers in the TCP/IP protocol and what purpose does each one serve in the communication process?

Networks – connections

This chapter is concerned with how nodes are connected in a network and how messages are transmitted. There are various technologies in use that are based on some of the protocols mentioned in earlier chapters.

Ethernet

Ethernet is a very common set of technologies used to implement LANs. It is essentially a standard used for connecting computers that are located fairly close together.

Ethernet has been around in various forms since 1980, having been developed in the 1970s. During its lifetime, it has been refined many times, largely to improve transmission speeds and the distances over which it is effective. Ethernet is still the dominant local area network standard except where it has been replaced with wireless technologies.

Ethernet is most often implemented using UTP (unshielded twisted pair) or fibre-optic cabling, with connections made using hubs or far more often, switches.

Currently ethernet networks are mostly capable of transmission rates of up to 100 Gbits per second. There is every reason to expect this to be improved further in the future.

Ethernet networks are subdivided into segments. Each segment is a group of devices on a shared medium such as a UTP cable.

If you have a few linked computers at home, they are likely to be part of just a single segment. Larger networks commonly are divided in order to improve performance, for example in a school all the computers in the computer lab might belong to one segment and the computers in the admin department will be in another.

Large networks benefit from segmentation because the nodes on a segment are chosen to be those that are most likely to be sharing information. They can still communicate with other segments but most of the traffic is likely to be local. This reduces the occurrence of data collisions. The fewer data collisions, the fewer requests there will be for resends and so the performance of the network is improved.

Key Points

- Ethernet is a standard used for connecting devices in LANs.
- Copper wire or fibre-optic cabling forms the transmission media.
- Networks are often divided into segments.

Extension Activity

Find out how many segments there are on your school or college network. If possible, find out what each one is used for.

What cabling connects your PCs in class to the network? What alternatives are there?

Frames

Ethernet networks divide data, when sending it, into units called *frames*. This is done by the network hardware such as NICs and routers.

There are rules that control the maximum and minimum sizes of frames. Each frame contains the data itself plus source and destination MAC address and error-checking data. If data becomes corrupted as it is sent, this is detected and can be corrected, normally by requesting a resend. The addresses used by ethernet to send frames are the MAC addresses of the connected devices.

A frame is broadcast on an ethernet network. This means that it is sent to all connected devices in a segment. If the destination address is not the same as a device address, the frame is discarded.

CSMA/CD

Networks based on ethernet often experience errors. A common error results from two data frames being transmitted at the same time so that they collide.

CSMA/CD (carrier-sense multiple access with collision detection) aims to prevent such collisions. What happens is, if a node is ready to transmit a message it first 'listens' to find if there is any traffic on the link. If it is quiet, it transmits its message.

Sometimes two nodes transmit at the same time on a particular network segment. Because this will result in a data collision, a single segment is sometimes called a *collision domain*. A collision results in corruption of the data just as when two people speak at the same time, the talking gets garbled. If this happens in a network with CSMA, the sending nodes detect that their messages bounce back in a corrupted form. They then wait a random length of time before retransmitting. This random delay is to try to avoid both nodes retransmitting again at the same time.

Ethernet has some built-in drawbacks because of its design. The length of cabling for a segment is limited (although this is improving all the time) and a limited sized segment tends to lead to more data collisions, which reduce the performance of the network. Also, CSMA collision detection systems cannot work optimally if there are too many devices connected to a single segment. This problem can be alleviated to an extent by separating networks into more segments with switches.

To get round the problem of finite and limited lengths of cable that are practical on an ethernet network, repeaters are sometimes used. These are devices that listen for signals and resend them onto other segments.

Simplex and duplex

Some network connections only allow data transmission in one direction. An example is the old ring standard (see page 40). One direction communication is called *simplex*.

Half-duplex communication is a method of communication that allows data transmission in both directions between two nodes but not at the same time. It is like the old radio communications where fragments of conversation were transmitted one way, then the other way, for example:

Alice: I have news for you. ... Over.

Bob: Message received, what is it? ... Over.

and so on.

Full duplex allows data to be sent in both directions at the same time.

Packets

On TCP/IP networks, data is divided up into packets. These packets are created by software, not by hardware as in the case of frames. These packets are then encapsulated into frames for sending.

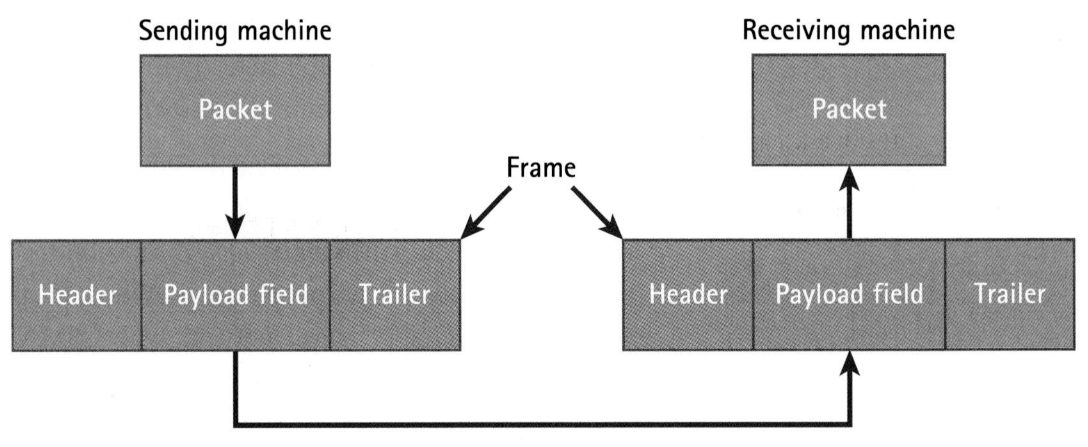

Figure 8.1 *Sending and receiving packets*

A packet typically contains the following three parts:

Part of packet	Contents
Header	Sender's IP address Receiver's IP address Protocol Packet number Length of packet
Payload	Data
Trailer	End of packet marker Error correction data

The protocol is needed in order to determine what sort of data is being sent such as email, video or a web page.

The packet number is needed because the data is usually split into many packets that may get sent by different routes. The packet number allows the receiving computer to reconstruct the whole message in the correct order.

The payload is the actual data that is being sent. Sometimes, in order to make sure that all packets have the correct number of bytes, it might be padded with dummy information.

The trailer contains a small number of bytes that indicate that the packet has come to an end. It also contains some error-checking data, which is normally used by a mechanism called the *cyclic redundancy check* or *CRC*.

CRC

CRC (cyclic redundancy check) is an error-checking process used in many networks.

- A mathematical expression is applied to the data, which generates a code.
- This code is sent along with the data.
- The receiving device performs the same check.
- If the results match, then the data has been sent correctly.
- Otherwise, the receiving device requests a resend.

Key Points

- The IP protocol determines the nature of data packets.
- The IP protocol delivers data to IP addresses.
- The data packets are inserted into frames created by the network protocol such as ethernet.
- The ethernet protocol delivers frames to physical devices based on their MAC addresses.

Routing

There are two basic ways in which data can be sent between two nodes on a network: circuit switching and packet switching.

Circuit switching

Circuit switching is the older method. This is sometimes referred to as *connection mode transmission*.

A physical link is established between two network entities. The data is sent in a stream until the end of the message, then the connection is released.

This is the typical method used on most traditional telephone networks. A link is made between the people who are having a conversation. This used to be achieved by telephone operators in a telephone exchange plugging cables into a plug board, but this was superseded by automatic switching.

Circuit switching is also suitable for remotely operating a computer from a distant terminal.

Circuit switching has the disadvantage that a link is tied up for the whole of a communication session and cannot be used by any other network traffic. Also, it is open to disruption if a fault occurs in the circuit. For these reasons, packet switching is the dominant technology in most network operations.

Packet switching

A packet-switched network is an example of connectionless mode communication. In other words, there is no single fixed connection between the sender and receiver of the message. In a packet-switching network, the message is divided into packets as already explained. The packets are sent to a router, which forwards them on to the next router.

The pathway is decided according to a table of nearby routers that it has built up and uses a routing algorithm to select the best path.

If one route is unavailable, another can be used.

Questions

1. What is *ethernet*?
2. Explain how a cyclic redundancy check helps to ensure that data sent on a network is not corrupted.
3. Explain the concept of *packet switching* and how it differs from *circuit switching*.
4. State four items that are commonly found in a data packet.
5. Explain what is meant by *half-duplex data transmission*.

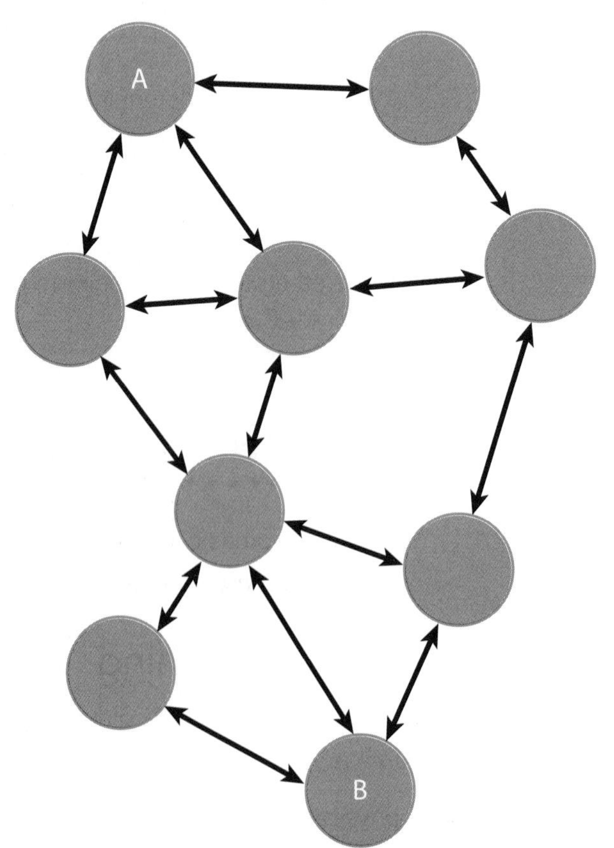

Figure 8.2 *Sending a message from A to B, using many routers*

Networks – security

Networks are inherently vulnerable to being accessed by the wrong people. By their very nature, they cover an extensive, sometimes immense, area and they have numerous access points. This means that there are plenty of potential ways in for snoopers and others who want to steal or damage data.

Hacking

There are endless arguments about the use of the term *hacking* and whether the term *cracking* is preferable but it does not really matter. The point is that most people understand that hacking is an attempt to get round computer security mechanisms.

The reasons why some people do this are various. They cover such motives as:

- **Theft:** Some cases of hacking are straightforward attempts to steal money or saleable information. This might involve attempts to contravene copyright laws in the theft of intellectual property.
  Often hacking involves attempts to defraud individuals or organisations.
- **Malice:** In order to do damage to some person or organisation with whom they have an actual or imagined grievance. Sometimes this involves making some political point.
- **Fun:** Some hackers break into computer systems just to prove that they can.
- **Ethical reasons:** Some hacking attempts are a genuine attempt to expose security weaknesses so that they can be fixed.

Whatever the reason, unauthorised access to a computer system is illegal in most countries and the penalties can be severe, often involving jail sentences.

Security weaknesses

Network managers try to keep their networks secure. After all, the survival of their organisations sometimes depends on it. They use various methods to maintain the safety and privacy of the data in their care but there are always vulnerabilities for hackers to exploit. Often the vulnerabilities are because of the careless behaviour of the people who work with the systems. The weakest aspect of many systems is the people who use it. The best security strategies can easily be defeated if the staff do not adhere to proper procedures.

Security policies

The objective of any network manager is to support the survival and success of the business by implementing and maintaining effective computer networks. This will include securing the network but it goes beyond that. A business needs to have in place security policies that drive the thinking and behaviour of all employees.

Security policies need to be simple so that they are well understood. Policies should state these basic points:

- **what:** what needs to be done
- **how:** how the policies are to be implemented
- **why:** the reasons for the policies
- **when:** the timing of actions such as backups and updates
- **who:** who does what.

If staff understand the basic security processes and why they are in place, they are more likely to adhere to them. Lack of clarity and understanding makes any security policy weak. If people do not know who is responsible for security procedures, then they will not be carried out.

Security policies need to be updated regularly. Bad guys change their tactics so security policies need to change too.

Example areas of a security policy

There are certain questions to ask when formulating any network security policy:

- What services are required for the business?
- Do employees need internet access to do their jobs?
- Do they need email? Can email be provided securely?
- Do users need access to the internal network? Is this dependent on their job function? How can this be secured?
- Access to which parts of the internal network are needed by each employee? How are they restricted to just the parts that they need?
- Do customers need to access your data via the internet?

For any network operation, the organisation needs to ask: 'Is it necessary for the operation of the business?'

The policy will normally cover the following areas:

Policy area	Explanation
Acceptable use	A position needs to be taken on the general use of computer equipment that is required for the business and is reasonable.
Passwords	Rules are needed regarding the nature of passwords and how often they should be changed. How are the rules enforced? Often users require more than one level of password checking. Passwords should be long enough and random enough not to be guessed. They also should include variations such as upper and lower case letters, numbers and special symbols.
Email	What may or may not be sent/received via email.
Web	Configuration of browsers and what categories of websites are allowed to be visited.
Mobile devices	What devices are allowed and how they are configured and supported.
Remote access	What can be accessed from outside the network and from what devices.
Internet	Rules for what is allowed in and out.
Wireless	How wireless access points are managed and secured, who is allowed to use them and under what circumstances.
Servers	What services are provided by the organisation's servers and under what circumstances.
Incident response plan	What to do if there is a security failure. Who is responsible for implementing the plan.

Network policies have to be fit for purpose, for example, it is dangerous to allow a junior employee on work experience to have unlimited access to the salary records of all other employees.

It is possible with database management systems to assign appropriate privileges to each user so that they can access only the data needed for their own job role.

Also, network operating systems can be fine-tuned to give each user access to certain programs and certain directories (see page 80).

Computing in context

ABC PLC is a large company that has thousands of employees. It has an extensive LAN with servers that store the company database.

The database contains industrial secrets as well as the personal data of its employees.

In order to safeguard the data, the networking team has introduced a number of rules. They include:

- all staff must use dual credentials for logging in. This means that they have two passwords
- all staff must change their passwords every month
- all passwords must contain upper and lower case characters plus numerals and special characters
- different passwords are to be used for different areas of functionality, for example the finance records require a different login from the personnel records
- members of staff have access only to functionality that relates to their jobs.

The managing director likes to look through the reports that are stored on the system. He has trouble remembering his password so he wants to have just one password that never changes. The network manager does not like this, but the managing director insists.

The managers of different departments often tell their staff their passwords so that they can do work when the managers are not there.

When technicians from outside are called in to fix problems, they are often given high-level passwords to access the system.

Many staff write their passwords on sticky notes and stick them to their computer screens.

Recently, members of staff were stopped on their way home and asked by a stranger what their passwords were. Amazingly some staff members gave them.

Questions

1. Describe some likely security incidents that might take place in ABC PLC.
2. What should the network manager do about some of these weaknesses?

Malware

Malware is malicious software. It comes in many forms. It is software that is installed on a computer system with the intention to cause damage or to steal information.

Examples of malware

Malware	Description
Viruses	A computer program, often hidden in another program. It replicates itself and usually causes some sort of damage such as deleting files.
Worms	Another form of self-replicating malware that does not necessarily need to embed itself in another program. It often spreads through networks.
Trojan horses	A malicious program that the user is tricked into installing under the pretence of it being useful.
Ransomware	Malware that either interferes with the user's operation of a computer or threatens to do so unless a sum of money (ransom) is paid. Some types encrypt the contents of the computer's storage; others are just empty threats to scare the user into payment.
Spyware	Software that gathers information about a user or organisation and sends it to the originator. This includes programs such as key-loggers that record and/or send all the user's keystrokes, thereby possibly obtaining passwords.
Rootkits	Malicious software that modifies the host operating system to avoid detection.
Back doors	An approach whereby the malware opens an access channel to outsiders that can bypass normal security checks.

Protecting against malware

Any good network policy will have strategies in place to avoid damage caused by malware.

- At the very least there will be anti-malware software in place, which can examine incoming network traffic and also perform periodic scans. New malware is being produced all the time, so this software must be regularly updated.
- Make sure that the ISP (internet service provider) has good awareness of malware issues and carries out scans of traffic itself. Online email providers such as Yahoo and Gmail implement scans, thereby adding an extra layer of vigilance.

Extension Activity

Research a variety of utilities that claim to clean malware from a computer or prevent it gaining access in the first place.

1. List which ones are free and which require some payment.
2. Look at reviews to find what other people think of them. Remember, some malware 'cures' are in fact malware in disguise!
3. Find out why Linux users are much less likely to be troubled with malware than Windows users.

- Perform regular operating system updates. Some, such as Windows®, automatically update themselves from time to time. Part of this process is to install the latest fixes for vulnerabilities that have been discovered.
- Email attachments should be treated with caution. Malware can be passed into a network by attached executable files as well as by many seemingly innocuous documents, especially if they contain macros. Rendering of images should be turned off as malware can be embedded in image files.
- Care should be taken opening emails from unknown senders.
- Peer-to-peer file sharing (see page 34) is another common source of malware. It should be subject to scans just like any other incoming file.
- Browsers should be kept up to date. Browsers often have security weaknesses and they are regularly updated to deal with these. Some browsers have inbuilt capability to identify phishing and other suspect sites.
- Cell phones also need protection and care to be taken just as with more conventional networks and computers. New malware is being produced for mobile devices.
- Internet messaging can bring in malware. It should not fire up automatically when the computer is switched on.
- Websites that are not familiar should be treated with caution. If in doubt, check their reputation and ownership as well as many statistics using tools such as who.is, as shown in Figure 9.1.
- Finally, to guard against any number of different threats, all data should be backed up regularly, preferably off-site.

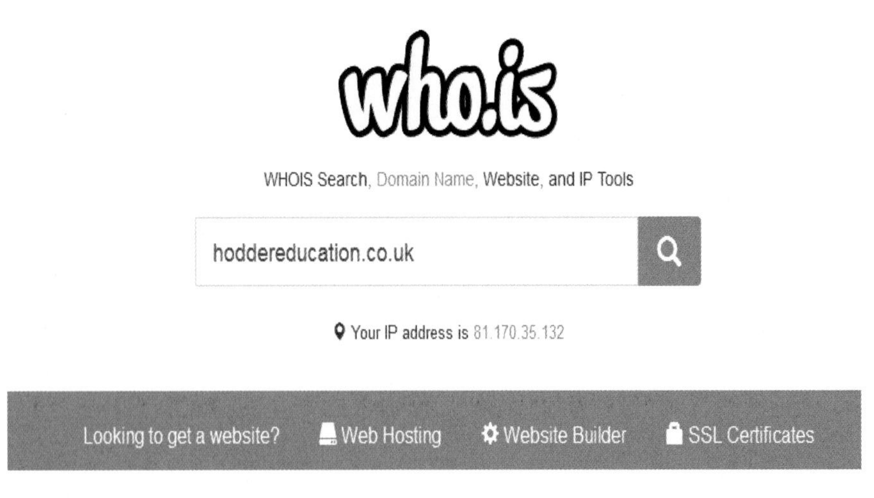

Figure 9.1 *Check unfamiliar sites*

Common hacking strategies

Most hacking involves getting hold of a password. Often the easiest way is simply to ask! People are very trusting and will often give up a password to anyone who asks for it, especially if that person seems to have a plausible reason to request it such as claiming to be a repair technician.

Brute-force attacks use software to try every possible combination of letters, numbers and characters until the correct one is found. Short passwords can be determined quite quickly but as the length of the password increases, the time taken to discover it by this trial-and-error method increases exponentially.

Another common technique is to try the common passwords that lots of people use, such as: password, 12345, letmein or even slightly altered versions such as p@$$word. Users' personal details can lead to their passwords if they are known, such as their children's or pets' names or birthdays. The easier a password is to remember, the easier it is to crack. That is why many password-requiring installations insist on passwords using upper and lower case letters, numbers and special characters.

Password strength checkers are commonly used to assess passwords of users, as shown in Figures 9.2 and 9.3.

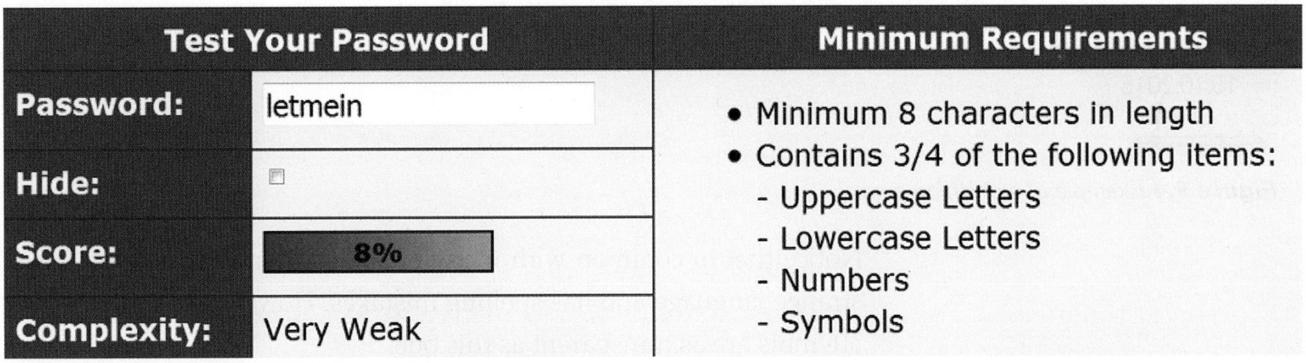

Test Your Password		Minimum Requirements
Password:	letmein	• Minimum 8 characters in length • Contains 3/4 of the following items: - Uppercase Letters - Lowercase Letters - Numbers - Symbols
Hide:		
Score:	8%	
Complexity:	Very Weak	

Figure 9.2 *This password is weak and would be easy to crack*

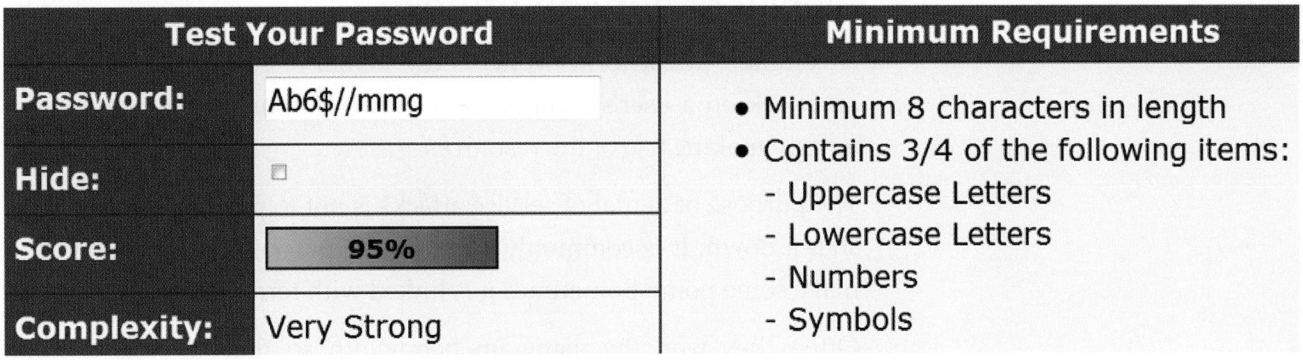

Test Your Password		Minimum Requirements
Password:	Ab6$//mmg	• Minimum 8 characters in length • Contains 3/4 of the following items: - Uppercase Letters - Lowercase Letters - Numbers - Symbols
Hide:		
Score:	95%	
Complexity:	Very Strong	

Figure 9.3 *This password is very strong and would be more difficult to crack*

Phishing

Phishing is a very common strategy for obtaining sensitive information. If you look in your email spam folder you are almost certain to find some examples of emails pretending to be from a bank or ebay or some other well-known site, pretending to need your credentials to fix some invented problem. Figure 9.4 is a fictional example of a phishing email.

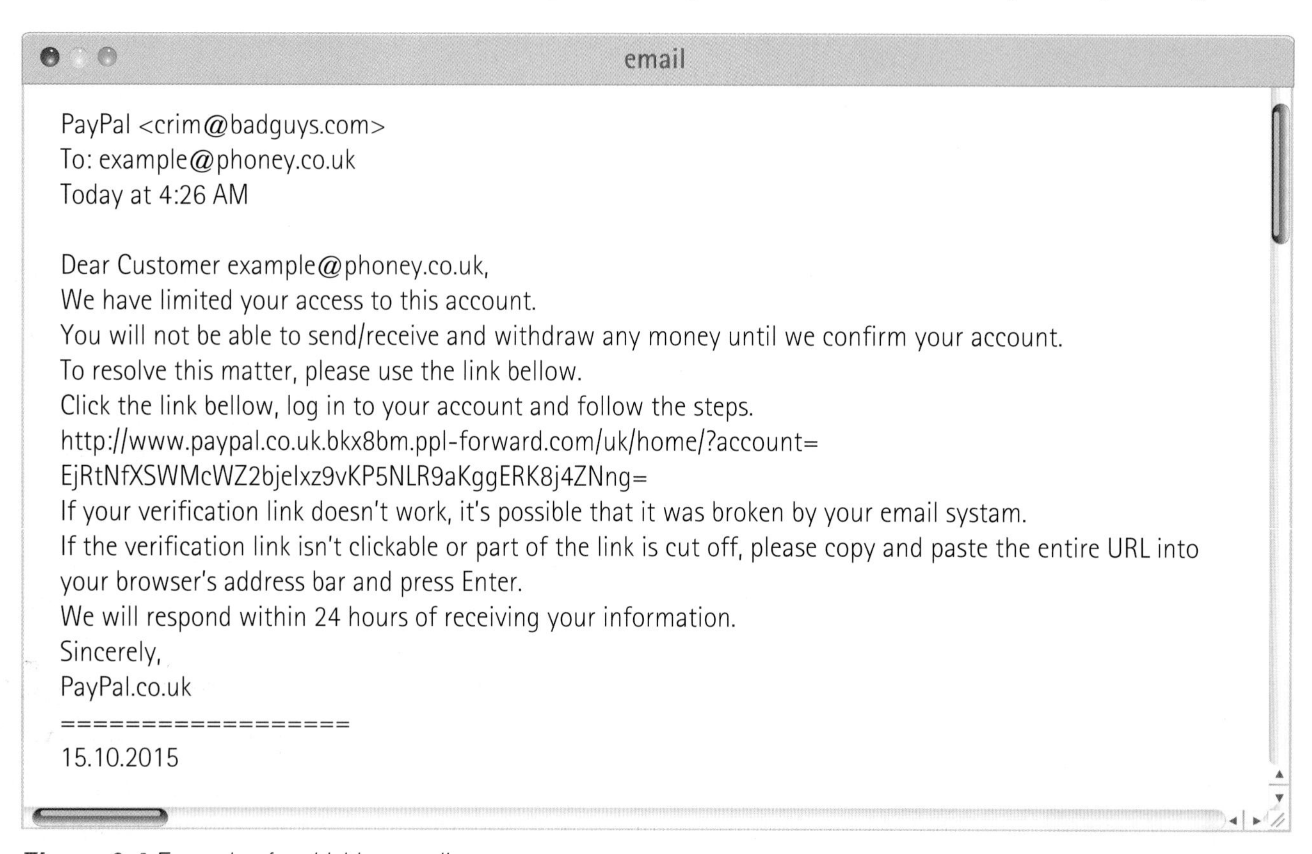

email

PayPal <crim@badguys.com>
To: example@phoney.co.uk
Today at 4:26 AM

Dear Customer example@phoney.co.uk,
We have limited your access to this account.
You will not be able to send/receive and withdraw any money until we confirm your account.
To resolve this matter, please use the link bellow.
Click the link bellow, log in to your account and follow the steps.
http://www.paypal.co.uk.bkx8bm.ppl-forward.com/uk/home/?account=
EjRtNfXSWMcWZ2bjelxz9vKP5NLR9aKggERK8j4ZNng=
If your verification link doesn't work, it's possible that it was broken by your email systam.
If the verification link isn't clickable or part of the link is cut off, please copy and paste the entire URL into your browser's address bar and press Enter.
We will respond within 24 hours of receiving your information.
Sincerely,
PayPal.co.uk
==================
15.10.2015

Figure 9.4 *Example of a phishing email*

Notice that in common with many phishing attempts, the email uses strange language and has spelling mistakes. However not all phishing attempts are as transparent as this one.

Denial of service attacks

A common threat to networks is the denial of service attack. This is an attack on a user's computers or network in an attempt to prevent anyone making use of the resources.

The purpose of denial of service attacks is not to penetrate a site but to shut it down. It is commonly done for the purposes of extortion or to make some point. Sometimes it is linked with terrorism.

Often they work by using up bandwidth so that services become unobtainable.

Sometimes a computationally intensive task is given to the target computers thereby taking up their processing power for a long time.

Another approach is to infect many innocent computers with malware that makes them into 'zombie computers' that simultaneously flood a website with too many requests for it to handle.

Routers can get damaged in these attacks and their routing tables disrupted.

Denial of service attacks are often perpetrated by individual vandals although they could be used as a form of cyber warfare.

It is difficult to counter denial of service attacks although traceback techniques can sometimes help in confirming the perpetrators of an attack once it has happened.

Data interception

Networks send data. Data can be intercepted *en route*. This can be done in a number of ways.

Packet-sniffing software examines data packets and checks them against predetermined parameters. A network switch can be configured to send all data that passes through it to a particular IP address where it can be examined.

Packet sniffing is often used legitimately by organisations in order to analyse network trends such as which addresses receive how much traffic. It is also sometimes used in order to detect intrusion attempts. Wireless LANs can use special WiFi adapters to sniff data from specific channels.

Wireless communications are vulnerable to data interception by malicious individuals who can sniff the packets of data quite easily as they are not constrained by physical cables. Intruders can access wireless signals from over 300 metres away so they can easily escape detection.

The best way to defeat data interception is to use some form of strong encryption. Wireless transmissions should make use of the WPA (WiFi protected access) protocol at least, where the transmissions are encrypted using keys of at least 128 bits, often applied to each packet and generated afresh for each packet. At least if such strong encryption is used, any intercepted data should be unintelligible.

SQL injection

Many database servers store huge enterprise-wide databases in order to underpin their businesses. Very often, the databases are created and maintained by a DBMS (database management system), which is controlled using SQL (structured query language) code. SQL can be used to perform most database operations and this includes operations that are not intended by the database owners. Fake SQL operations can be produced by a technique called *SQL injection*.

SQL statements often operate on data input into fields on online forms, so input data can be passed to the processing SQL scripts. This data can itself be SQL code, thereby causing the scripts to behave in a totally different way from how they were intended to.

Example

A simple example is the following SQL statement on a server script to retrieve user details:

```
txtSQL = "SELECT * FROM Users WHERE UserId
= " + txtUserId;
```

The intention of this statement is to retrieve all the data (* is a wildcard that means 'everything') from a table called 'Users' where the user ID is data that was input onto an enquiry form. It is put into the variable `txtUserId` and added to the SQL statement.

So, if a user enters data into a web form such as '150' the SQL will retrieve everything about user 150.

If a user enters `150 OR 1=1`, the server interprets this into an SQL statement like this:

```
SELECT * FROM Users WHERE UserId = 105 OR 1=1
```

Now, `1=1` is TRUE, so the SQL will retrieve everything from everyone.

Question

3 Describe how a validation check could be applied to avoid the SQL injection 1=1 technique.

SQL injection can be more sophisticated than this and exploit a range of vulnerabilities.

A range of validation techniques can be used to filter out 'clever' data entries.

Penetration testing

In order to test the security of a network, a penetration test may be carried out in order to mimic a possible attack. This is used as part of a security audit. Typically, it tries out a variety of possible attacks on a network or system and determines whether these attacks are likely to succeed. It also tests the ability of the network and its staff to detect and counteract such threats.

Penetration tests normally involve:

- looking for a possible vulnerability
- setting up an attack
- carrying out the attack
- testing the ability to recover any compromised data after the attack.

There are software tools to automate this process.

Firewalls

Key Term

Firewall Software that limits access to and from a computer system.

Firewalls consist of software and/or hardware placed between one network or node and another in order to control inbound and outbound traffic. Firewalls make use of predetermined rules in order to exert control over the flow of data.

The name *firewall* derives from the old practice of erecting barriers between buildings to prevent the spread of fires. Typically, computer firewalls are used as protective barriers between one's own network and the internet, where traffic can be unpredictable and possibly unsafe. Firewalls can be installed in servers, client computers or routers, depending on where the control is required.

Firewalls are the principal defence against Denial of Service (DoS) attacks. These are when a user or group of users saturate the service with requests in order to make the service unavailable to others. The intention can be to blackmail the organisation or to make a political point.

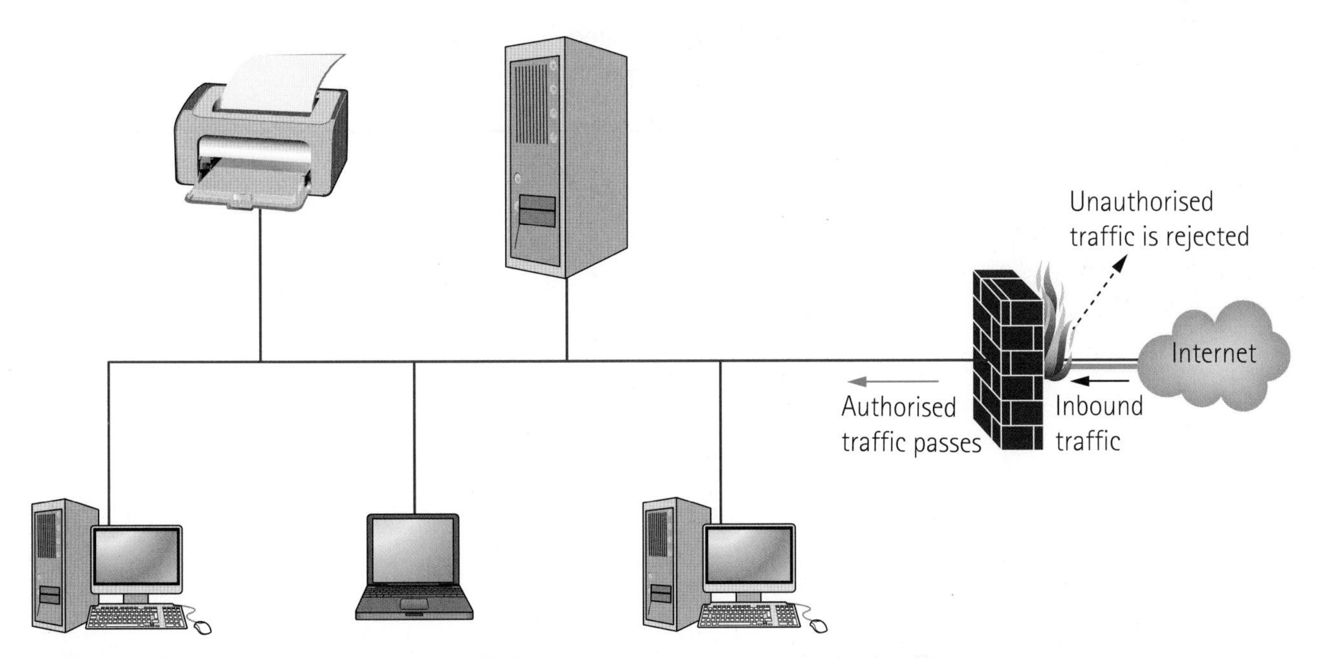

Figure 9.5 *A firewall allows authorised traffic but denies access to unauthorised traffic.*

Packet-filter firewalls inspect each data packet and assess it for certain characteristics that, if not met, result in the packet being 'dropped' and not allowed through.

Firewalls can also make decisions based on the originating IP address of a message or the protocol used, which can be useful to reject, for example spam email messages.

Questions

4 What is the purpose of a firewall?

5 (a) What is the role of SQL used by an online vendor?

(b) How can SQL be exploited by a criminal to extract sensitive data?

6 What is the meaning of the term *malware*?

7 What is a *Trojan horse*?

8 Give two precautions that a network manager can take against dishonest employees stealing company data.

9 Assess the following passwords for strength. Give reasons in each case.

(a) 3gr8kids

(b) 12november

(c) secret

(d) secret 2015

(e) 123

(f) manchesterunited

(g) 45%^vGGtT**

10 The internet

The nature of the internet

The internet is the biggest network of all; it is a network of networks. Each participating network can be very different. The standards adopted by the internet have made it possible for very diverse installations to communicate with each other. As we have seen (on page 49), the family of protocols called TCP/IP underpin the workings of the internet.

The internet is an infrastructure. That is, it is a facility for sending data between computers. Numerous applications 'sit' on this infrastructure and make it useful for us. Examples of services that run on the internet are the worldwide web and email.

A typical user on the internet uses a computer of some sort as a client in order to access data from a server. Clients can also be hardware or software. A hardware client can be any of a wide variety of microprocessor-controlled devices such as a desktop or laptop computer, a tablet or a mobile phone. All sorts of automated devices also connect to the internet in order to obtain 'services' from a server somewhere, for example smart devices in the home such as a smart television or a burglar alarm connect to servers over the internet.

Note

The internet is not the same as the worldwide web, which is the collection of billions of web pages that are hosted on servers connected to the internet.

Clients can also be software, for example a web browser is client software and so is an email program. Many apps on phones and tablets such as those that look up rail timetables are examples of client software. Other common examples are chat applications, ebook readers and online learning resources such as Hodder's Dynamic Learning (see Figure 10.1).

Likewise, the word *server* can refer to an item of hardware or the software residing on it that responds to client requests.

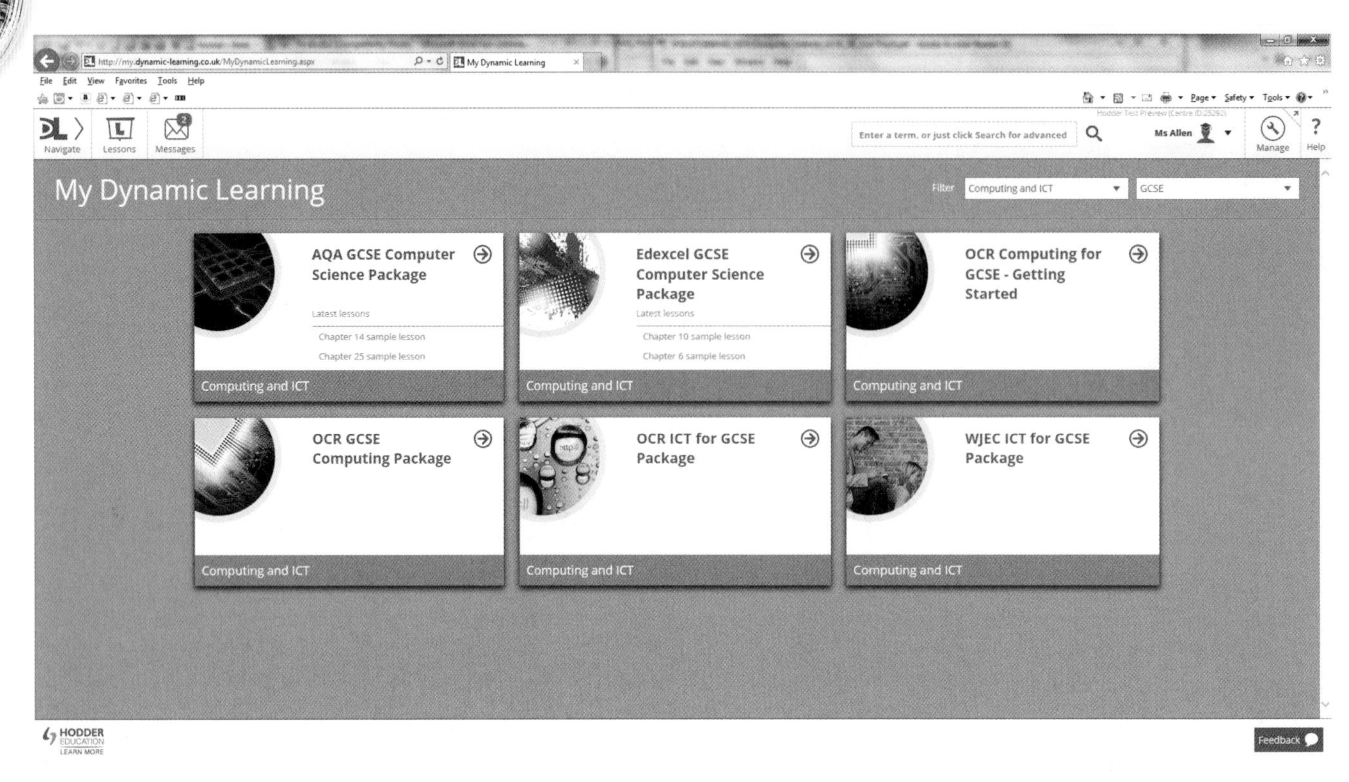

Figure 10.1 *Hodder's Dynamic Learning*

DNS

DNS stands for domain name system or sometimes domain name server, depending whether you are talking about the overall facility or one of the computers used to implement the system.

As we have seen on page 45, computers and other resources on a TCP/IP network are identified by an IP address such as 69.172.201.167. This is hard to remember for most people, so servers are set up to store these IP addresses alongside an easier-to-remember domain name such as might be used as a uniform resource locator (URL). A domain name is the name given to a set of web pages such as hodder.co.uk. Many files and other resources may be stored under the one domain name, for example:

www.hodder.co.uk/Books/detail.page?isbn=9781473621176

www.hodder.co.uk/newsletters.page

If we run a traceroute program on a domain name, we can see its IP address along with the IP addresses of the routers passed through to reach it from our own IP address.

Figure 10.2 Mobile apps

Task

Find where the traceroute program is on your computer or try out an online traceroute service such as http://ping.eu/traceroute/.

Every domain name ends with a suffix that indicates which top-level domain it belongs to, such as:

- **gov:** government agencies
- **org:** non-profit organisations
- **com:** commercial businesses
- **uk:** based in the United Kingdom.

Task

Find out the top-level domains of some of the websites that you have recently visited.

The domain name system is its own network. If the server that you connect to when you have entered a domain name does not know the particular domain you requested, it will forward the request to another and so on until the name is found (or not).

When you type in a domain name or the complete reference for a resource into the URL box in a browser, the name is forwarded to a domain name server.

Host

A host is a computer that stores a particular resource, so the computer that stores the newsletters at the URL:
www.hodder.co.uk/newsletters.page
is hodder.co.uk, which is, of course, actually found by looking up its corresponding IP address on a DNS server.

The domain name system is hierarchical, which means that the name of a resource is built up from several layers of domains, each name separated from the next by a dot.

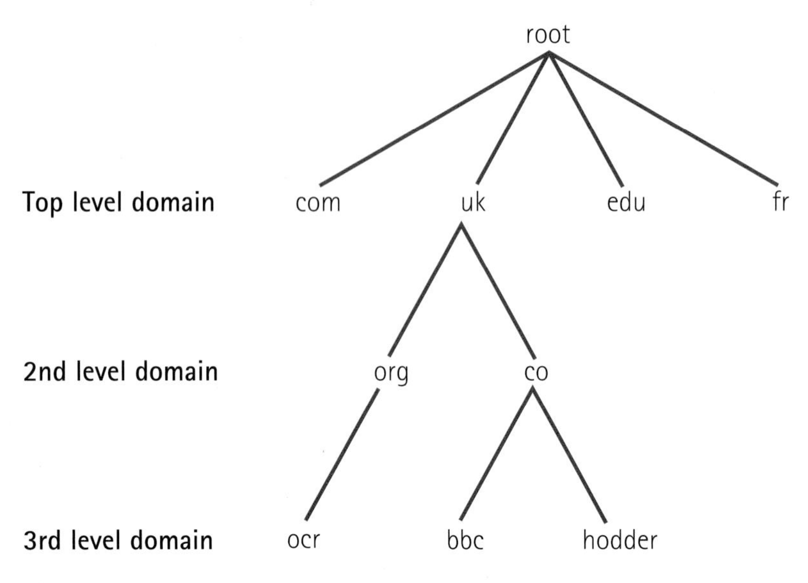

Figure 10.3 *A hierarchical naming system*

In the Figure 10.3 example, you can build a full URL by working down through the domains and creating the full URL reference by working from right to left.

Question

1 Construct a hierarchical diagram to show how the following URLs form part of a naming system:
   (a) yahoo.com
   (b) bbc.co.uk
   (c) hodder.co.uk
   (d) microsoft.com

Key Points

- The internet is an infrastructure.
- The internet hosts a wide variety of services.
- Many phone and other apps work through the internet.
- Resources on the internet are given domain names to make them easy to remember.
- Domain names are translated into IP addresses by domain name servers.

The cloud

Increasingly, we are all using the 'cloud' for our computing needs. That is 'we' as individuals and also organisations, large and small.

The *cloud* is a term that denotes the remote provision of storage and increasingly software resources that we can access from our own devices. In physical terms, it refers to servers and data centres that can be anywhere in the world and are connected to the internet.

The point is that we as users, do not normally care where the servers are (although perhaps we ought to, given certain laws that are being passed allowing access to locally stored data by the security organisations of some countries).

Cloud services have certain great benefits.

- There is no need to update application software if what you use is remotely provided.
- There is no need to maintain your own network system to store your data.
- There is no or reduced need for an organisation to employ expensive network managers and other technical staff.
- Backup is not a worry because the service provider takes care of this.
- It becomes easy to share files with colleagues anywhere in the world.

However, there are some drawbacks such as that we:

- entrust our data, which may be sensitive to an outsider
- trust that our data will be stored safely
- trust that the service will always be available when we need it.

Extension Activity

Research the term *PaaS (platform as a service).*

1. Find out what is provided by a typical PaaS provider.
2. To what extent would such a service benefit your school or college?

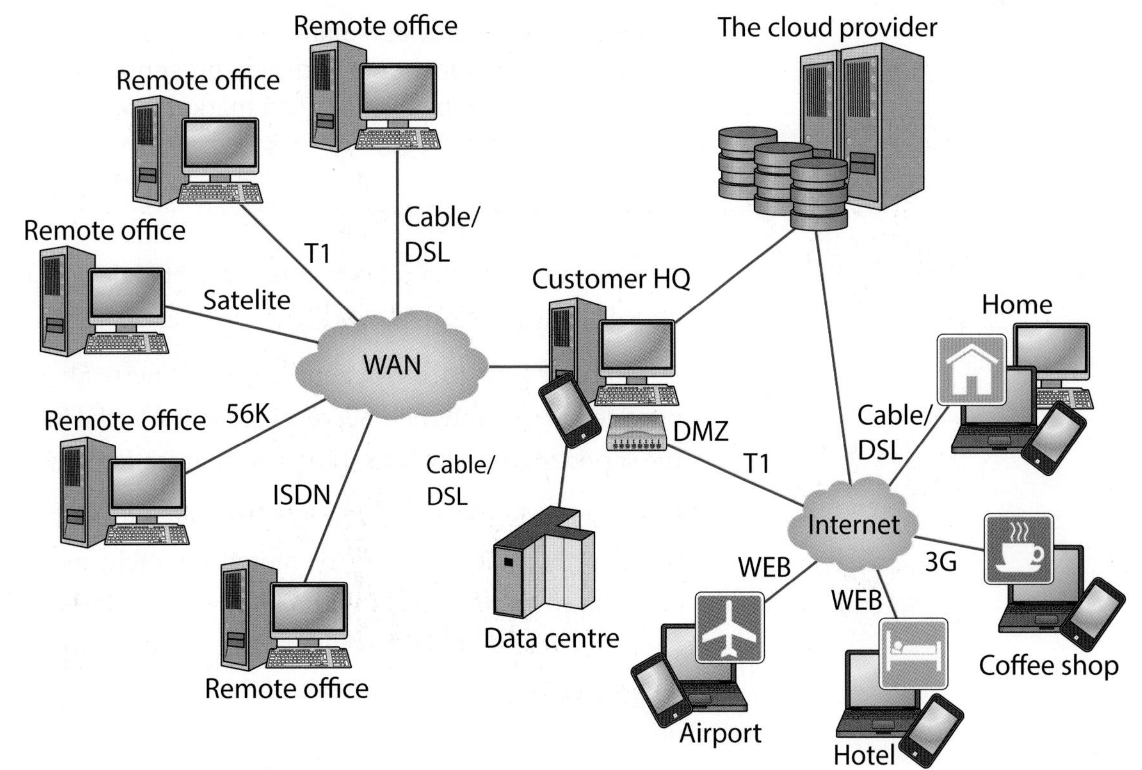

Figure 10.4 *Cloud computing*

Note

It is a big advantage if you use cloud services in your computer science (and other) exam studies.

- There is no worry about losing work.
- You can work on your studies at school, college, at home or in a library.
- A drawback is that some schools do not allow access to cloud services.

Some cloud services such as Dropbox™ will allow you to work locally but when you save your work, it is copied to the cloud. The advantage of this is that there is no worry about losing work in the unlikely event that you cannot access the provider; you have a copy on your own computer as well as stored remotely. Also, if you accidentally delete an important file, the provider will normally keep several previous copies that you can get back.

Computing in context

This book has been produced with the help of various cloud services.

- The text was written in numerous locations and was stored remotely.
- The authors collaborated remotely as needed.
- Editors and reviewers were brought in as needed to give their opinions.

Cloud software provides many standard applications such as word processing, spreadsheets and slide presentations. These are all more or less compatible with the market leaders.

Virtual networks

A virtual network is a collection of connected devices that do not make up a discrete physical network.

A common way to implement a virtual network is to use services provided on the internet. Servers connected to the internet can provide the services normally located on an organisation's own hardware.

Some services are not really feasible on a virtual network, such as printing, but data files can be stored remotely, as can software. The advantages are exactly as with cloud services but care must be taken (as with cloud services) to ensure that an organisation's data is secure. Given that the physical location of the data is theoretically available to others who are connected to the physical infrastructure, much use is made of privacy controls such as strong encryption.

Key Points

- Cloud computing is the remote provision of data storage and often software too.
- Cloud computing has many advantages over local computing.
- Virtual networks are a private sub-part of a public network such as the internet.
- Cloud computing and virtual networks provide many convenience and cost benefits, although care has to be taken with security and availability issues.

Questions

2 What is a *domain* on the internet?
3 What is a *top-level domain*?
4 What is a Domain Name Server used for?
5 Give two definitions of the term *client* in the context of the internet.
6 Give two advantages to a student of using cloud services.

Software – an overview

What is software?

In 1937, Alan Turing described an imaginary device that could carry out any computable task as long as it was supplied with instructions. Given that no such device existed at that time, this was a big leap of the imagination. It was a big step in the history of computing because it showed that it was possible for a single machine to perform various tasks as long as it was able to respond to instructions. The instructions could be changed in order to perform different tasks.

This required the use of an algorithm in order to give the instructions. People had been using algorithms for years to solve mathematical problems, such as long division or working out averages, and to perform physical tasks, such as making a meal or building a house. But this time it was shown that a machine could follow an algorithm too. Also, a single machine could perform a variety of tasks by being given different algorithms.

Modern computers evolved from Turing's idea and now, of course, we have electronic machines that can store a program in primary memory (the RAM) having loaded it from a secondary storage device such as a hard disk (see Chapter 2).

A set of instructions to perform a particular task or set of tasks is called a *program* and in general, programs are known as software, to distinguish them from the hardware on which they run.

Computers have proved so useful, indeed fundamental to modern life, that a huge range of software has been produced and continues to be produced. The popularity of mobile devices has increased the demand for software yet further. It does not stop there either. More and more devices are being developed that contain embedded systems (see page 14) and these need software too.

Key Term

Platform A combination of hardware and operating system that supports the running of particular applications.

Computing in context

There is a huge demand for people with suitable technical and business skills to develop new apps for the Android ™platform, Mac iOS and whatever **platforms** will appear next. This represents a great opportunity for those with these skills or the willingness to develop them.

It is a particular success story in the UK, with much work going on to develop embedded systems as well as larger scale enterprise computer systems; for example there is a cluster of firms and universities in Bristol and the West Country where much pioneering work on embedded systems is taking place.

Students taking Computer Science courses now have an unparalleled chance to develop the skills that will enable them to pursue successful, lucrative and fun careers in some of the most dynamic economies of the world. You can be part of a continuing success story in all sorts of locations.

Task

Do an online search for such terms as 'app development jobs' and 'embedded system jobs' and see just how numerous, varied and lucrative the opportunities are.

Much of what you are doing right now in your GCSE studies is already in demand. Look at this extract from a recent advertisement:

We have job vacancies for software engineers with experience in embedded Linux®. The following skills and experience are particularly valued:

- familiarity with the Linux kernel and basic concepts such as scheduling
- familiarity with Linux device drivers, in development and/or debugging
- familiarity with other key Linux concepts and sub-systems such as the TCP/IP network stack, inter-process communication, memory management
- knowledge of POSIX and Linux system calls and common libraries (such as threads)
- debugging and fixing common program errors from, for example, those that cause segmentation faults
- kernel-level debugging
- experience in identifying, fixing and preventing resource problems such as memory leaks, resource or I/O contention, and so on.

Key Terms

Application Software designed to carry out a useful real-world task.

Utility A single-purpose program normally used in the maintenance of computer systems.

Program A self-contained set of instructions that can be stored and used by the processor.

Software The general term for computer programs.

Programming language A means of writing programs in a form that can be passed to a computer to process.

Instructions A set of commands that a processor can recognise and act upon.

Software is of course immensely diverse but there are two major categories that help to make some sense of it all. They are **applications**, **utilities** and system software.

System software is the software that makes the computer hardware easily available to users and applications. Applications are what users buy the computers for; they are the **programs** that are task-oriented, they deal with real-world issues, whereas systems software looks inwards at the machine.

The people who write computer **software** are called *programmers* and they normally follow the plans of analysts or other developers. Some programmers design the software themselves, usually in consultation with the intended users. Programmers use a variety of **programming languages** in order to set down the **instructions** that the computer will run. These are written in either high- or low-level languages depending on the needs of the particular project (see page 179).

Computing in context

The British catering company J. Lyons & Co. was the first company to use a computer for commercial purposes. The company contributed £3000 (approximately equivalent to £80 000 in today's money) to a team at Cambridge University to help them develop their EDSAC (Electronic Delay Storage Automatic Calculator). They then constructed their own computer based on EDSAC and called it LEO – Lyons Electronic Office. This was ready in 1951 and was used to produce valuations of production runs. Later it was also used for payroll and inventory applications.

Programmers wrote applications in assembly language and also a high-level language called CLEO (Clear Language for Expressing Orders).

By 1961, Lyons had improved its LEO computers and developed a multi-tasking operating system for them.

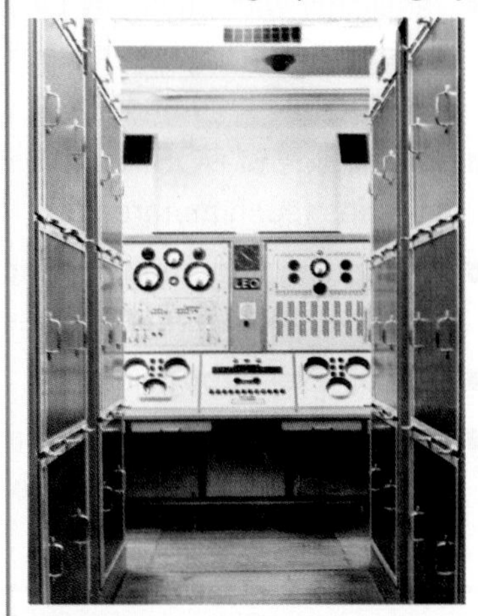

Figure 11.1 *LEO1*

Extension Activity

Some operating systems come with applications provided.

Find out what applications come bundled with:

1. the latest version of Windows®
2. any Debian Linux distribution.

Comment on any advantages or disadvantages of relying on bundled software for everyday applications.

Procurement of software

Individuals and organisations have to make decisions about what sort of software they need and where to get it from. This can be a trivial decision if you are looking at apps for your phone. You will probably go to Google™ Play Store or the Apple App Store.

Choosing a phone app is not usually a big decision because there is just one individual involved and quite often it is only required to do a simple one-off job. Getting software online from one of these stores is also a fairly safe way to get software because it is supplied, if not written by, either Google or Apple and so is unlikely to contain malware.

In contrast, choosing software for a whole organisation is a big task that normally involves long negotiations with suppliers and visiting reference sites to see how the software works in real life.

Standard applications are needed by everyone, both in their workplace and also as private individuals. Most users need word-processing and spreadsheet software along with presentation and other packages. These can be bought 'off the shelf'. This means that they are ready made and can be obtained immediately. They are also probably well tested and reliable, with plenty of advice online about how the user can get the best out of them. Off-the-shelf software has to be paid for and this is sometimes an issue, especially for individuals with limited funds.

Businesses often have very specific requirements and so need custom-made software. Custom-made software is often an adaptation of a big, expensive system that has already been developed for others. Obtaining this can be a lengthy process and with only a few customers, there is a greater chance that there will still be some bugs in it although the contract will normally cover bug fixes for a period of time.

Software repositories

Many organisations maintain servers where free or open source (OSS) software is available for download. A good example of this is in the case of Debian versions of Linux. Package management software can be used in order to download all the files need for say, a word processor, and also to update it when necessary.

Package managers are particularly desirable because they will download and update software from a source that is normally reliably malware-free. If you are running such a version of Linux, you probably will not need any anti-virus software.

Questions ?

1. What is a *computer program*?
2. Explain the difference between an application and system software.
3. Explain what a *software repository* is.
4. Explain the advantages of obtaining software from an online repository.
5. State two actions that are carried out by a package management utility.

Systems software

The early pioneers in computing worked directly with the hardware, using switches and patch leads to connect items of hardware in order to program the computer (see Chapter 2). This made programming very specialised, difficult and extremely slow. These early computers, and many that followed, were only able to run one program at a time. Data was provided for the computer each time it ran the program using punched cards or paper tape.

Operating system

In time, operating systems were developed to enable the programmers to ignore the hardware and concentrate their efforts on developing programs to meet the customer's needs.

Operating systems are collections of programs that tell the hardware what to do. They are necessary on most computer systems, other than simple self-booting systems devoted to performing a single task. They are found in nearly all computing devices, from video game consoles to mobile phones and devices to large data servers and super computers such as those used by NASA and the Met Office.

The operating system looks after and oversees such things as:

- managing the computer hardware and peripherals
- managing programs installed and being run
- managing data transfer between memory locations, the CPU and secondary storage
- providing the interface between the hardware and the applications
- providing an interface between the computer and user, and managing the video display on screen
- managing security and organising data so that it is not overwritten
- providing a file system for the storage and retrieval of files.

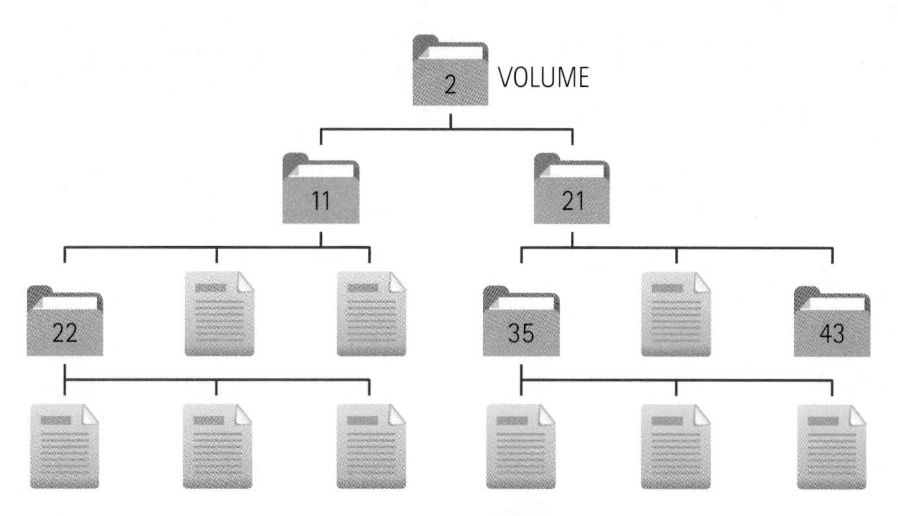

Figure 12.1 *A hierarchical files system*

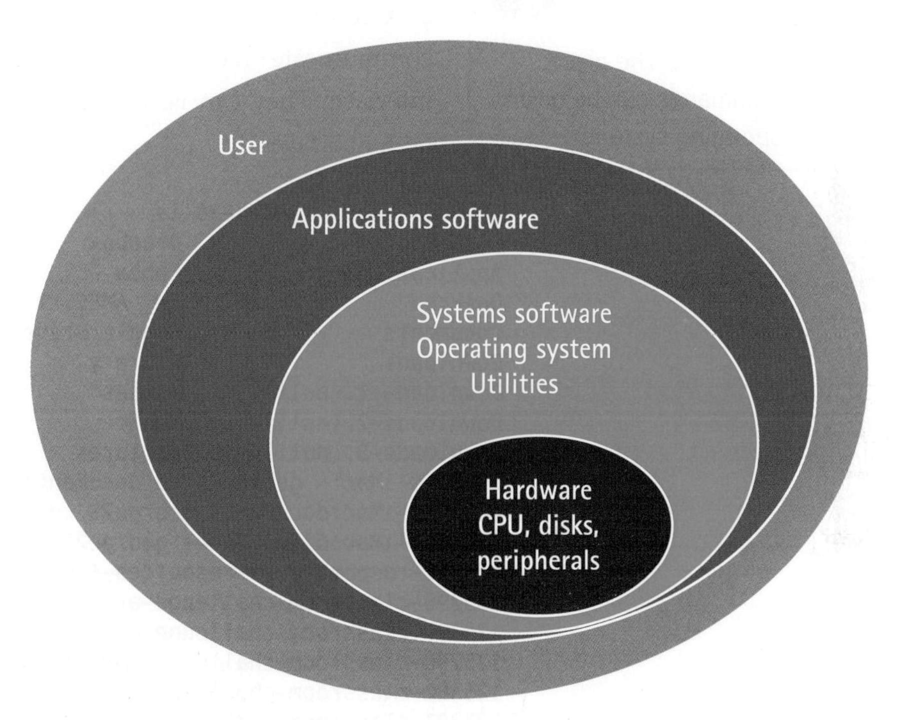

Figure 12.2 *The operating system is the interface between the hardware and the user and applications*

Applications

Kernel

CPU | Memory | Devices

Figure 12.3 *The operating system kernel connects applications to the hardware*

Operating systems are developed in layers, with each layer interfacing with the one above it and the one below it. At the heart of all operating systems is the kernel. The kernel deals with the low-level hardware operations. Any application that needs to run on a computer must interface with the operating system kernel in order to operate the hardware. This ensures applications do not issue hardware commands directly and helps to minimise the possibility of the application causing problems with the hardware and basic memory operations.

User interface

The user interface provides a means of communication between the user and the operating system. The user-interface layer is above the kernel so one operating system kernel can provide a range of user interfaces. Linux, for example, is technically the kernel for an operating system and various user interfaces can be used with the Linux kernel without affecting the rest of the set up for the operating system.

Command line

Key Term

Command line The place where commands can be given to the operating system.

Most operating systems will allow the user to type commands directly at a command prompt. Typically network technicians will prefer to communicate with the operating system using a **command-line** interface. They can issue single, powerful commands to manage the system efficiently.

```
GEORGEs-iMac:~ george2$ ls
Accellion              Dropbox             Public
Applications           Ephox               hello.sh
Desktop                FW_ AMEC.rtfd       mysql
Documents              Google Drive        records.txt
Downloads              Library             scores.txt
Downloads-1.(null)     Movies              weightwatch.csv
Downloads-2.(null)     Music               weightwatch.txt
Downloads-3.(null)     Pictures            words.txt
GEORGEs-iMac:~ george2$ cd documents
GEORGEs-iMac:documents george2$ cd piresources
GEORGEs-iMac:piresources george2$ ls
125292-raspberry-pi-resources-link.pdf
125296-classroom-challenge-architecture-learner-sheet.pdf
125297-classroom-challenge-architecture-teacher-sheet.pdf
125299-classroom-challenge-connecting-to-a-network-learner-sheet.pdf
125300-classroom-challenge-connecting-to-a-network-teacher-sheet.pdf
125301-classroom-challenge-simple-animation-learner-sheet.pdf
125303-classroom-challenge-simple-animation-teacher-sheet.pdf
GEORGEs-iMac:piresources george2$
```

Figure 12.4 *Unix commands on an Apple Mac; the commands used are ls (list) and cd (change directory)*

For commonly used sequences of commands, network technicians will collect these sequences up into batch files or shell scripts so that single commands can cause multiple actions.

Extension Activity

Research command line instructions for an operating system that you can access and explore some of the commands. If you do not have access to the command line then there are applications that simulate the UNIX/LINUX environments on the internet, for example Patrice Bellard's Linux simulator (http://bellard.org/jslinux/).

This simple shell script, called hello.sh, asks for a name then says: hello, 'name', nice to meet you.

```
#!/bin/sh
printf "What is your name? -> "
read NAME
echo "Hello, $NAME, nice to meet you"
```

```
Last login: Mon Jan 18 12:02:48 on ttys000
GEORGEs-iMac:~ george2$ ./hello.sh
What is your name? -> Fred
Hello, Fred, nice to meet you
GEORGEs-iMac:~ george2$
```

Figure 12.5 *Shell script running*

Graphical user interface (GUI)

Most personal computers and devices will use a graphical user interface with small icons (pictures) that represent the applications and actions that can be performed. The use of icons reduces the need to learn commands and is particularly suited to touchscreen devices such as mobile phones and tablet computers. The use of icons, however, provides limited scope for customisation of the actions that can be performed.

Figure 12.6 *The graphical user interface on a Mac OS X operating system*

Smartphones are particularly suited to the graphical user interface with icons.

Figure 12.7 *A smartphone showing its graphical user interface*

Voice input

Voice recognition technology has improved significantly in recent years and many mobile devices provide voice input facilities able to decipher simple commands and provide a suitable response. These voice-recognition interfaces are able to answer such questions as 'where is the nearest post office?', take dictated notes or record events in a diary. Call centres also commonly use voice-recognition interfaces, where spoken responses to specific questions can be successfully interpreted by the computer system. Typically these systems require yes or no responses, or numeric responses, but are now capable of dealing with increasingly more complex ones, including names and addresses.

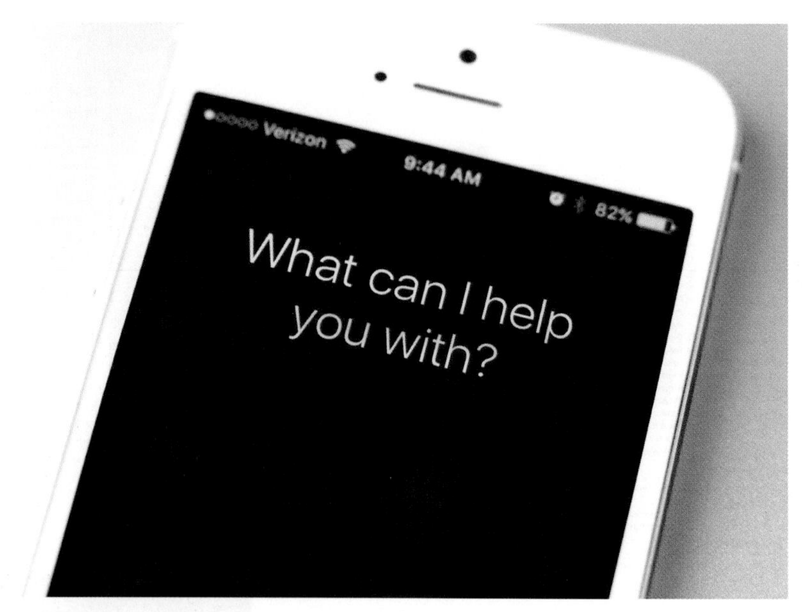

Figure 12.8 *Voice input on a mobile phone*

Key Point

- Operating systems:
  - help to control the hardware
  - provide facilities for other software to run
  - manage file handling
  - provide a user interface
  - manage security
  - manage memory.

Computing in context

In 1956, the Prime Minister, Harold Macmillan, introduced Premium Bonds as an incentive for people to save. Each Premium Bond, then as now, is entered into a prize draw each month. Bonds are selected at random using the output from a computer known affectionately as ERNIE (Electronic Random Number Indicator Equipment). The numbers are genuinely random, unlike the common random functions available in programming languages and most applications.

The first ERNIE was invented by one of the original Bletchley Park code breakers, basing it on the first electronic computer, Colossus, which was used in the Second World War code-breaking efforts. There have been four generations of ERNIEs, making use of advances in computer technology so that currently the draw takes place at about 500 times the speed it did on the original computer.

The original ERNIE, which is the size of a van, can be viewed in the Science Museum in London.

Figure 12.9 *ERNIE*

Some typical operating systems

Many operating systems have been developed over the years. They have all evolved to cater for changing needs and to take advantage of improvements to hardware. The approach to operating systems also varies between developers, with Microsoft® including the user interface as part of the operating system while Unix® and Linux restrict the operating system to dealing with the hardware, leaving others to add a suitable user interface.

Operating system	Description
Android®	Developed by Google to run on mobile devices. It is based on Linux.
Mac OS	Apple's mobile device operating system used on iPhones, iPads and Apple TV.
Unix	Originally developed in the 1970s, Unix is widely used and is the basis of many other operating systems including Apple's Mac OS X and Linux.
Linux	Available in many distributions, Linux is an open-source operating system based on Unix.
Mac OS X	Operating system on Apple computers based on Unix.
Windows®	Probably the best known and most widely used operating system developed by Microsoft. It is found on laptop and desktop PCs and on a range of mobile devices.

Most personal computers run on a version of Windows, a powerful proprietary multi-tasking operating system. Windows is developed by Microsoft and incorporates a huge range of features that go way beyond the basic requirements for an operating system. The Windows graphical user interface makes all applications running under Windows look very similar. This familiarity makes learning how to use each application and locating features within each application much simpler. The reason why they all look so similar is that when a developer writes new software the buttons or menus are called up from Windows and used in the application.

Many Windows features are stored on the disk as DLL files. DLL means dynamic linked library. These DLL programs can be utilised by the developer to produce applications that have the Windows look and feel. These DLLs also save the programmer a lot of time and effort. Routines can be linked into the application at run time, reducing the size of the application and reducing the amount of code that needs to be written and tested.

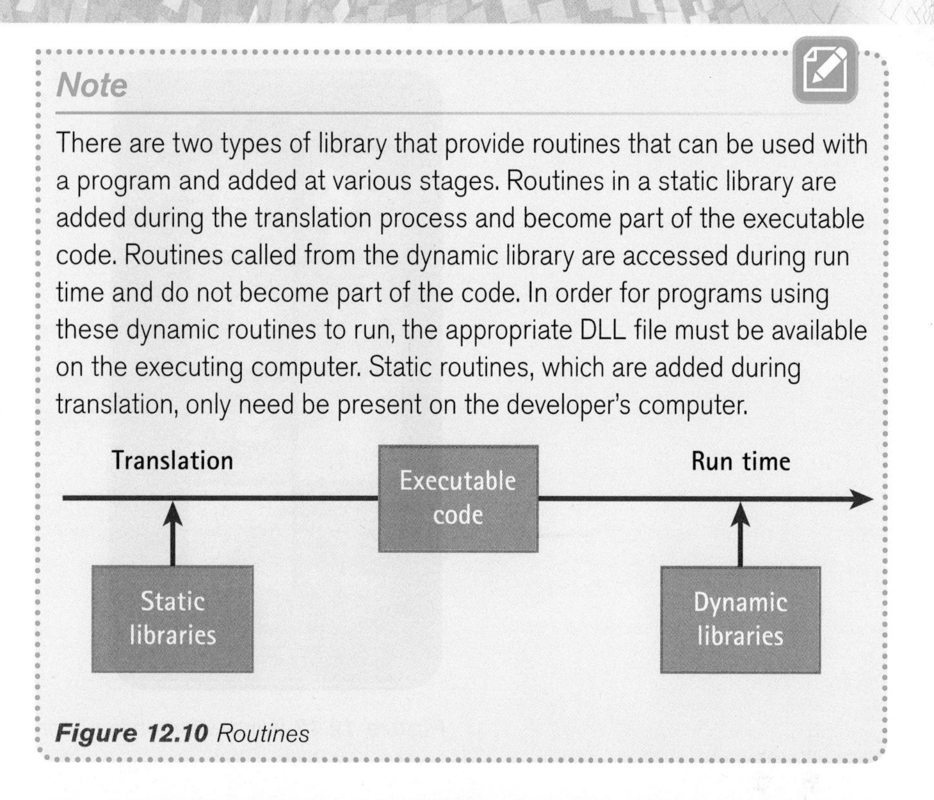

Note

There are two types of library that provide routines that can be used with a program and added at various stages. Routines in a static library are added during the translation process and become part of the executable code. Routines called from the dynamic library are accessed during run time and do not become part of the code. In order for programs using these dynamic routines to run, the appropriate DLL file must be available on the executing computer. Static routines, which are added during translation, only need be present on the developer's computer.

Figure 12.10 *Routines*

Figure 12.11 *Windows apps*

Unix is a family of operating systems found on high-end servers as well as on workstations. Unix is often customised by hardware manufacturers for their systems and will only run on their hardware. Unix was developed in conjunction with the C programming language. Unix is very popular with professional users because of its security and robustness. Apple's Mac OS, used on the iMac desktop and laptop computers, is a variant of Unix. Mac OS includes networking and internet features and works seamlessly with cloud computing.

Figure 12.12 *Windows mobile phone graphical user interface*

The Mac OS and Android™ platforms are operating systems designed to work with mobile phones and portable devices. They are designed to be used with a touchscreen so they can accept input from finger movements such as dragging, pointing and pinching. These operating systems also incorporate interfaces to the built-in features on the devices, such as accelerometers to respond to the movement of the device. Windows 10 Mobile® is a system for mobile devices that provides a familiar environment for mobile and desktop devices in the Windows environment.

Figure 12.13 *The Xfce graphical user interface for Unix*

Linux is similar to Unix but is a separate development. It was initially developed by Linus Torvalds and is open source, so anyone can have access to the code and modify it. Linux is a popular operating system kernel that has been adapted to run on computer systems from super computers to mobile phones. It is particularly popular as a server operating system, including many web servers. Google's Android smartphone operating system is based on the Linux kernel.

There are many versions of Linux available for desktop and laptop computers, for example Red Hat, Debian, Ubuntu and GNU. Linux is gaining popularity in this market because it is a relatively small operating system and is therefore quite fast and economical with memory. The constant development and testing has made it largely bug free with some significant security features built in rather than added on later. The fact that it is free of charge is also an important consideration.

Firmware

Key Term

Firmware Software that is stored permanently in a device.

The operating system used on a home computer or a large system is loaded from a disk. In a small, embedded system or on a portable device, such as a mobile phone and tablet, there is no requirement for a disk and the operating system is stored permanently on ROM or in flash memory chips. Software stored on memory chips like this is called **firmware**. It typically consists of small programs used to control the device. Larger computer systems also have firmware that is used to control the boot up operations.

Multi-tasking

Originally computers could only have one process running at a time. Modern CPUs work much faster than RAM and other components meaning they can cope with more than one process at a time. It makes sense to keep the CPU as busy as possible to get the most out of the computer system. If the current program is loading data from a slow peripheral device, rather than allow the CPU to stand idle it will turn its attention to another process. This is known as multi-tasking.

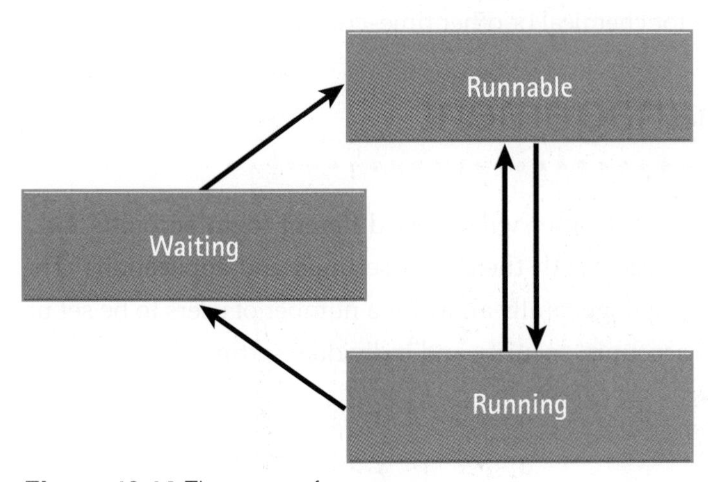

Figure 12.14 *The states of a process*

End users often make use of this feature to enable several programs to run at the same time. They will have several applications open at once, their email program will be receiving mail and they might have music playing. While in reality there is still generally only one process running at a time, the CPU is able to switch its attention to each of these tasks in turn fast enough for the user not to notice that they are not running simultaneously.

Multi-tasking operating systems allow several processes to be resident in RAM at any one time. These processes are in different states – running, runnable or waiting.

If a process that is running is terminated, because its allocated time has run out or it is interrupted by an external event, the CPU can now turn its attention to a runnable process. Processes that are waiting have to wait for a signal to set them to runnable before they can be dealt with.

Key Term

Scheduling The process of arranging, controlling and optimising work and workloads.

The multi-tasking operating system ensures that these processes get dealt with efficiently by **scheduling** them in some way. There are various ways these processes can be scheduled; they might take it in turns, the shortest job may go first or the one waiting longest may be dealt with first. Managing this is part of the operating system's role in a computer system.

Other types of operating system

Multi-user

On larger computer systems, many users may login and use the system simultaneously. In this case the operating system is responsible for allocating access to memory, storage and CPU time to a number of users simultaneously. This type of operating system is called *multi-user*.

Real time

Any safety-critical system will require very short and guaranteed response times. These times are generally fixed at a small fraction of a second. This type of system, where the response from the operating system is guaranteed, is called a *real-time system*. Typical examples are autopilots or control systems for chemical or other time-critical manufacturing plants.

User management

The typical home computer will allow different login accounts for a number of users, each with their own settings and applications. The operating system will generally allow for a number of users to be set up with their own accounts, security and individual settings.

```
Last login: Mon Jan 18 12:05:59 on ttys000
GEORGEs-iMac:~ george2$ ls -l
total 2912
drwxr-xr-x    4 george2  staff     136  1 Mar  2015 Accellion
drwx------    4 george2  staff     136 24 Oct 13:52 Applications
drwx------+  77 george2  staff    2618 18 Jan 12:13 Desktop
drwx------+ 239 george2  staff    8126 23 Dec 13:14 Documents
drwx------+  96 george2  staff    3264 15 Jan 18:00 Downloads
-rw-r--r--@   1 george2  staff  347029  1 Oct  2012 Downloads-1.(null)
-rw-r--r--@   1 george2  staff  347029  1 Oct  2012 Downloads-2.(null)
-rw-r--r--@   1 george2  staff  769116  9 Jul  2013 Downloads-3.(null)
drwx------@  20 george2  staff     680 11 Jan 15:21 Dropbox
drwxr-xr-x    2 george2  staff      68  8 Jun  2015 Ephox
drwxr-xr-x@   4 george2  staff     136 12 Oct  2013 FW_ AMEC.rtfd
drwx------@  10 george2  staff     340 20 Dec 11:31 Google Drive
drwxrwxrwx@  72 george2  staff    2448 17 Dec 12:41 Library
drwx------+  19 george2  staff     646  4 Apr  2015 Movies
drwx------+  22 george2  staff     748  7 Sep 15:31 Music
drwx------+ 240 george2  staff    8160 24 Oct 15:35 Pictures
drwxr-xr-x+   5 george2  staff     170  2 May  2012 Public
-rwxr--r--@   1 george2  staff      89  8 Oct 19:07 hello.sh
-rw-r--r--    1 george2  staff       0 17 Dec 12:14 mysql
-rw-r--r--    1 george2  staff      98  2 May  2012 records.txt
-rw-r--r--    1 george2  staff      36  2 May  2012 scores.txt
-rw-r--r--    1 george2  staff      34  2 May  2012 weightwatch.csv
-rw-r--r--    1 george2  staff      56  2 May  2012 weightwatch.txt
-rw-r--r--    1 george2  staff      79  2 May  2012 words.txt
GEORGEs-iMac:~ george2$
```

Figure 12.15 *File permissions*

In Figure 12.15 the file permissions are shown on the left for each file or folder:

- The first group of three is for owner permissions.
- The second group of three is for group permissions.
- The third group of three is for all users permissions.

The letters mean:

- **d:** directory
- **r:** read
- **w:** write
- **x:** execute.

For example, the file hello.sh can be read, written to and executed by the owner, but other users only have the right to read this file.

Memory management

One of the key roles for the operating system is to manage the available memory. The primary memory will contain the programs and data currently in use. The operating system makes sure the programs and data are stored safely and efficiently. Each program will have its own data and the operating system makes sure that no program can change the data for another program by restricting each program to accessing and amending only its own area of data. It is, of course, possible that two programs will require legitimate access to the same data; it is the role of the operating system to manage this.

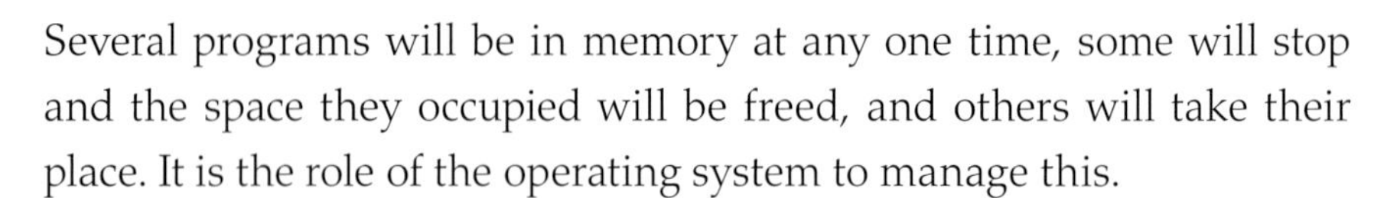

Several programs will be in memory at any one time, some will stop and the space they occupied will be freed, and others will take their place. It is the role of the operating system to manage this.

For example, three programs are in memory, A, B and C.

B finishes and is removed from memory.

D is to be run but will not fit into either of the free spaces:

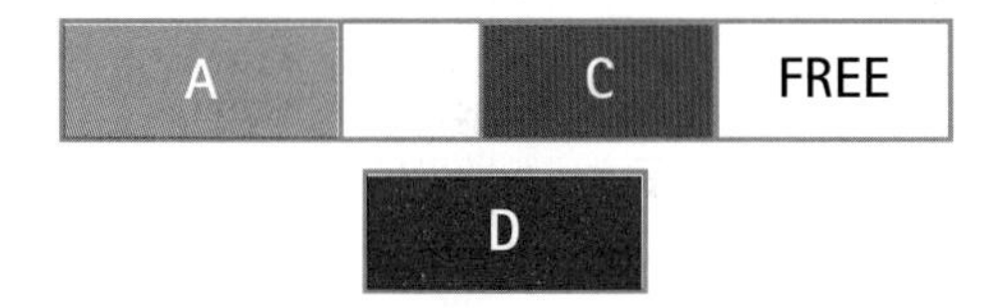

However, D will fit if the program and its data is split between the two free spaces. The operating system can separate the data into two segments.

The operating system will now keep track of these two segments.

Alternatively the operating system can split all programs into equal-sized pages (typically several kilobytes) and keep track of all the pages in a table.

When using paging, programs are split into equal-sized blocks, and these blocks are allocated to a suitable free space in the memory. The program pages can be distributed through memory, with the operating system keeping track of the separate blocks or pages.

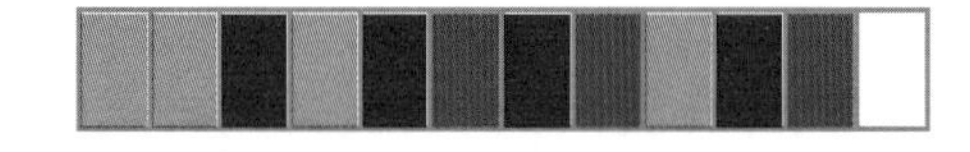

Typically, operating systems use both paging (splitting programs into equal-sized pages) and segmentation (splitting programs into blocks to fit the available gaps) to manage memory.

Peripheral management

Peripheral devices are essential for a computer system to input, output and store data. These devices need to communicate with the rest of the computer system. This communication is controlled by signals produced by the device drivers. Device drivers are required for each peripheral and are generally written by the device manufacturer or provided as generic device drivers by the operating system. These device drivers take care of the peripherals so that the application programmers need not concern themselves with the details of each device they are using. The application needs simply to pass on a request to the driver, which will then translate it into the codes specific to the device.

The device drivers are specific not only to the device but also to the operating system. A printer will require different device drivers if used on an Apple Mac from those required if used on a Windows-based system. This is because the communication with the peripheral device is triggered by a signal, an interrupt.

An interrupt is a signal to the operating system to tell it to stop running the current program and turn its attention to the program that is looking after the peripheral device. These interrupts are codes, which are different for each operating system. When the job requiring the peripheral is finished the CPU returns to the original program at the point where it was interrupted.

Most operating systems allow the user to make minor modifications to the way the peripheral behaves. The device manager utility allows the user to change settings such as the display settings.

Figure 12.16 *Setting the screensaver settings on an iMac*

Utility software

Key Term

Utility A small program designed to carry out a limited maintenance task.

Most computer systems have many **utility** programs installed alongside the operating system. Utilities are small programs that perform a limited range of functions. Programs that are supplied alongside operating systems, or those added by the user to manage aspects of the system, are maintenance utilities. Operating systems always come with disk organisation tools. These tools allow the user to do various disk management functions such as format the disk, move files, copy files or rename files.

Note

Using auto updates is generally the best option for most users. The machine is updated without the need for user interaction, and security loopholes, bugs and performance issues can be resolved. There are some updates that are not necessary and, if asked, the user may not want. There are also updates that are incompatible with other software on the system, leading to issues with running that software.

Auto update

Operating systems rely on many small utility programs alongside the kernel. These programs are being constantly developed to improve the performance of the system, to fix bugs and to eliminate any security loopholes. The auto update facility ensures that the latest versions of these utilities are downloaded on to the computer.

Disk utilities

Defragmentation utility

Over time the files on the hard disk get broken up into fragments scattered across the surface of the disk. This happens because files are deleted, leaving gaps of varying sizes. This can result in larger files being stored in a number of locations in the available spaces on the drive.

Key Term

Defragmenter Software that brings together fragments of files on a disk and collects all the free space in one area.

Because the read/write heads on the drive will have to move a lot to locate all the segments of the file, fragmentation will slow down access quite considerably. Defragmenting tools (**defragmenters**) reorganise the files on the surface of the disk so that individual files and free spaces are put together.

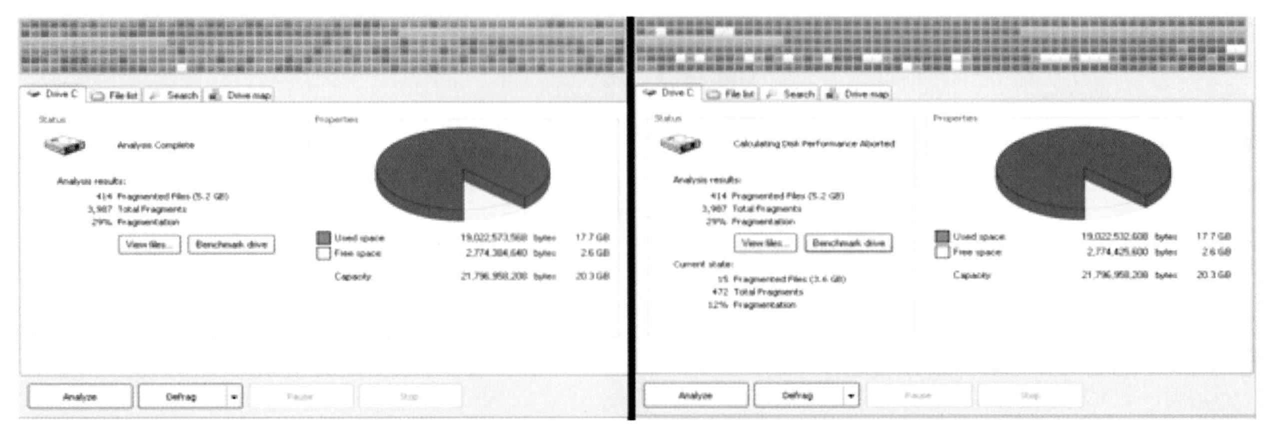

Figure 12.17 *Defragmenting a disk to improve access to the files, using Defraggler®*

Disk checking and repairing

There are also utilities that can be used to locate and solve problems, for example ScanDisk® on Windows. This checks for and fixes bad links between file fragments and identifies bad sectors on the disk, keeping a record of where the problems are located. This way, damaged sectors can be avoided in the future.

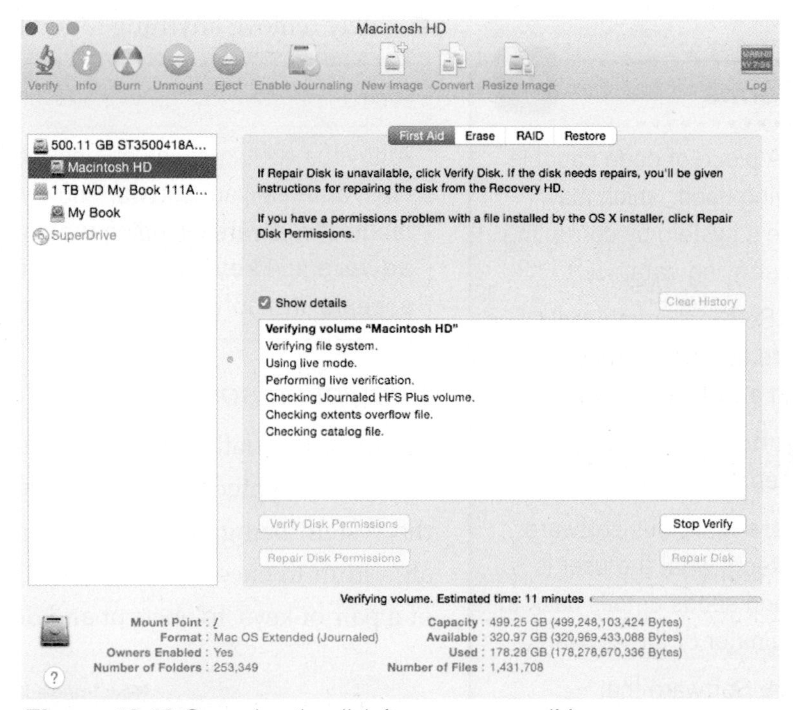

Figure 12.18 *Scanning the disk for errors on an iMac*

System cleanup

There are commercial programs such a MacKeeper and CCleaner that will identify temporary files, cached copies of files and unused files that can be removed safely, leaving more free space on the hard disk.

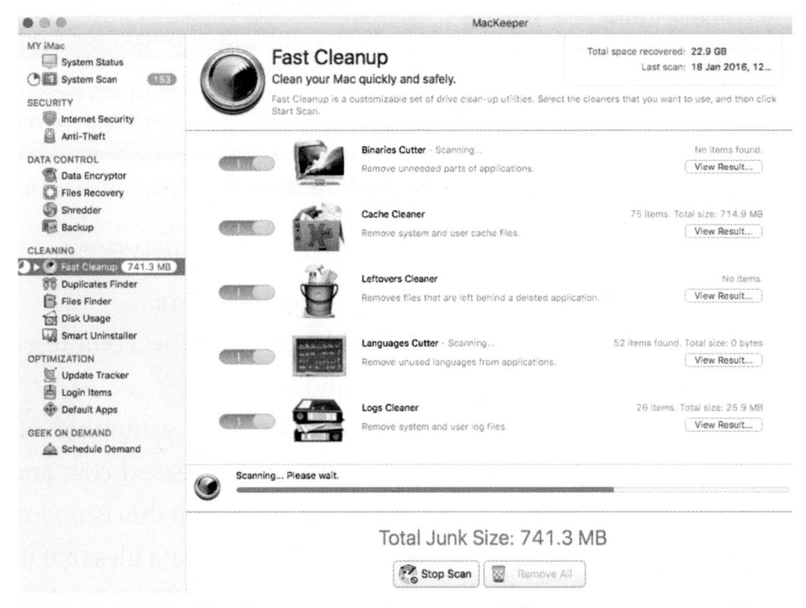

Figure 12.19 *MacKeeper removing unused files to recover space on the hard disk drive*

Anti-virus or anti-malware software

Anti-virus or anti-malware software is used to:

- minimise the danger from malicious software (malware) being introduced onto the system
- detect, prevent and remove malware by scanning incoming files or scanning the hard drive to identify threats
- safely remove anything found that is considered a threat.

Note

Anti-virus software was originally designed to prevent **viruses** but most anti-malware software now will protect the system from a wide range of malware including **worms**, **Trojan horses**, **spyware**, **adware** and **keyloggers**. Given the speed at which new malware appears, this software is only really useful if it is kept up to date.

Key Terms

Virus A piece of code capable of copying itself, which may damage a system by corrupting it or destroying data.

Worm Self-replicating, malicious software that can spread through a system or network.

Trojan horse Harmful software disguised as something useful.

Spyware Malicious software that detects what the user is doing and sends details back to the originator of the spyware.

Adware Software that automatically displays advertising when a user is online.

Keylogger A program that records every keystroke of the computer user; often used to gain confidential information in order to commit fraud.

Encryption software

Securing the data on a computer from outside threats is important. Data is encrypted to prevent anyone gaining unauthorised access to the system being able to read this data. Encryption software uses an algorithm to encode the data so that it cannot be read and uses a key, or a pair of keys, to encrypt and decrypt the data. (See also Chapter 6.)

***Figure 12.20** Adding encryption to a folder on the hard disk drive*

Compression software

Compression software:

- enables data to be compressed into a smaller file by removing redundant data
- is supplied with a number of operating systems to save on disk space. (The decreased cost and increased availability of large hard disk drives means this is no longer necessary.)
- is used for large data files that need to be moved to a smaller medium, such as CD or DVD, or for data that is transmitted electronically.

(See also Chapter 16.)

Other utilities

Other typical utilities include:

- disk free-space calculator
- calendar
- clock settings
- email clients
- file search facilities
- image editing
- help
- basic text editor.

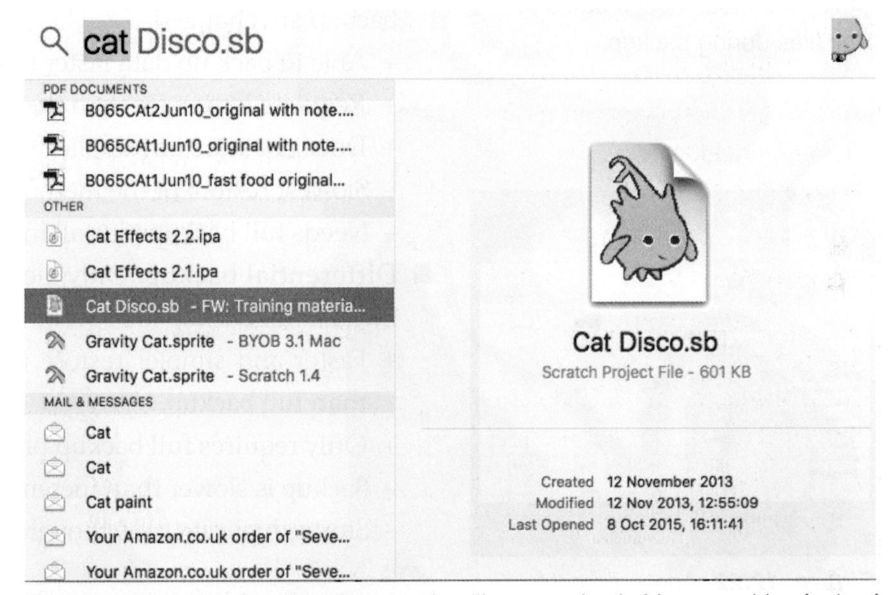

Figure 12.21 *The Spotlight file search utility on an Apple Mac searching for 'cat'*

Backing up data

(See also Chapter 9.)

Key Term

Backup A copy of the data and programs on a drive used to restore them if they are lost or damaged.

Data stored on the hard disk drive is potentially at risk from loss or damage and important data should be **backed up**. There are a number of options:

- back up important files
- back up the whole drive
- use an external backup device such as a flash drive or an external hard drive
- use a remote data storage service; that is, a cloud server.

> **Note**
>
> Apple Time Machine uses an incremental backup process. The system records when each directory is modified on the hard drive. This means that it only needs to scan the directories that have changed for files to copy. This differs from the approach taken by similar backup utilities, which examine modification dates of all files during backup.

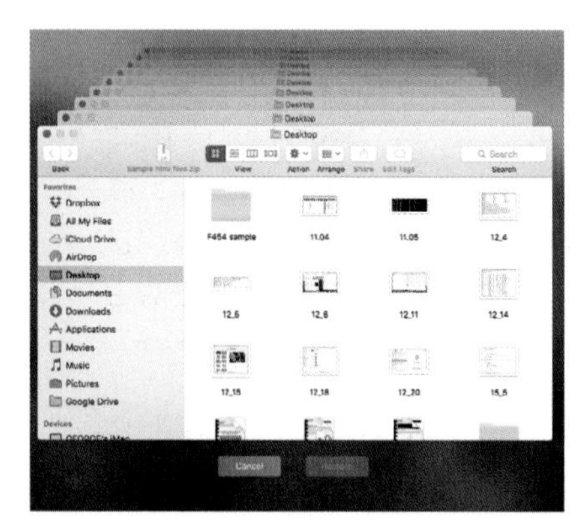

Figure 12.22 Apple Time Machine backup and restore facility

Once the medium for saving the data is decided, the backup regime needs to be considered.

- **Full backup:** All files and folders on the drive are backed up every time a backup happens.
  - \+ Able to restore data faster than other methods.
  - \+ Only requires the last backup to restore data.
  - – Slowest backup of the methods.
  - – Requires the most storage space.
  - – Inefficient storage with lots of duplicated data stored.
- **Incremental backup:** Make an initial backup and back up changes regularly. Only new files or files that have changed since the last backup are changed.
  - \+ Able to back up data faster than the other methods.
  - \+ Requires less space than the other methods.
  - \+ Does not store any duplicated files.
  - – Slowest restore of the methods.
  - – Needs full backup plus all incremental backups to restore data.
- **Differential backup:** Only files that are new or have changed since the last full backup are saved.
  - \+ Faster and simpler restore than incremental backup but slower than full backup.
  - \+ Only requires full backup plus latest differential backup.
  - – Backup is slower than incremental but faster than full backup.
  - – Stores duplicate files, though not as many as full backup.

Questions

1. What are the main functions of an operating system?
2. Explain why multi-tasking is needed in an operating system.
3. Describe the following utility programs:
   (a) device drivers
   (b) anti-virus software
   (c) defragmenter
   (d) system clean-up.
4. Describe the advantages and disadvantages of a using a full backup system compared to an incremental backup system.
5. What are the advantages of setting auto update for an operating system?
6. Describe two utilities that are available to improve the performance of the hard drive in a computer.

13 Computational thinking and algorithms

What is computational thinking?

Computational thinking is thinking like a computer scientist. It means applying the methods of computer scientists to problem solving.

In the very short period since computers were first developed, there has been enormous progress in finding new uses for computers and also in making better software for them. We are used to ever more reliable and fast computers and much of this progress has been down to the development of better and more efficient algorithms.

Remember, this has come from a more or less standing start. People who worked with the early computers had to 'feel' their way in getting the machines to do useful things. There were no rules or precedents.

Making software was, and still is, difficult. It is difficult because:

- often the software is being made to do something that has never been done before
- software is intangible – it can be extremely difficult to determine if it is behaving exactly as intended or in the most effective way
- software does not obey physical laws in the same way that steel used to make a car does. Steel has physical properties, such as density, conductivity and hardness, that can be observed and measured, and always behaves in exactly the same way.

Over the years, computer scientists developed ways to make the production of software more predictable and reliable. Techniques and methodologies have been developed, such as the discipline of software engineering and structured program design, which make it more likely that software will do what is intended or expected. Testing software has become a more formal discipline too.

Note

For the GCSE, you should look carefully at problem solving using computational thinking because:

- you may well see exam questions that ask specifically about it
- there may be questions that you can tackle better by applying these methods
- you can apply these skills to dealing with your NEA (non-examined assessment).

More recently, it has become apparent that the disciplines developed and used by computer scientists have wider application and can be deployed usefully in all sorts of spheres. Understanding exactly what methodology is used in software engineering has proven to be useful and indeed we now see that the development of computer solutions has actually helped us to think more efficiently.

In summary, computational thinking helps us to:

- look at a complex problem
- understand it
- formulate a solution that can be implemented by either a computer, a human or a combination of both.

There is a clear cut methodology that we can use to apply computational thinking to problem solving.

Problem solving

Stages of problem solving

When solving a problem. there are some well-defined stages that are helpful to go through.

1 **Understand the problem.** You cannot begin to solve a problem unless you clearly know what you are trying to solve.
   - Do you have all the data you need to understand the problem? If not, can you get it?
   - Is the problem possibly unsolvable? Remember, not all problems can be solved.
   - Could you solve just some of the problem and still be better off?
   - Is it possible to divide the problem into sub-problems?

2 **Devise a plan.**
   - Has this problem been solved before? Can you learn from what has previously been solved?
   - Make a list of things to do.
   - Are there patterns that could allow some of your solutions to be reused? Can you borrow ideas from other solved problems?
   - Can maths help? Quantifying a problem can often help to describe a situation with precision and numerical methods may be helpful.
   - Look at similar problems and their solutions.
   - Can you see any scope for using or reusing algorithms?

3 **Carry out the plan.**
   - Check that what you are doing is in fact correct.
   - Ask the questions 'Am I doing the right thing?' and 'Am I doing it right?'

4 Look back over what you have done.
- Can your solution be improved, for example are the algorithms the most efficient that you could use?
- Is any of the solution likely to be reusable in the future?
- Is the problem now properly solved?

Extension Activity

Someone has an idea for a new app such as finding the quickest and cheapest train route between any two stations in the UK.

In an attempt to find how to do this, work through stages 1 and 2 of the problem-solving strategy in this chapter.

Here are some of the common aspects to solving a problem in a computational way.

Abstraction

Abstraction is the taking of a real-life situation and modelling it so that we can analyse it and think more clearly about it.

We are making abstractions when we use symbols to represent reality. When we have symbols, we can carry out actions virtually, which is usually a lot easier and more realistic than solving a problem by actually carrying out a physical experiment.

Abstractions let us see the component parts of a large problem. They often help us to realise what parts are important and those that are unimportant and can be ignored. They make it easier for us to see how the parts of a problem fit together.

Examples of abstractions

- Variables in a program: these represent values.
- A function in a program: these represent a coherent group of actions designed to produce a particular result.
- Layers in a network: these separate the functional aspects of a network so that they can be worked on separately.
- Tables in a database: these store data about real-life entities so that we can organise and find the facts we need.
- A map: a representation of part of the Earth's surface; we can use it to plan journeys before we actually make them.
- A company: a representation of the buildings, people, products and processes that work together to make or do something for a profit.
- Money: has no intrinsic value in itself; it is an abstraction that allows us to value goods and services and to interact with each other in a fair and agreed way.

Questions

1. Make a list of three other abstractions in addition to those given on this page.
2. Make a list of two or three problems that face humans and for which no solution is likely.
3. Describe a problem that can be solved, at least in part, by the combination of human and computer resources.
4. Describe a problem that can be completely solved by using a computer.

Example

The well-known map of the London Underground is a particularly good example of the power of abstraction.

The London Underground is, in reality, a subterranean network of tunnels and tracks, trains, staff and services. The full details are too complex to be useful for someone who just wants to plan a journey across the capital city. All users want to know is the best way to get from A to B. The map is designed to make it easy to plan a journey within the system.

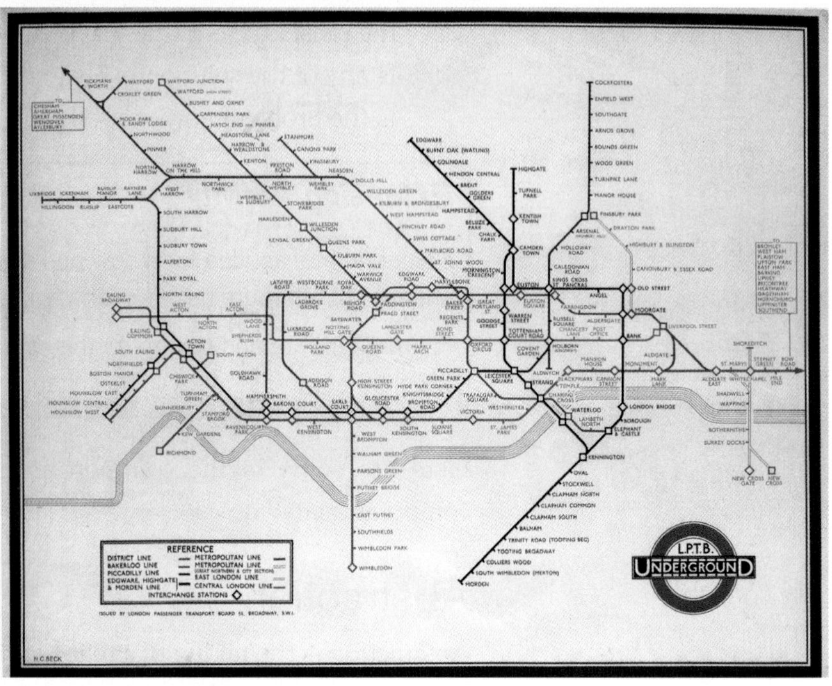

Figure 13.1 *Abstraction: Henry Beck's map of the London Underground*

The famous map designed by Harry Beck in 1931 displays the system as an abstraction that pays little attention to the actual geographical positions of the stations in real life. Instead, it shows which places each line provides access to (station names) and how the different lines interconnect (a different colour for each line/service). The passenger does not need to know much about the streets that pass overhead and so they are left out.

A more realistic map is not as easy to comprehend without looking much more closely.

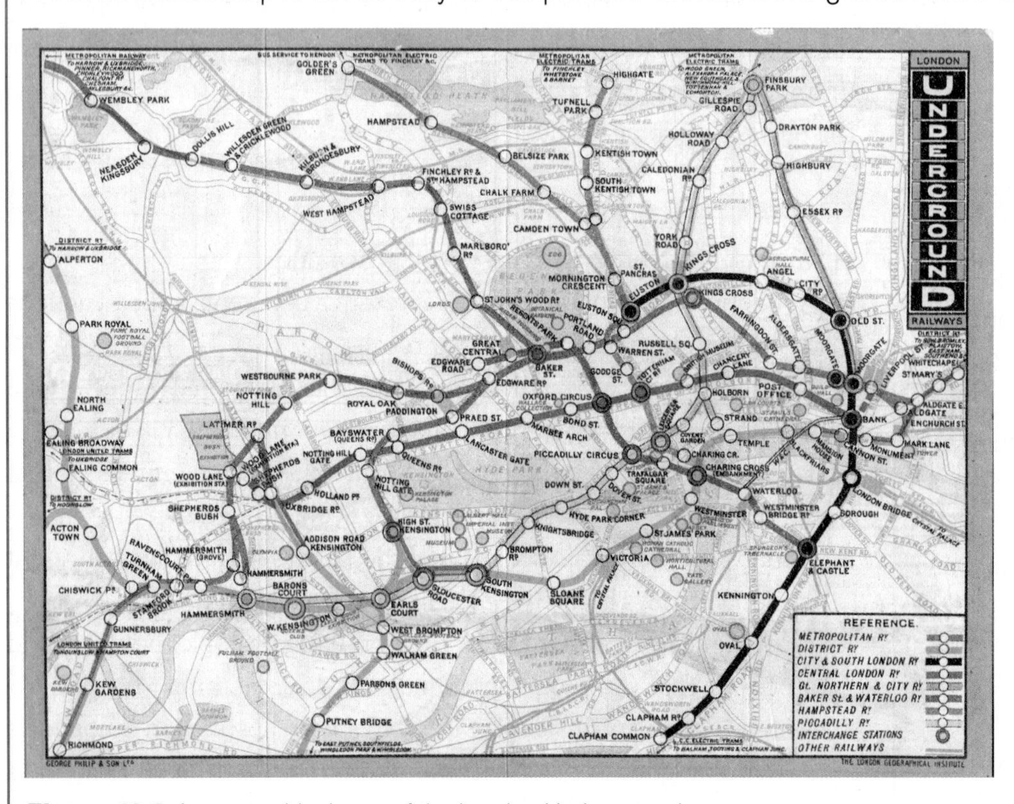

Figure 13.2 *A geographical map of the London Underground*

Decomposition

Another essential part of computational thinking is decomposition. This is the breaking down of a complex problem into small parts. These small parts should each be easier to solve than the large problem.

For example, suppose a car manufacturer needs to develop a new model. It would make no sense to attempt to design a whole new car from scratch. It makes more sense for the manufacturer to have a good idea of the overall objectives of the project and then to look at the sub-problems. In the case of a new car, it would make sense to concentrate separately on the body shape, the engine and the braking systems.

Also, in the case of developing a new car, there is the long history of previous cars from which lessons can be learned. It may be that some of the sub-problems do not need solving at the present time. Old solutions can be brought into the new overall plan.

Another advantage of decomposition is that different people or teams can work on separate parts, which helps to spread the workload.

Task 

Take a complex problem such as planning a school trip.

Break the problem down into sensible steps that make it easier to plan the whole event.

Are there alternative ways you could break the problem down?

Pattern recognition

It is often helpful to spot trends and patterns in problems. This is particularly useful if you can see a pattern that has been identified and solved before. You can often reuse the old solutions to save effort.

If you are producing software to handle an online store selling books, it may be useful to look for similar examples selling other merchandise, for example the process of asking for credit card details and validating them has probably already been solved.

Algorithms

Algorithms are at the heart of computational thinking. An algorithm is a series of steps to solve a problem. This is most easily applied to the solving of mathematical problems but it is also applicable to other, less well-defined problems.

Example

It is possible to apply algorithmic thinking to many everyday activities such as finding your way to school or college:

- Leave house through front door
- Turn right
- Walk to end of road
- Wait at bus stop
- Repeat until number 130 arrives
- Get onto bus
- Sit on bus until arrival at school
- Get off bus
- Walk down the school drive

This algorithm has been expressed here as a series of statements. This can be done in a slightly more formal way when planning software by using pseudocode. Alternatively, you could use a flowchart to map out the steps.

Figure 13.3 is a flowchart to show the algorithm above.

This algorithm might not be the most effective one. Algorithms should always be reviewed in order to test whether there may be a better solution. Perhaps it would be better to ride your bike to school.

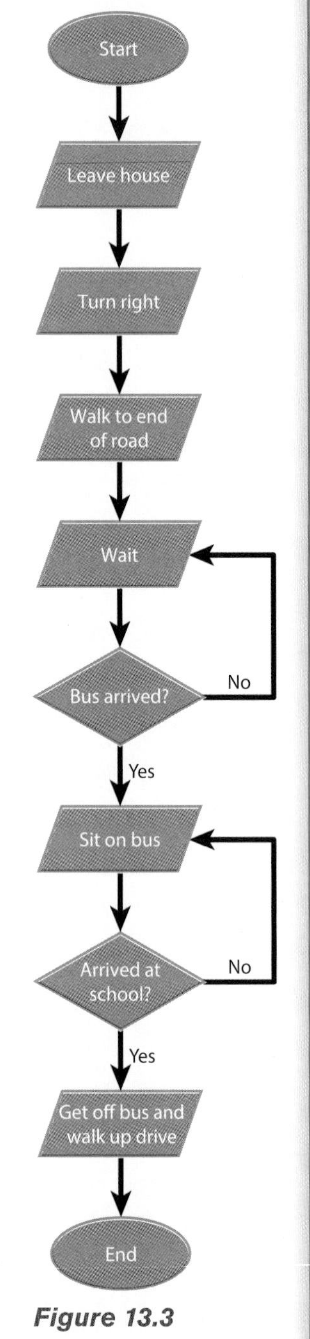

Figure 13.3

Questions

5 Write a simple algorithm for making a cup of tea.

6 (a) How could you test the effectiveness of the example algorithm above for making your trip to school?

(b) Describe what data you would need to compare it with an alternative algorithm to achieve the same result.

So, when solving a problem, you should try to envisage the steps necessary to solve it. Once you have done that, you should review your algorithm for effectiveness. Ask yourself:

- Is the problem solved?
- Is the problem solved as well as it could be?

Expressing algorithms

Flowcharts or pseudocode can be used to express algorithms. Pseudocode is often preferable because it can lead more directly to the actual source code when the program is written. On the other hand, flowcharts can give a more immediate visual impact.

Pseudocode

Pseudocode is a way of setting out an algorithm in concise statements. There are no rules for pseudocode. You can devise your own way of expressing the algorithm but it usually approximates to real program code.

Example

Here is an example of pseudocode. It is not any particular version of pseudocode but it is clear enough to follow.

```
Set total to zero
Set counter to one
While counter is less than or equal to twenty
   Input the next weight
   Add the weight into the total
   Add 1 to counter
   Set the average weight to the total divided
   by twenty
Print the average weight
```

Note

Any pseudocode presented to you in an exam will be in a form as set out in the OCR guide to pseudocode. You can answer questions about algorithms in any concise format. You will not be penalised for making slight syntactic errors. It is important that you set out your algorithms clearly and include all necessary steps.

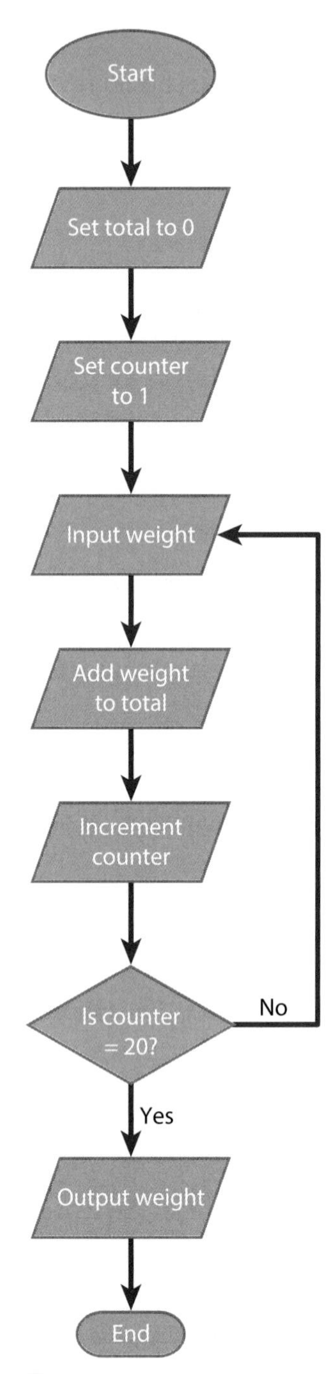

Figure 13.4

Flowcharts

When using a flowchart, it is best to use specially designed software to create it. There are plenty of examples online including free ones such as draw.io.

Figure 13.4 is the same algorithm as in the previous example, expressed as a flowchart.

Often, students misuse flow charts and produce something that is unclear or messy. Here are some basic rules about using flowcharts to show a process or algorithm:

- keep it simple
- if a flowchart is beginning to look complex, break it into smaller sections
- be careful with decision boxes.

Decision boxes will normally have one entry point and two exits although sometimes there can be more exits.

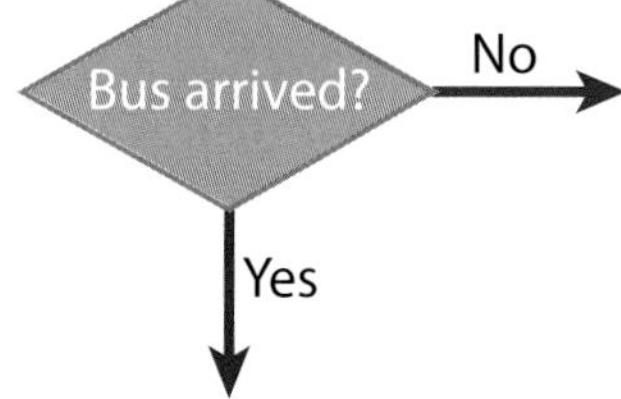

Figure 13.5 *A decision box*

Standard algorithms

There are many well-known algorithms that have produced already to solve common problems. So, when you have a problem to solve, it makes sense to look to see if there are pre-existing algorithms that can do the job. But of course, it is sensible to ask whether the algorithm is the most efficient that could be used. Maybe it could be improved by adapting it.

Searching for something

Often a computer system needs to search for something. You go online to find a pair of trainers and you are faced with a huge variety of vendors and products. Somewhere along the line you will use a search algorithm, even if you do not know you are using one.

Linear search

The linear search is the simplest way of searching a list for something. It is a process for finding something in a list of items that are arranged one after another.

Example

Imagine that you have a collection of anything, such as a shuffled pile of playing cards. Suppose you want to find the ace of spades. There are various approaches.

You could just cut the cards, dip into the pile and hope that you find it. This hit-and-miss approach might get lucky but it probably will not. You have only a 1 in 52 chance of finding the card on each dip. If the card is not there at all, you will not know any better.

A more methodical approach, like linear search, will at least guarantee a result. You could lay the cards out in a row, start at one end, then examine each one in turn, moving on if you do not find the one you want. If you reach the end of the deck of cards and have not found it, at least you know that it is not there.

You might find it straight away, but you might have to wait until you have examined all of the cards. It is clearly not a particularly fast way of finding the card.

To show how the linear search works in pseudocode, instead of looking through a list of 52 items, we will keep it short and search for a letter in a list of six items.

The list is called `List` and its contents are shown in the following diagram.

F	C	D	E	A	B

You can express this search in pseudo code like this:

```
position=0
len=LengthOfList
while position<len AND list[position]!=itemsearchedFor
    Add 1 to position
endwhile
if position>=len then
    print("Item not found")
else
    print("Item found at position "+position)
endif
```

We now work through this algorithm with the list shown, looking for the letter A.

We start at the beginning, in other words `position=0`. The letter there is F, so we have not found A.

We add 1 to the variable `position`.

We look at `position 1`. It is still not A.

We add 1 to `position` again.

We then try `position` equal to 2, 3 and 4 in succession.

When `position=4`, the value of `List[4]` is A, so we have found it.

The algorithm reports that A is found and the location in the list where A is.

position	0	1	2	3	4	5
item	F	C	D	E	A	B

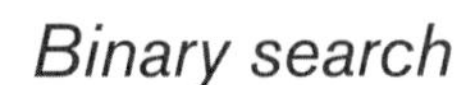

Binary search

You can imagine that if we are searching for something in a huge list, the algorithm will have to potentially examine every single item in the list. For many real-life databases, this could mean millions or even billions of comparisons being made. Even a very fast computer would take a long time to do that. The reality is, we would not use a linear search unless we knew that the data set was small.

A much more efficient and fast algorithm is the binary search. This uses what is called a 'divide and conquer' approach. The problem, in this case the data set, is successively split into pieces and the algorithm is applied in turn to smaller and smaller pieces of the data.

There is one important condition if the binary search is to do its job: the list must be in order.

The binary search works like this:

- The item being searched for is first looked for at the midpoint in the list.
- If it is the item required, all well and good, the item is found.
- If the searched-for item is more than the one at the midpoint (or later alphabetically) then the upper half of the list is examined at its own midpoint. The lower half cannot contain the searched-for item so it is not searched any more.
- The process then continues, halving the remainder of the list each time.

This process quickly reduces the size of the data being searched and so the algorithm is much faster than a linear search.

The algorithm can be expressed in pseudocode like this:

```
item=input("Enter the item wanted")
lowerBound =0
upperBound=LengthOfList -1
found=false
while found==false AND lowerBound!=upperBound
  midPoint=round((lowerBound+upperBound)/2)
  if list[midPoint]==item then
    found=true
  elseif list[midPoint]<item then
    lowerBound=midPoint+1
  else
    upperBound=midPoint-1
  endif
  endwhile
```

```
if found==true then
  print("Item found at" +midPoint)
else
  print("Item not present")
endif
```

Here is an ordered list of nine items.

position	0	1	2	3	4	5	6	7	8
item	A	B	C	D	E	F	G	H	I
	lower Bound				midPoint				upper Bound

Suppose we are searching for B.

Look at the midpoint, that is (0+8)/2 = 4.

The item there is E, so our item is not found. B is lower in the alphabet than E, so next we look to the lower half.

	Lower half								
position	0	1	2	3	4	5	6	7	8
item	A	B	C	D	E	F	G	H	I
	lower Bound				midPoint				upper Bound

Take the midpoint of the lower half. This is position (0+3)/2 = 1.5, which rounded is 2.

	Lower half								
position	0	1	2	3	4	5	6	7	8
item	A	B	C	D	E	F	G	H	I
	lower Bound		midPoint	upper Bound					

Look at position 2. This is C. B is lower so repeat the process for the lower half of this segment. This is (0+2)2/2 = 1.

	Lower half								
position	0	1	2	3	4	5	6	7	8
item	A	B	C	D	E	F	G	H	I
	lower Bound	midPoint	upper Bound						

Look at position 1. There we find B.

Sorting data

We often want computers to sort data into some order. We use this feature in lots of standard examples of generic software such as in spreadsheets and word processors.

As with most problems, there are various possibilities. When it comes to sorting things, there are choices of approach. There are various well-known sorting algorithms that vary in their efficiency.

Suppose you dropped a pack of playing cards on the floor and they got scattered. How could you put them back in order?

You could pick them up and place them in the right position on the floor.

Alternatively, you could gather them all together and go through them one at a time and see if two successive cards are in the right order. If they are not, you swap them. Then you move on and do it again.

Question ?

7 Which of the two methods of ordering playing cards described to the right seems to be the more efficient? Why?

Bubble sort

The bubble sort is the easiest sorting algorithm to understand. It is also famously inefficient. Suppose you have an unordered list of items, for example letters.

position	0	1	2	3	4	5
letter	B	D	C	A	E	F

You start at the beginning and compare the first two items. If they are out of order, you swap them. You make a note that a swap has been made so that later you can check that you still need to continue the process.

The algorithm can be written in pseudocode as follows:

```
swapflag = true
while swapflag == true
  swapflag = false
  position=0
  for position=0 TO listlength-2 //that is the
  last position but 1
    //Compare the item at current position with
    the next one ahead.
    //if they are out of order then
    //Swap items and set swapflag to true

    next position
endwhile
```

Applying the algorithm to the list above, we get this sequence:

`swapflag=false`

B and D are in order: no action required.

D and C are out of order, so swap them and set `swapflag` to true.

0	1	2	3	4	5
B	C	D	A	E	F

`swapflag=true`

D and A are out of order so swap them.

0	1	2	3	4	5
B	C	A	D	E	F

`swapflag=true`

D and E are in order so no action required.

E and F are in order so no action required.

Check swapflag. It is true so we need to start again at the beginning, which of course resets `swapflag` to false.

`swapflag=false`

0	1	2	3	4	5
B	C	A	D	E	F

B and C are in order so no action.

C and A are out of order so swap and set `swapflag` to true.

`swapflag=true`

0	1	2	3	4	5
B	A	C	D	E	F

The rest of the list is in order so when the algorithm works through it, no more changes are needed, but `swapflag` was set to true so we start again. Notice that immediately `swapflag` is set to false again.

`swapflag=false`

B and A are out of order so we swap and set `swapflag` to true again.

0	1	2	3	4	5
A	B	C	D	E	F

We have to start yet again because `swapflag` is true.

`swapflag` is immediately reset to false.

`swapflag=false`

0	1	2	3	4	5
A	B	C	D	E	F

Now when we go through, all the items are in order so no more changes are made and `swapflag` remains false and the algorithm can end.

You will see that for a really small list like this, the checking process happens many times. For a large list, the algorithm is very inefficient and would take a long time, even on a fast computer.

Merge sort

This is another divide and conquer algorithm in which a large data set is divided into smaller sets and the same process is applied repeatedly to the sets.

If we start with two lists that are in order, we can merge them into a single, ordered list using the following algorithm:

```
while list1 is not empty and list2 is not empty
  if the first item in list1 < the first item in
  list2 then
    Remove the first item from list1 and add it
    to newlist
  else
    Remove the first item from list2 and add it
    to newlist
  endif
endwhile
if list1 is empty then
  Add the remainder of list2 to newlist
else
  Add the remainder of list1 to newlist
endif
```

Example

Suppose we have the following lists, already in order.

List1	List2
3,4	5,6

Look at 3 and 5. 3 is smaller than 5 so we remove 3 from List1 and add it to a new list:

Old lists	
List1	List2
4	5,6

New list
3

Now look at the two old lists. 4 is smaller than 5 so remove it and add it to the new list:

Old lists	
List1	List2
(empty)	5,6

New list
3,4

List1 is now empty, so add the remainder of List2 to the new list.

Old lists	
List1	List2
(empty)	(empty)

New list
3,4,5,6

New list now contains all of the original data in order.

Example

This process can be used on an unsorted list if we first divide the unsorted list into individual elements; that is, lists of one item each.

Suppose we have a list such as this one:

2	3	5	4	6	8	7	1

Divide into eight lists of one item each:

2		3		5		4		6		8		7		1

Go through the lists, taking a pair at a time. In each case, merge the pair into a new list, this time each new list will have two items in order.

2	3		4	5		6	8		1	7

Repeat the process, this time making two lists each of four items, each will be in order.

2	3	4	5		1	6	7	8

Repeat the process to merge these two lists into one new list of eight items.

1	2	3	4	5	6	7	8

Insertion sort

This algorithm uses the sort of approach you might use yourself if you are sorting playing cards on a table. You might use it if you have a pile of bills that you want to sort into date order.

What you essentially do is take an item from the unsorted pile and put it into its correct place in a blank space or working area somewhere else on the table, so you have two collections of cards or bills, the sorted one and the unsorted one.

In pseudocode it looks like this:

```
Make the first item the sorted list and the
remaining items are the unsorted list.
while there are items remaining in the unsorted
list
  Take the first item from the unsorted list.
  while there is an item in the sorted list
  which is smaller than itself
    swap with that item
  endwhile
endwhile
```

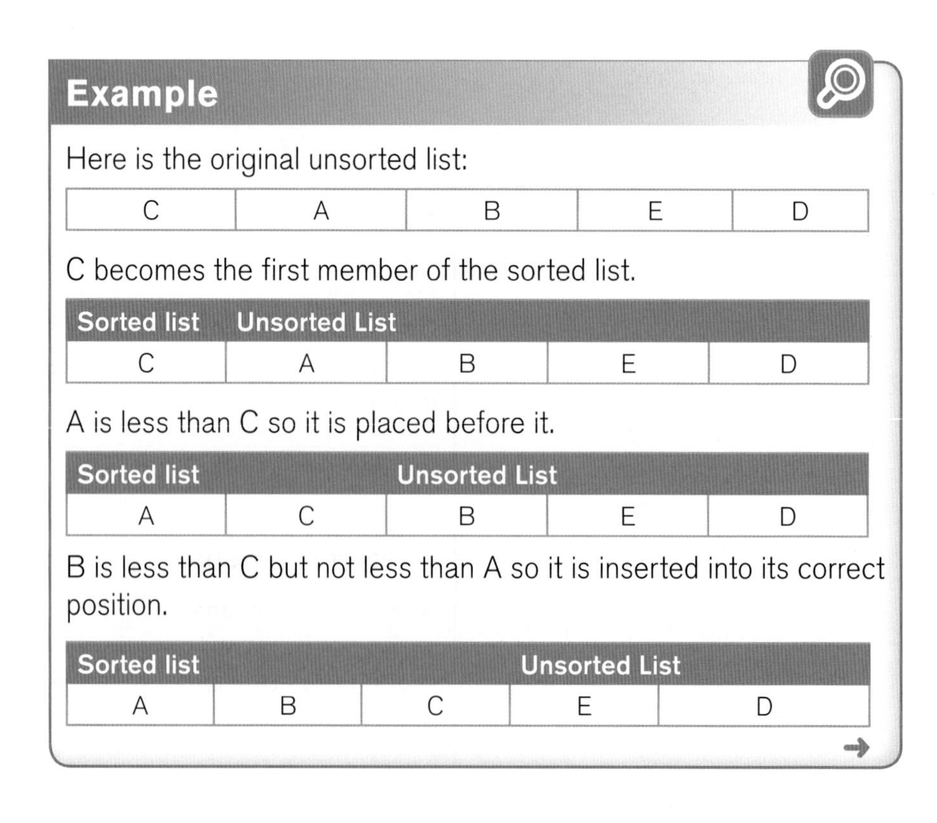

Example

Here is the original unsorted list:

C	A	B	E	D

C becomes the first member of the sorted list.

Sorted list	Unsorted List			
C	A	B	E	D

A is less than C so it is placed before it.

Sorted list		Unsorted List		
A	C	B	E	D

B is less than C but not less than A so it is inserted into its correct position.

Sorted list			Unsorted List	
A	B	C	E	D

E is in its correct position so does not get moved.

Sorted list				Unsorted List
A	B	C	E	D

D is less than E but not less than C so it is moved to its correct position.

Sorted list				Unsorted List
A	B	C	D	E

E is in its correct position so it is not moved and the list is now sorted.

Sorted list				
A	B	C	D	E

Questions

8 Show the stages of the bubble sort when applied to the list:

DCBA

9 For a binary search to work, what state must the data list be in?

10 In a binary search, which data item in a list is examined first?

11 A linear search is used on a pack of 52 playing cards. How many comparisons must be made in order to prove that a certain card is not present?

12 Show how an insertion sort can place in order the names: London, Cambridge, Birmingham, Manchester, Leeds.

13 What is meant by the term *abstraction*?

14 Explain why a bubble sort is rarely used in commercial applications.

More algorithms

In an exam you may be asked to interpret what an algorithm does or maybe spot and correct some errors in one.

Common errors that you might be asked to spot are those where a loop is not set correctly and iterates the wrong number of times.

Task

Here is an algorithm that is intended to take the names of those going on a trip. Only twenty people are allowed to go.

```
array names[5]
number=0
while number<20
    names[1]=input ("input name")
    number=number+1
endwhile
print("The total number of names entered is
"+number)
```

1 Identify the mistakes in this algorithm.

2 Rewrite the algorithm so that it does what is intended.

3 Add to the algorithm so that it outputs all the names entered.

Programming techniques

Variables and constants

Computer programs are essentially an abstraction of reality. They often use symbols to represent the components of the problem. Consider the following maths problem.

Example

John has some sweets. He gives three to his friend Mark. Mark had two sweets already. John now has three times as many sweets as Mark. How many sweets did John have originally?

We solve this problem by replacing the unknown quantity, the number of sweets John had originally, by a variable, for example *x*.

$x - 3 = 3(2 + 3)$

$x - 3 = 15$

$x = 18$

Answer: John had 18 sweets originally.

A simple problem but the use of variables helps us express problems in a way they can be dealt with by a computer program.

Variables are labels we use to represent values stored in the computer memory. When we declare a variable, the computer allocates a location in memory to store any values assigned to that variable.

Constants are labels we use to represent fixed values, for example the value of pi used to calculate the circumference of a circle.

Key Terms

Variable A label that refers to a location in memory containing a value that can be accessed or changed by a program.

Constant A label referring to a location in memory containing a value that can be accessed but not changed by a program.

Example

```
pi=3.14159
radius=0
radius=input ("Enter the radius")
print ("The circumference is", 2*pi*radius)
```

Key Term

Assignment Setting the value of a variable or constant.

In the example the command pi=3.14159, the = sign is being used to **assign** a value to the constant pi. The value we enter at the keyboard when asked to 'Enter the radius' will be assigned to the variable radius.

Note

In some programming languages, = is used to assign a variable and == a constant.

Data types

In order for the program to prepare a memory location for the data, it needs to know what type of data is to be stored so that the right amount of space can be reserved. The main types of data we need to deal with include:

- **Integer:** Whole number values, positive or negative, used to store data that will never have a decimal or fractional value, for example quantities.
- **Real:** Numbers that may store decimal or fractional values, for example prices.
- **Boolean:** Named after the English mathematician, George Boole. Boolean variables only ever store one of two values, TRUE or FALSE. These are often used as flags to indicate the result of a condition.
- **Character:** A single character from the character set of the computer, for example A, k, 9, & or ø.
- **String:** Stores a string of characters such as names, telephone numbers, and so on.

Key Term

Declaration Identifying a variable, constant or array to a program so that memory can be allocated for it.

Many programming languages require that variables and their types are **declared** at the start of the program. Declaring a name for a variable or constant identifies a storage location in memory of the right size so that the program can locate the values.

We usually initialise the variables at the start of the program so that we clear the memory location of anything that was previously stored there. If the variables are not initialised, the program may use data left over from a previous program and not work as expected. In the example program on page 116, the value of radius is initialised to 0.

Key Term

Typecast Casting a variable using str, int or float.

Note

In most languages a constant is declared at the start, for example:

```
PublicConstPi As Double = 3.14159
```

This prevents the value from being accidentally modified during the execution of the program.

In the Python programming language, variables are assigned a type by the first data that is put into them. These variables can be **typecast** using the commands `str`, `int` or `float` to make them string, integer or floating point.

For example, if we wish to allocate an integer to an input we can use the following:

```
number =int(input('Enter a number'))
```

The amount of space reserved differs for the variable type; a Boolean variable only requires one bit but string variables can be extremely large. Typical allocations are:

- **Integers:** Usually 2 or 4 bytes but they can also be set to other values (for example 1 to 8 bytes).
- **Real numbers:** Usually 4 or 8 bytes.
- **Character:** 1 byte.
- **String:** As many bytes as the longest string they are likely to contain.
- **Boolean:** 1 bit.

It is important to select the correct variable type. A string can contain a price but it will not be possible to perform any arithmetic on it. A telephone number may just contain numerical digits, 0–9, but these are not numbers in the real sense and we would not perform any arithmetic on them, they are best stored as strings.

Sizing a data file

To estimate the size of a data file, we add together the data size for each field based on its type and multiply by the number of records in the file.

Example

A file containing the customer reference, name, address, email and telephone number of 2000 customers might have the following fields:

Field	Type	Size
Customer reference (5 digits)	string	5 B
First name (typically up to 20 characters)	string	20 B
Family name (typically up to 20 characters)	string	20 B
Address 1 (building number and street)	string	30 B
Address 2 (district)	string	30 B
City (typically up to 30 characters)	string	30 B
Postcode	string	8 B
Email (typically 30–40 characters)	string	40 B
Telephone	string	11 B
Number of orders placed	integer	4 B
Account balance	real number	8 B
Adding these we get a maximum for each record		**206 B**
Multiply by 2000		**412 KB**
Add 10% for overheads (approximately 41 KB)		**453 KB**

For strings, we calculate the size at 1 byte per anticipated character.

Input and output

In the example about the circumference of a circle on page 116, we include input and output statements.

When designing a computer program one of the first things to do is to determine what outputs are required. This determines what inputs are necessary to make those outputs possible. Once these have been decided it is possible to start thinking about how to process the input data to get the desired output.

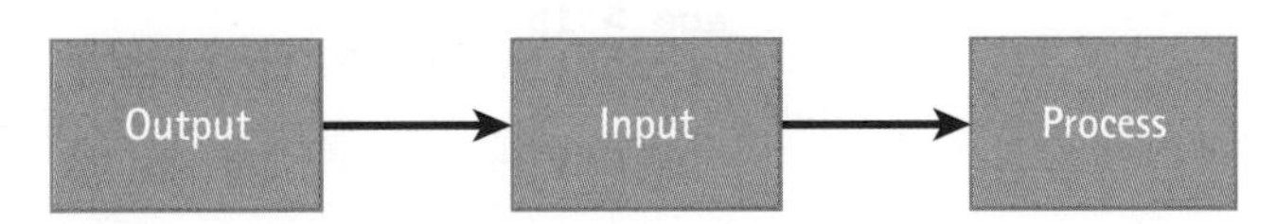

Figure 14.1 *Define outputs, then inputs to identify what processing is required*

> **Note**
>
> When executing the program, the process is to input the data, process it and output the results.
>
> Input → Process → Output

Program structures

Despite all the advances in computer science, the basic approaches to programming and building blocks for creating a program have remained largely unchanged. Any program can be written using just three constructs: **sequence**, **selection** and **iteration**.

1 **Sequence:** This is the execution of statements or functions one after the other.

2 **Selection:** The path through the program is decided by looking at a condition and then taking one of a set of alternative paths based on the result, for example IF THEN ELSE.

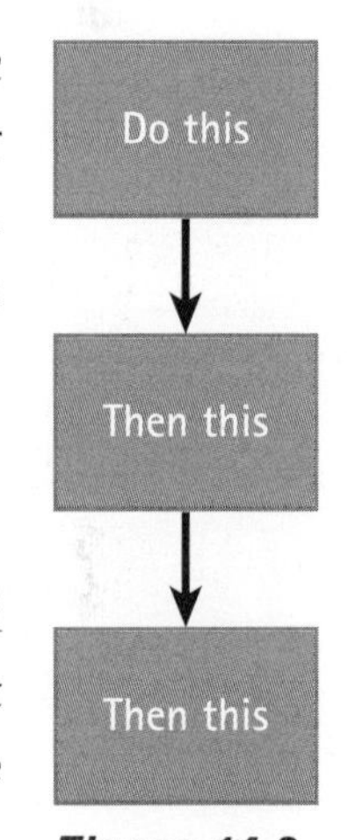

Figure 14.2 *A sequence*

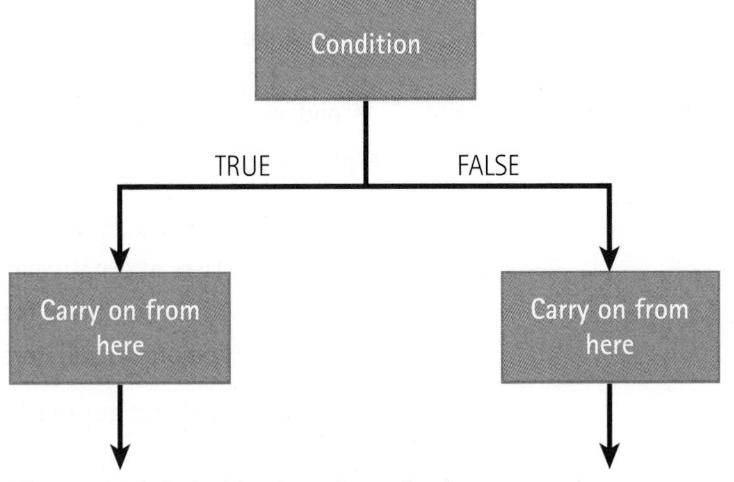

Figure 14.3 *A decision based on a Boolean expression*

> ***Key Terms***
>
> **Sequence** When a list of instructions is carried out in order, one after the other.
>
> **Selection** A condition to decide the path through the program and which set of instructions to execute next.
>
> **Iteration (repetition)** Where a group of instructions is executed repeatedly until a condition is met, or while a condition is true (a loop).

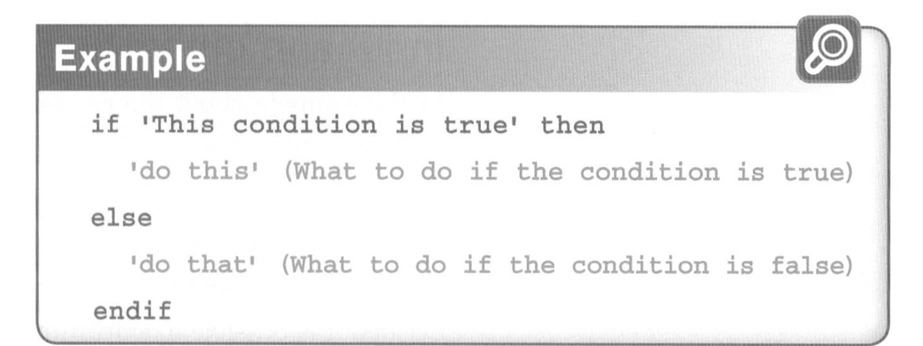

Example

```
if 'This condition is true' then
   'do this'  (What to do if the condition is true)
else
   'do that'  (What to do if the condition is false)
endif
```

```python
age = int(input("enter age"))
if age > 15:
    print("Allow on to ride")
else:
    print("Do not allow on to ride")
```

Figure 14.4 *A Python program using an IF–ELSE structure*

We can nest conditions inside other conditions to test for more complex situations, for example a heating system that turns on if the temperature is below 19 °C and off if the temperature is over 21 °C.

```
Get temperature
if temperature < 19 then
   Switch heating on
else
   if temperature > 21 then
      Switch heating off
   endif
endif
```

Two IF ELSE structures, one **nested** inside the other on right

Notice how we indent the conditions so that we can see that there are two conditions, one inside the other.

```python
temp = int(input("enter temperature"))
if temp < 19:
    print("Turn heating ON")
else:
    if temp > 21:
        print("Turn heating OFF")
    # end of second condition
# end of first condition
```

Figure 14.5 *A Python program with a nested IF–ELSE structure*

3 **Iteration:** In the previous example we use a condition to decide which of two alternative paths to follow. If we need to repeat a process while a condition is true, or until a condition is true, we need another type of control, iteration.

There are three basic approaches to creating a loop.

1 By counting a set number of loops.

2 By repeating a set of instructions until a condition is met.

3 By repeating a set of instructions while a condition is true.

The FOR–NEXT structure allows the program to repeat a set of instructions between a 'for' command and a 'next' command a set number of times, for example the standard multiplication table for the number 7 from 1 up to 12:

```
for k = 1 TO 12
  print (k, "times 7 is " ,k*7)
next k
```

In this example the FOR–NEXT loop uses the index value k. Each time it reaches `next` it adds 1 to k and repeats the loop until k is 12. Note it adds 1 to k on the last time through so when leaving the loop, k is in fact 13.

The structure assumes a step of +1 each time, but it is possible to select other values for the step, for example counting down lives in a game:

```
for lives = 10 to 0 step -1
```

will count down from 10 to 0.

Note

Choosing certain combinations of start value, stop value and step can lead to a loop that will never end, for example `FOR index = 5 TO 10 step -1` will never reach 10. Most programming languages will trap this error by comparing the end point with the current value of the index. It will note that the step is negative and halt the loop after one iteration.

The step can be any value, integers or real numbers, for example 3, –5, 0.5, and so on.

If the number of times the loop is to be executed is not known, the loop needs to use a condition to determine when to stop.

The REPEAT UNTIL loop repeats a set of instructions until a condition is true. It checks the condition at the end of the loop so it must execute the instructions at least once.

The WHILE DO loop repeats a set of instructions if a condition is true. The condition is checked before the loop starts so it may not be executed at all.

```
count = 0
total = 0
repeat
  value=input ("Enter a number")
  count= count + 1
  total = total + value
  more=input ("more numbers ? " )
until more != "yes"
print (total, total/count)
```

```
count = 0
total = 0
more = "yes"
while more="yes"
    value=input ("Enter a number" )
    count= count + 1
    total = total + value
    more=input ("more numbers ? ")
endwhile
print (total, total/count)
```

Note

Some programming languages do not support both of these structures, but by planning carefully, this is not an issue and either can be used to solve the same problem.

Task

Using your chosen programming language, code these programs using whichever loop structures are supported.

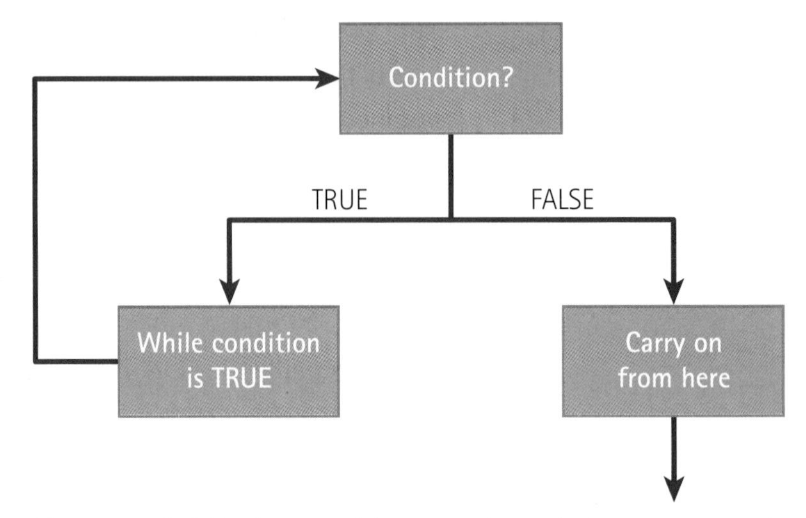

Figure 14.6 *A Boolean condition determines whether to repeat code or not for a WHILE loop*

Extension Activity

1 Write a pseudocode program or a program in your chosen language to take in values from the user until they indicate there are no more, then output the highest and the lowest values.

2 Write a pseudocode program or a program in your chosen language to calculate the sum of the first five positive odd numbers.

3 Write a pseudocode program or a program in your chosen language to output the squares of the positive integers from 1 to a number selected by the user.

Save your programs so that you can use them when you reach Chapter 15.

Operations

In the examples, we have used + and * operations. These are standard mathematical operations that can be applied to numeric data types, the results of such operations being assigned to a variable. Depending upon the language being used, the assignment operator is =, or :=, or ::=, but these all mean the same. The result of the operation is to be stored in the variable on the left-hand side of the assignment.

The standard operators are:

Operator	Name	Example	Comment
+	Add	total =num1+num2	Adds the values represented by the variables num1 and num2 and stores the result in the variable total.
–	Subtract	value = num1–num2	Subtracts the value represented by num2 from the value represented by num1 and stores the result as value.
*	Multiply	value = num1*num2	Multiplies the value represented by num1 by the value represented by num2 and stores the result as value.
/	Divide	value = num1/num2	Divides the value represented by num1 by the value represented by num2 and stores the result as value.
^	Exponentiation	value =num1^x	Raises num1 to the xth power, e.g. 3^3 is 3*3*3 = 27, and stores this as value.

Note

If num1 and num2 are integers, the result after addition, subtraction and multiplication will also be an integer, BUT the result after division may not be, it could be a real number. If num1 and num2 are real numbers then the results for all operations could be either a real number or an integer.

Some operations only apply to integers.

Operator	Name	Example	Comment
MOD %	Modulus	value = num1MODnum2 e.g. if num1 = 14 and num2 = 3 value = 14MOD3 = 2	MOD returns the remainder after division. 14/3 = 4 rem **2**
DIV //	Quotient	value = num1DIVnum2 e.g. if num1 = 14 and num2 = 3 value = 14DIV3 = 4	DIV returns the whole number part of the division. 14/3 = **4** rem 2

Comparison operators

When looking at conditions, we checked if a variable had a certain value. In the examples for iterations, if more= "yes". This comparison returns either TRUE or FALSE. The = sign is being used not as an assignment but as a comparison operator.

- If we use the command num1=3 then we are assigning the value 3 to the variable num1.
- If we use the command IF num1=3 we are asking if num1 is equal to 3.

Programming languages often use slightly different symbols for assignment and comparison to clarify the difference.

Comparison operator	Meaning
= =	Is equal to
>	Is greater than
<	Is less than
!=	Is not equal to
<=	Is less than or equal to
>=	Is greater than or equal to

```
num1=int(input("enter first number "))
num2=int(input("Enter second number "))
if num1>num2:
    print("TRUE")
else:
    print("FALSE")
```

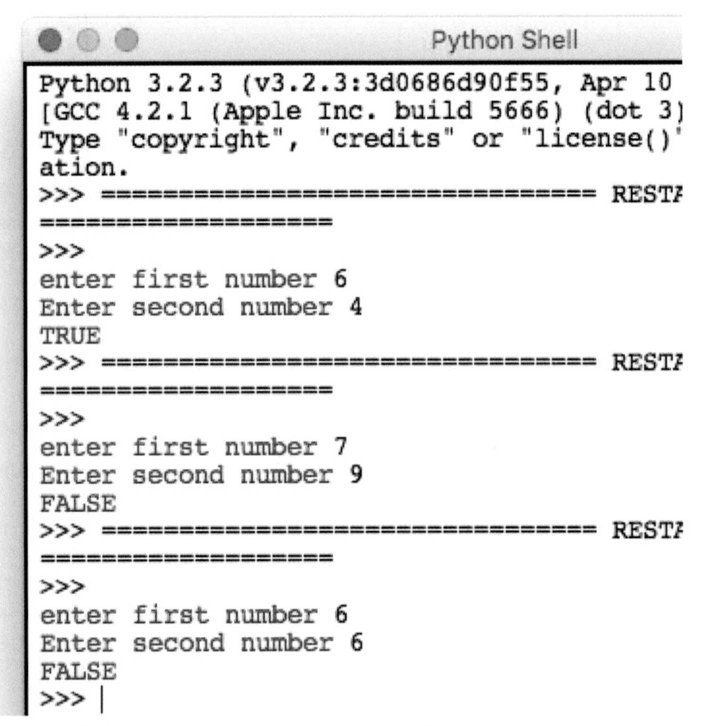

Figure 14.7 *A Python program to compare values using >*

Here are some examples:

Variables	Condition	Comment	Value returned
a=5, b=7	a>b	5 is NOT bigger than 7	FALSE
a=5, b=7	a!=b	5 is NOT the same as 7	TRUE
a=5, b=7	a<=b	5 is less than 7	TRUE
a=3, b=3	a>=b	3 is the same as 3	TRUE
a=3, b=3	a!=b	3 is NOT different from 3	FALSE

These conditions can be combined using the Boolean operators AND and OR or reversed using NOT.

- NOT would simply reverse the output from FALSE to TRUE or TRUE to FALSE.
- Combining with AND means that both conditions must be TRUE for the value returned to be TRUE.
- If combined with OR, then just one of the conditions needs to be TRUE to return TRUE.

Here are some examples:

Variables	Condition	Comment	Value returned
a=5, b=7 c=4, d=2	(a>b) AND (c>d)	5 NOT greater than 7 FALSE 4 greater than 2 TRUE	FALSE
a=5, b=7 c=4, d=2	(a!=b) AND (c>=d)	5 is not the same as 7 TRUE 4 is greater than 2 TRUE	TRUE
a=5, b=7 c=4, d=2	(a>b) OR (c>d)	5 NOT greater than 7 FALSE 4 greater than 2 TRUE	TRUE

When using arithmetic operators, it is important to apply them in the correct order, for example:

3*5–2 means 15–2 = 13

But:

3*(5–2) means 3*3 = 9

In the first example, the multiply operator takes priority over the subtract operator, but in the second example the brackets take priority over the multiply operator, making these two very different statements.

The order in which operators are applied is:

Operations inside brackets are dealt with first.	( )
Unary operations (e.g. signs) are next	– (negative sign e.g. –5), NOT
Exponentiation and roots	^, √
Multiplication and division	* ,/ , DIV, MOD
Add and subtract	+, – (e.g. 5–3)
Comparison operators	<, >, <=, >=, =(equals), !=
Boolean operators	AND, OR
Assignment	= (e.g. x=3 or x=3+5)

Questions

1 What is the value assigned to the variable x for the following?

(a) x= 23−2*3
(b) x= (12−2)*3
(c) x= 6*2/4
(d) x= 8/(3−1)
(e) x= 19MOD4
(f) x= 22MOD5*2
(g) x= 28DIV5
(h) x= 23DIV 2*3

2 What will be returned by the following comparisons?

(a) a!=b if a=6 and b=5
(b) a>=b if a=6 and b=5
(c) a>b OR c<d if a=3, b=3, c=4, d=2
(d) a<=b AND c!=d if a=4, b=4, c=2, d=3

Arrays

When using variables, it is good program design to make obvious the purpose of each variable. If the program requires a large number of variables all of the same basic description, such as a list of names, then we use an array.

Note

Most programming languages number lists and arrays starting at 0, not 1.

An array uses a single identifier (or variable name) with an index value to provide a set of variables, for example we might use a list of 10 names. This can be declared as an array with 10 spaces: `Names(10)`. This will reserve 10 spaces in memory called Names(0), Names(1), and so on to Names(9).

We can reference the contents of the array by name and index value, so in the following array, Names(3) is Abigail.

Names

0	1	2	3	4	5	6	7	8	9
Henry	Abid	Jaswinder	Abigail	Mikael	John	Umar	Hannah	Li	Keith

The content of the array can be changed by providing new values for the array items, so the instruction Names(2)=Ruben will modify the array to:

Names

0	1	2	3	4	5	6	7	8	9
Henry	Abid	Ruben	Abigail	Mikael	John	Umar	Hannah	Li	Keith

If we need to store more than just a name, for example the names for students divided into their work groups for a project, with a class of 20 and four groups of five, we could choose an array with dimension (5,4).

Note

In the Python programming language, lists are often considered equivalent to one-dimensional arrays, but there are some notable differences:

- Arrays can only store one data type.
- For arrays, it is normal to declare the maximum size of the array.

The Python programming language does have an array structure, but its use is quite specialised. It is possible to declare a two-dimensional array in the Python programming language by making each item in a list another list.

Extension Activity

Using your chosen programming language, declare an array and populate it with data.

Modify the program to be able to output data from a specific location and modify data at a specific location.

Save your program so that you can use it when you reach Chapter 15.

Names

	0	1	2	3
0	James	Helen	Frida	Umar
1	Ruben	Abigail	Mikael	Li
2	John	Hannah	Abid	Daniel
3	Jayne	Keith	Jaswinder	Henry
4	Kyle	Sheila	Thomas	Jin

In this case we identify a specific entry by giving two coordinates, for example Names(3,2) is Jaswinder.

We can populate an array by collecting the data from a user using a simple FOR NEXT loop.

```
Names(9)
for index = 0 to 9
  Names(index)=input ("Enter name " )
next index
```

To populate a two-dimensional array we can nest FOR NEXT loops to run through all the possible locations.

```
Names(3,4)
for x= 0 to 3
  for y = 0 to 4
    Names(x,y)=input ("Enter name ")
  next y
next x
```

Questions

3 The following shows values stored in an array at the start of a process:

	0	1	2	3
0	Apple	Cherry	Banana	Pear
1	Lemon	Orange	Raspberry	Damson
2	Grape	Pineapple	Peach	Plum

The value in `fruit(0,3)` is Pear.

(a) What is the value of `fruit(1,2)`?

(b) What location stores the name *grape*?

(c) Redraw the table after the following series of commands has been executed:

(i) `fruit(2,3)='Lime'`

(ii) `delete fruit(1,1)`

(iii) `fruit(1,0)='Strawberry'`

Files

Key Term

File Stored data saved on a suitable medium.

An array is just a set of indexed variables and, when the program is closed, all the data is lost. If the data needs to be kept then the data must be written to a **file** and stored.

In order to use a data file, the program must identify the name of the file, its location, whether the file is to be read from or written to and a communication channel. The commands to do all of this vary between programming languages, but there will be commands to:

- open the file for write access (this will often create a file if it does not already exist)
- open a file for read access
- close a file
- identify the end of a file.

Extension Activity

In your chosen programming language, write a program to get data from a user until they say they have finished entering data, and store this in a file. Modify the program so that it can retrieve this data into an array or list.

Save your program so that you can use it when you reach Chapter 15.

To save the data stored in a one-dimensional array with 10 locations we would need to:

```
open for write access savednames.dat
for i = 0 to 9
  write to file names(i)
next i
close savednames.dat
```

To read them back:

```
open for read access savednames.dat
j=0
while NOT end of file
  read from file names(j)
  j=j+1
endwhile
close savednames.dat
```

Records

Arrays and lists store data by index values, so to identify a specific value we need to know the index. This is not always the easiest way to identify what we are looking for. Records store data by attributes, or field names. To create a record we must first define the attributes. For a simple address book these might be:

- First_name
- Last_name
- Telephone
- Email

The data file with this record structure will have to be initialised with these attributes before any data can be stored.

Populating the data file is then achieved by creating a new copy of the record for the address book stored under these attributes. This structure is used by database management systems such as Microsoft Access®. We refer to the data structures formed by the process as tables.

Structured query language (SQL)

Data stored in tables can be queried by the name of the field or attribute using structured query language (SQL). SQL commands can be quite complex, but are essentially used to isolate and display a subset of the data.

For the table of data `tblAddress_book` defined above, the table may contain the following data:

First_name	Last_Name	Telephone	Email
Bill	Wilson	02223334445	bw@notreal.cod
Graham	Mills	02232232232	gw@notexist.cot
Harry	Smith	01223123123	harry@home.vid
Sheila	Jones	01212121212	SJ@home.vid

The SQL command SELECT can be used to select data from the table, for example:

```
SELECT "First_name", "Telephone" from "tblAddress_book"
```

would return the data:

Bill, 02223334445

Graham, 02232232232

Harry, 01223123123

Sheila, 01212121212

The data selected can have conditions applied to it using the WHERE command, for example:

```
SELECT "First_name", "Email" from "tblAddress_
book" WHERE "Last_name" = 'Mills'
```

will return the matching data:

Graham, gw@notexist.cot

The conditions applied can be modified using wildcards, for example * means 'everything'.

```
SELECT * from "tblAddress_book"
```

returns all the data.

% means 'any string of characters' and is useful for looking for anything with a particular element in the field. It is particularly useful when used with the LIKE command, for example:

```
SELECT "First_name", "Email" from "tblAddress_
book" WHERE "Email" LIKE '%vid'
```

will return the matching data:

Harry, harry@home.vid

Sheila, SJ@home.vid

_ can be used to replace a single character, for example:

```
SELECT "First_name", "Email" from "tblAddress_
book" WHERE "Email" LIKE 'co_'
```

will return:

Bill, bw@notreal.cod

Graham, gw@notexist.cot

Note

Find a version of SQL (Access or Libre Office for example, have SQL commands available), and try using SQL commands on a data set.

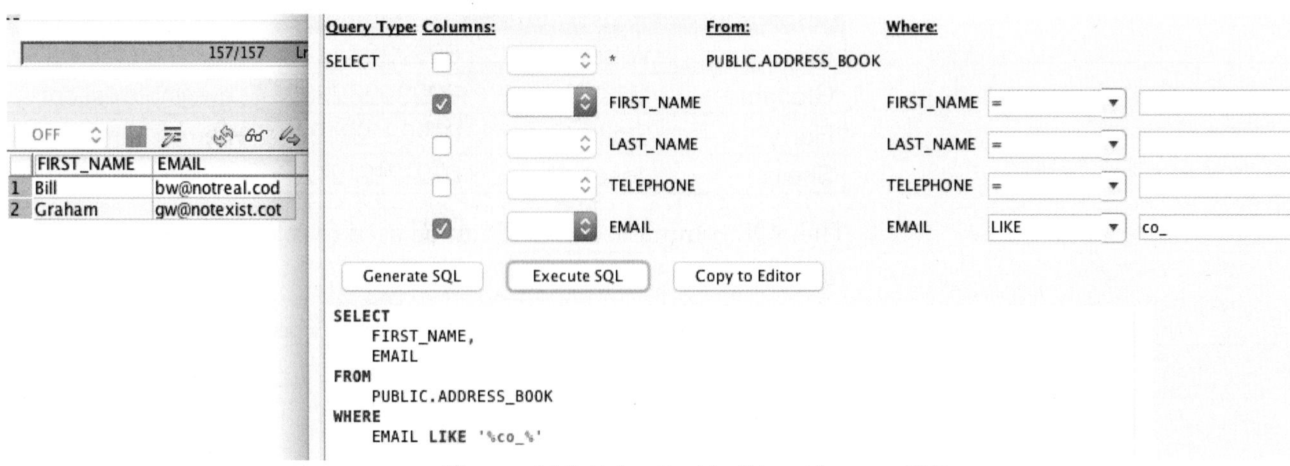

***Figure 14.8** Using the '-' wildcard in razor SQL*

Other useful SQL commands include:

- **CREATE:** This command can be used to create a table.
- **INSERT:** This command can be used to insert data into a table.
- **DELETE:** This command can be used to remove data from a table.

Questions

4 This is the data table `tblsales`.

Record_ID	Item_name	Supplier	Price	Quantity_stock
231	Plastic fork	Hodden	0.25	3000
311	Metal tray	Bilton	8.50	10
232	Plastic plate	Hodden	0.12	1200
421	Wooden spoon	Caddon	1.20	55
331	Metal dish	Bilton	6.35	15

(a) What will be returned by the following queries?

(i)
```
SELECT "Item_name", "Price" from "tblsales"
WHERE "Supplier" = 'Bilton'
```

(ii)
```
SELECT "Record_ID", "Item_name", "Supplier"
from "tblsales" WHERE "Price"<'1.00'
```

(iii)
```
SELECT "Record_ID", "Item_name", from
"tblsales" WHERE "Item_name" LIKE
'Plastic%'
```

(b) Write a query to print out the `Record_ID`, `Item _ name` and `Supplier` for all items where the stock level is less than 50.

(c) Write a query to print out the `Record_ID`, `Item _ name` and `Quantity _ stock` for all items where the `Record_ID` starts with a 2.

String manipulation

String variables simply store a string of characters. It is possible to manipulate the contents of a string using a range of commands. Typically we can:

1 Return the length of a string as an integer.

Note

In the Python programming language, `text[2:3]` means from the 3rd character to the 3rd character in the text and would return a single character, `'m'`. We can achieve the same result in the Python programming language by using `text[2:5]`.

Example

If text = "Computing", len(text) = 9

We can separate and return parts of the string, for example:

- text[3] would return the fourth character of the text, "p".
- text[0:4] would return the first four characters, "Comp".
- text[2:3] would return from character 3 for 3 characters, "mpu"

2 Locate sub-strings within strings returning TRUE if it exists or locating the start position.

Example

text = “Computing"

searchstring = “put"

searchstring in text would return TRUE.

In the Python programming language, the location of the sub-string would be found using a search function. Other languages have built in features to do this.

Example

VB.net has a function called InStr:

InStr(text,searchstring) would return 4.

Note

In the Python programming language, the string command '`find`' will return the starting location for a substring. Python treats strings as lists, so the first character in the string is in position 0 not 1. In this case, it returns the value 3 when searching for '`put`' in the string '`Computing`':

```
text="Computing"
searchstring="put"
print(text.find(searchstring))
```

```
Python Shell
Python 3.2.3 (v3.2.3:3d0686d90f55, Apr 10 2012, 1
1:25:50)
[GCC 4.2.1 (Apple Inc. build 5666) (dot 3)] on da
rwin
Type "copyright", "credits" or "license()" for mo
re information.
>>> ================================ RESTART ====
==============================
>>>
3
>>> |
```

Figure 14.9 *The code for this in the Python programming language*

3 Concatenation, simply combining two strings into a single one, often simply by using the + sign.

Example

text1= "red"

text2= "blue"

text1+text2 will return "redblue"

Questions

5 A programming language has the following string-handling commands:

- len where, for a string variable, 'text' len(text) returns the length of the string
- text[start,number] will return the substring starting at the start position indicated by start for the number of characters identified by the variable number.

(a) If text is 'Computing is fun', what is returned by:

(i) len(text)

(ii) text[3,3]

(iii) text[9,5]

(b) What command returns the string 'fun'?

(c) Use the variables: text1 'cat', text2 'sat', text3 'the', text4 'on', text5 'mat' to make the string 'the cat sat on the mat'.

Functions and procedures

Apart from the simplest linear ones, programs consist of several modules, each performing part of the task. If these tasks are completed more than once then, to avoid typing the same code over and over again, these modules can be written as subprograms, functions or procedures.

Functions and procedures are an invaluable tool when writing well-structured programs because:

- they can reduce the overall size of the code as the code need not be repeated in several places
- the use of named subprograms can make the code much more readable for maintenance purposes
- using them can reduce the time taken to produce the code since the routines only need to be written and tested once
- use can reduce debugging time since the code need only be checked in one place
- there are many pre-written and thoroughly tested procedures and functions that can be reused as building blocks for a program, saving time and reducing the chance of errors.

Functions

Functions are subprograms that can be called whenever they are required. They are called with some data. This data is input into the function, which then returns appropriate outputs. The typical process is:

1 The program reaches a line of code containing a call to a function.
2 The program passes control to the function.
3 The instructions inside the function are executed until they are either completed or there is a code that passes control out of the function.
4 Control is returned to the line with the function call in the main program.
5 Any results calculated by the function are returned to the main program and used in place of the function.

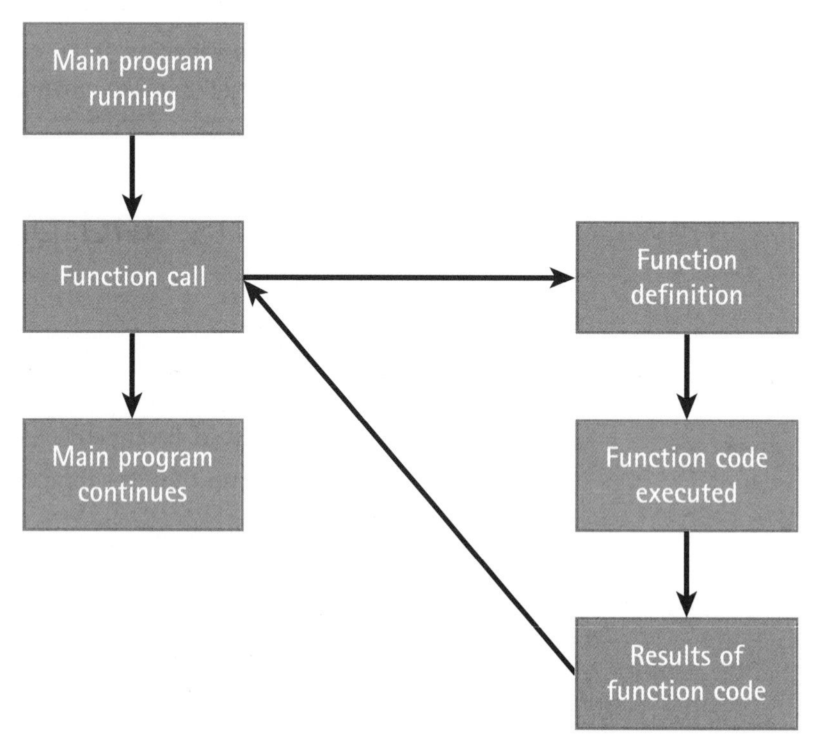

Figure 14.10 *Calling a function*

Functions are defined outside the main body of the program. To define a function we need:

- a function name
- any parameters (data to be passed to the function)
- the code for the function
- the outputs (the value returned to the main program).

Example

A simple function to calculate the area of a circle given the radius:

- function name 'area'
- parameters to be passed 'radius'
- the code area= 3.14159*radius*radius
- the output returned to the main program 'area'.

```
# the function definition
def area(radius):
    area=3.14159*radius*radius
    return area

# the main body of the program
value=int(input("Enter the radius for the circle"))
print("Area of circle is")
print(area(value))
```

Figure 14.11 *The code for this in the Python programming language*

Procedures

Procedures like functions are also subprograms defined outside the main body of the program. The only real difference between a procedure and a function is that a function should return a value. Procedures do not have to do this. They are subprograms that act independently of the main program.

Note

While functions should return values to the main program, several languages do not have the concept of a procedure and allow for functions that do not return values.

Example

A procedure to print out some text a number of times:

- The procedure 'multiprint' is passed two parameters, 'text' and 'times'.
- It prints the text as many times as it is told to, then returns control to the main program, but no values are returned.

```
# the sub program to print out text several times
def multiprint(text,times):
            for i in range(0,times):
                print(text)



# Main program
sampletext=input("input text to be printed")
value=int(input("number of times to be printed"))
multiprint(sampletext,value)
print("Now control is back with the main program")
```

Figure 14.12 *A procedure in the Python programming language to print text several times*

Questions

6 What is a *function*?

7 What is the difference between a procedure and a function?

8 What are the advantages of using procedures and functions in a program?

Writing reliable programs

When going on holiday, few people simply turn up at the airport and get on whatever flight is available. This sort of approach would result in many problems to solve. Where is the traveller going to stay when they arrive at their destination? They may have packed for hot weather and ended up in Iceland in the winter, or have lots of US dollars but be in a Eurozone country. This approach shows poor planning and will ultimately lead to a poor experience.

Generally, when we go on holiday we plan ahead, we organise flights, hotels, currency and transport to, and possibly from, the airport in advance. We think about the climate and pack accordingly. This does not mean there will not be any other problems, but we have identified (and mitigated) those we can anticipate and will be better placed to deal with any others as they arise.

Programming is similar; planning ahead and trying to anticipate all the things that can go wrong will lead to a much simpler and more effective development and a product with fewer problems left to sort out at the end of the process.

Syntax errors

Key Term

Syntax error When the rules of the programming language are broken.

Good program design with properly constructed and checked algorithms will eliminate many errors in a program. Using an integrated development environment (IDE) will also help to reduce errors by identifying **syntax errors** in the commands used in the code. Despite this, there may still be errors in the code that prevent it from working as anticipated.

Programming languages require very precise use of the instructions. Unless the correct language rules (syntax) are used the program will generate an error message.

```
a=int(input('Enter the first number'))
b=int(input('Enter the second number'))
c= a+b
print('The answer is '+c)
```

```
Python Shell
Python 3.2.3 (v3.2.3:3d0686d90f55, Apr 10 2012, 11:25:50)
[GCC 4.2.1 (Apple Inc. build 5666) (dot 3)] on darwin
Type "copyright", "credits" or "license()" for more information.
>>> ================================ RESTART =====================
============
>>>
Enter the first number5
Enter the second number7
Traceback (most recent call last):
  File "/Users/george2/Desktop/GCSE CS Book/add.py", line 4, in <
module>
    print('The answer is '+c)
TypeError: Can't convert 'int' object to str implicitly
>>>
```

Figure 15.1 *Error because variable types incompatible in print line*

Syntax errors occur when the programming language has not been used properly. In this example the variable c is an integer but the print line tries to concatenate it with a string.

Some examples of syntax errors include:

- variables not declared before use
- variables not declared properly before use
- incompatible variable types
- using assignments incorrectly, for example 3 + 4 = x rather than x = 3 + 4
- variable names incorrect, for example incorrect spelling or formatting.

Logic errors

Key Term

Logic error When the logical structure of a program produces unexpected results.

Eliminating syntax errors will allow the program to run, but this may still lead to unexpected results because of **logic errors**. These errors may be generated by values in variables not being as expected, for example division by zero.

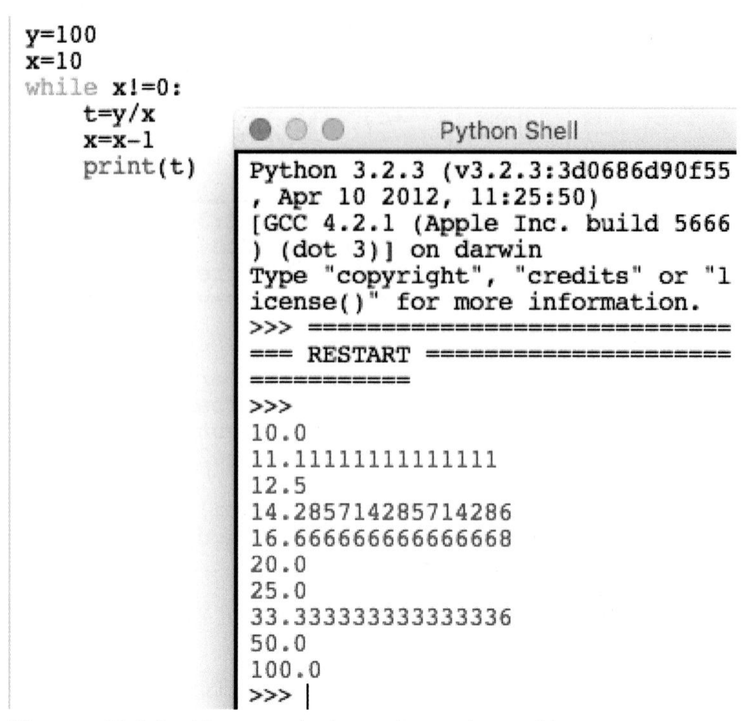

Figure 15.2 *In this example the code produces this output*

However, if the fourth and fifth lines are typed in the wrong order, the syntax is still correct but the logic leads to a division by zero and we get the following output:

```
y=100
x=10
while x!=0:
    x=x-1
    t=y/x
    print(t)
```

```
Python Shell
Python 3.2.3 (v3.2.3:3d0686d90f55, Apr 10 2012, 11:25:50)
[GCC 4.2.1 (Apple Inc. build 5666) (dot 3)] on darwin
Type "copyright", "credits" or "license()" for more information.
>>> ================================ RESTART ================================
==
>>>
11.11111111111111
12.5
14.285714285714286
16.666666666666668
20.0
25.0
33.333333333333336
50.0
100.0
Traceback (most recent call last):
  File "/Users/george2/Desktop/GCSE CS Book/loopy2.py", line 5, in <module>
    t=y/x
ZeroDivisionError: division by zero
>>> |
```

Figure 15.3 *The logic leads to a division by zero and we get this output*

Logic errors can generate a range of problems including:

- division by zero
- programs that do not complete
- the memory is filled with data and creates a stack overflow
- incorrect outputs
- the program crashes.

The main causes of logic errors are:

- conditions that cannot be met in conditional statements
- divisors that can reach zero
- infinite loops
- incorrect algorithm (it does not do what it is meant to)
- incorrect expressions (calculations that are incorrect or missing brackets).

```
c=10
while c!= 0:
    print(c)
    c=c/3
```

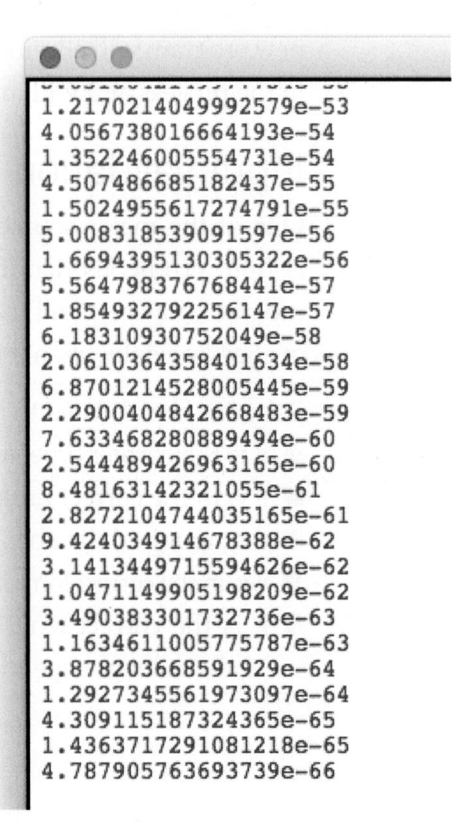

Figure 15.4 *An infinite loop*

In this example, c/3 will never be equal to 0 and the loop will execute forever, or until the program is halted by the user.

Questions

1. What is a *syntax error*? Give two examples of syntax errors.
2. What is a *logic error*? Give two examples of logic errors.
3. The following code segment will produce an error. What is the error and what type of error is it?

```
value = 10
for index = 1 to 0
   print value/index
next
```

4. The expression 'a + b = c' is incorrect. Explain the error and rewrite this to be a valid expression.

Defensive design

Thinking about potential problems before starting the development of a new program will eliminate many of the problems that could occur later in the process and will improve the reliability of the solution.

Input validation

One of the major sources of potential problems when programming is from erroneous data input. If data is entered incorrectly then the program may respond in an unexpected way. Validation is the process of checking data when it is entered to see if it conforms to a rule.

Data can be validated to make sure:

- it is the correct type, for example integer, real, string or Boolean
- it is in the correct range, for example between 1 and 10
- that required data has been entered, that is a presence check
- it is in the correct format, for example dates are in the form dd/mm/yyyy
- it is the correct length, for example telephone numbers are 11 or 12 digits long, depending on the format chosen.

```
number=0
while number<1 or number>10:
    number=int(input("Enter a number between 1 and 10   "))
print("You entered ",number)
```

```
Python Shell
Python 3.2.3 (v3.2.3:3d0686d90f55, Apr 10 2012, 11:25
:50)
[GCC 4.2.1 (Apple Inc. build 5666) (dot 3)] on darwin
Type "copyright", "credits" or "license()" for more i
nformation.
>>> ================================ RESTART ========
========================
>>>
Enter a number between 1 and 10   11
Enter a number between 1 and 10   -2
Enter a number between 1 and 10   0
Enter a number between 1 and 10   7
You entered  7
>>> |
```

Figure 15.5 *Validating a numeric input between 1 and 10*

Validating data does not guarantee that the data is accurate though; it merely checks that the data conforms to the rules for that input, for example a telephone number might have the correct number of digits to pass a validation check but the inputter may still have transposed some numbers so that the client cannot be contacted on that number.

Planning ahead

Note

Division by zero can be checked by calculating the divisor separately. If the divisor is zero then displaying a suitable error message and skipping to an appropriate point in the program will provide a smooth exit rather than a crash.

However carefully thought through the input validation is, there are situations and combinations of data that, during processing, will lead to unexpected results. It is almost impossible to consider all of these but having a plan B, a contingency plan, is always a good idea. When programming, we need to make sure the program can deal with unexpected results that might occur from previous processing stages, for example division by zero.

When we develop a program, we know how it should work, we use the correct sort of data and press the keys in the correct order but this may not be obvious to the end user. They may make different choices about which key to press and what data to enter at each prompt and this may lead to problems. Some users may even deliberately try to crash the system. These actions need to be anticipated. Planning for such contingencies is essential if we are to create a robust program. When writing programs we should:

- use meaningful prompts for each input
- trap unexpected inputs
- anticipate misuse of the system and build in error-trapping for these events
- consider the combined effect of valid input values that are atypical and might lead to errors
- for online systems, identify methods to authenticate the user.

Maintenance

Apart from the simplest programs, it is unlikely a program will be error-free in its first version so revisions will need to be made. Over time the requirements for a program may change and the program will require some modification. Therefore programs need to be well structured and documented to ensure they are easily maintained. A maintenance programmer's job can be made much more straightforward if the originator does the following:

- Keeps logs showing the tests that have been carried out and the results of these tests. This will enable the maintenance programmer to eliminate these as sources of error and simplify the process of tracking down bugs.
- In the code, using indents to show the program structure enables a maintenance programmer to follow the process more effectively, identifying loop entry and exit points more easily.
- Adds comments to the code to identify what each section does and how the program is intended to work.
- Uses meaningful variable names to help identify the purpose of each variable so that the maintenance programmer can see much more clearly what data should be expected at each point.

```
    print('Letters not in word:', end=' ')
    for letter in incorrectLetters:
        print(letter, end=' ')
    print()

    blanks = '_' * len(Word)

    for i in range(len(Word)): # replace blanks with correctly guessed letters
        if Word[i] in correctLetters:
            blanks = blanks[:i] + Word[i] + blanks[i+1:]

    for letter in blanks: # show the hidden word with spaces between each letter
        print(letter, end=' ')
    print()

def getGuess(alreadyGuessed):
    # Returns the letter entered. Makes sure a single letter has been entered.
    while True:
        print('Guess a letter.')
        guess = input()
        guess = guess.lower()
        if len(guess) != 1:
            print('Please enter a single letter.')
        elif guess in alreadyGuessed:
            print('You have already used that letter. Choose again.')
        elif guess not in 'abcdefghijklmnopqrstuvwxyz':
            print('Must be a letter')
        else:
            return guess

def playAgain():
    # Returns True if the player wants to play again otherwise False.
    print('Do you want to play again? (yes or no)')
    return input().lower().startswith('y')
```

Figure 15.6 *A section of the Python programming language code*

This Python code uses sensible variable names and comments to explain what each section does. Also, note how the Python programming language indents the loops.

Testing

The purpose of testing is to ensure the program functions as expected and as defined by the requirements specification. It is essential to find situations that could impact on the function, usability and maintainability of the program. There are various types of testing:

- **Functional testing** verifies that the program performs as expected by using a subset of the possible inputs carefully chosen to identify normal, abnormal and extreme conditions. This should ensure it not only deals with typical inputs but also unusual inputs and situations.
- **Parametric testing** should be applied to all subprograms such as functions and procedures. These should be tested individually with a range of possible typical, extreme and erroneous parameters and extreme combinations of these parameters.
- **Fault tolerance testing** should check how the program or subprogram copes with illegal or out-of-range values. Ideally the program should identify these and restart at a suitable point or exit gracefully if the data is illegal or out of range.
- **Integration testing** is used to check that once each subprogram has been tested that these subprograms integrate into the main program effectively. It should check that the data output from each module is handled effectively by the other subprograms or the main program.
- **Regression testing** is used to check the knock-on effects of any changes made to a subprogram or the main program; that is, changes in one part do not lead to unexpected results in another part of the program.
- **Iterative testing** is the process of testing the program at every stage of the development process. It is vital that programs are checked at a modular level during development to ensure the individual components of the program function as expected. As each new module is added to a program, the program should be tested to ensure that no errors have been introduced either in the new module itself or as a result of previous modules working with the new module. If programs are not tested at this level it is much more difficult to identify faults in an individual module later. Faults that appear to be the result of one process may be a consequence of inputs from another module. Testing at the modular level is often called *white box testing*.

- **Final testing** is to check that the modules are correctly assembled into a working solution. This is testing that the program functions as expected. This is often called *black box testing*. At this level, the testing is ignoring the detailed process and simply checking with a range of data that the program produces the required results.
- **User acceptance testing** follows on from the final, black box testing stage. Users will not have knowledge of how the program functions and may use it in ways and with data that were not anticipated by the programmer. User acceptance testing tests that the system will work as expected by the end user, with real data and with a typical end user. This is often called *alpha testing*.
  Testing to follow up modifications from this stage, once the product is considered functional, is often carried out with groups of end users and is called *beta testing*.

To test a program effectively, it is necessary to identify suitable test data and the expected outcome required for that data. Test data should cover the following situations:

- **Valid:** test data that is a typical input for the system.
- **Valid extreme:** test data that is valid but at the extreme end of the range of acceptable inputs.
- **Invalid:** test data that is out of range and should be rejected.
- **Invalid extreme:** test data that is invalid but only just outside the limit for being acceptable.
- **Erroneous:** test data that should be rejected because it is the wrong type of input.

Example

To test a system to find the cost of making a mobile phone call

In this case, the final costs for a system that charges 5p for a minute or part of a minute is being tested.

There are many possible combinations but some suitable test values include:

Test	Data	Reason	Expected
Valid whole minutes	120s	Whole minutes only	10p
Valid < whole minute	35s	To check if minutes rounded up	5p
Extreme value in range	60s	To check a boundary condition	5p
Extreme value in range	61s	To check if 1s greater than whole number rounded up correctly	10p
Invalid data	36.7s	To check input not in whole seconds is rejected	Error
Invalid data type	six	To check non-numeric data rejected	Error

It is important to check boundary values because this checks we have used the correct conditions, for example >=60 rather than >60 when checking for whole minutes. Non-numeric values are included because these are often treated as zero by a program, and should be rejected rather than producing unexpected results.

Questions

5 In a program that collects data about birds, there are variables for sex and wingspan. Identify one type of validation for each of these variables that can be used within the program.

6 Explain the difference between white box and black box testing.

7 Why is iterative testing during the development of a program important?

8 A system used at an ATM (automatic teller machine) uses the customer's PIN and available credit to decide whether or not to dispense cash.

Draw a test table including four tests that could be used to check that the code for this works as expected. Identify the test type, the test data to be used, the reason for the test and the expected outcome.

Test	Data	Reason	Expected

Extension Activity

If you completed the Extension Activities in Chapter 14, go back to these programs and:

1. annotate them to explain what each section does
2. identify suitable test data for each one to test that they work under normal, extreme and erroneous situations
3. if the programs fail under testing, add suitable validation or amend the code to make them more robust.

16 Data representation, conversion and arithmetic

Key Terms

Binary A number system based on 2, using just two symbols: 0 and 1.

Denary A number system based on 10, using ten digits: 0–9.

We have already mentioned how important the work of John von Neumann was – he proposed the principle used in all modern computers that data and instructions should all be stored in **binary** (see Chapter 2). It is easier to see how numbers are stored in this way, but what about images, text and sound? The principle is, of course, to convert images, text and sound into numbers before storing them. In order to understand how the computer stores all these forms of data in binary we need to first understand the concept of binary numbers and how values can be converted to binary.

The computer uses electronic circuits to store one of two values using a switch – the switch is either on (1) or off (0). Using a number of these switches provides us with many possible combinations of 1s and 0s, which we can use to represent numeric values.

In the common **denary** (or decimal) (base 10) system we all use every day, there are 10 different symbols: 0, 1, 2, 3, 4, 5, 6, 7, 8, 9. We use these symbols to write numbers, so 573 means 5 lots of 100, 7 lots of 10 and 3 1s. In primary school we may have seen this written in a table:

100	10	1
5	7	3

The column values are simply 10 times the previous value as we move from right to left.

In binary (base 2) we only have two symbols: 0 and 1. We can use a similar table, but this time we multiply the column values by 2 rather than 10.

128	64	32	16	8	4	2	1

So the binary number 101101 can be put into the table starting from the right-hand column.

128	64	32	16	8	4	2	1
		1	0	1	1	0	1

Using the same approach as we did for base 10, we can say we have:

1 lot of 32, no 16s, 1 lot of 8, 1 lot of 4, no 2s and 1 lot of 1.

That is 32+8+4+1.

This means that 101101 in binary is the same as 45 in base 10.

Note

1000 is not a very tidy number in binary, so we often use the closest approximation that is a power of 2: 2^{10} or $2 \times 2 \times 2 \times 2 \times 2 \times 2 \times 2 \times 2 \times 2 \times 2 = 1024$. In computing, there is set of names used to describe binary numbers as multiples of 1024. These are not in common use and you may well see 1024 bytes referred to as a kilobyte.

8 bits	byte
1024 bytes	kibibyte
1024 kibibytes	mebibyte
1024 mebibytes	gibibyte
1024 gibibytes	tebibyte
1024 tebibytes	pebibyte

Units

In base 10, we have some important numbers we give names to, for example 10 × 10 × 10 = 1000, which we call *thousand*. One thousand multiplied by 1000 is a million, and so on. We also use the metric system based on 10s and use the name *kilo* to refer to thousands, for example kilogram or kilometre. In binary there is also a system of names to describe key values.

The basic unit is 1 or 0 – a **bi**nary digi**t** or *bit*.

A group of 8 bits is called a *byte*. Half a byte (4 bits) is called a **nibble**. (Computer humour!)

In denary, we refer to multiples of 1000 using the prefix *kilo*, as in 'kilogram' or 'kilometre'. We do the same in binary.

8 bits (b)	1 byte (B)
1000 B	1 kilobyte (KB)
1000 KB	1 megabyte (MB)
1000 MB	1 gigabyte (GB)
1000 GB	1 terabyte (TB)
1000 TB	1 petabyte (PB)

Note

The symbol for *bit* is lower-case b; the symbol for *byte* is upper-case B.

1 Petabyte = 1,000,000,000,000,000 = 1 billion million bytes
1 terabyte = 1,000,000,000,000 = 1 million million bytes

Numbers

We have already seen how to convert a binary number to its base 10 (denary) equivalent. We add up the column values for every column containing a 1.

Example

Another example: 11000110

128	64	32	16	8	4	2	1
1	1	0	0	0	1	1	0

128 + 64 + 4 + 2

= 198 in base 10.

The process to convert from base 10 to binary is also straightforward. There are other approaches, but one simple process is to divide by 2 repeatedly, recording the remainder until the answer is 0, for example 199 in denary to binary is:

199	÷	2	=	99	Rem	1	This is the number of 1s
99	÷	2	=	49	Rem	1	This is the number of 2s
49	÷	2	=	24	Rem	1	This is the number of 4s
24	÷	2	=	12	Rem	0	This is the number of 8s
12	÷	2	=	6	Rem	0	This is the number of 16s
6	÷	2	=	3	Rem	0	This is the number of 32s
3	÷	2	=	1	Rem	1	This is the number of 64s
1	÷	2	=	0	Rem	1	This is the number of 128s

OR

128	64	32	16	8	4	2	1
1	1	0	0	0	1	1	1

199 in denary is therefore 11000111 in binary.

Note

Another method that is useful for doing these conversions in your head is to search for the largest multiple of 2 that can be subtracted from the number, take it away and repeat the process with the remainder, for example:

199 – 128 = 71	(put 1 in the column under 128)
71 – 64 = 7	(put 1 in 64 column)
7 – 4 = 3	(put 1 in 4 column)
3 – 2 = 1	(put 1 in 2 column)
1 – 1 = 0	(put 1 in 1 column)

All of these examples have been limited to 8 bits but the computer deals with significantly larger numbers. While the arithmetic becomes a little harder the process remains the same.

Adding binary numbers

Adding binary numbers is very similar to the way we add denary numbers.

Example

Adding 256 and 165

```
2 5 6
1 6 5
-----

-----
```

6 + 5 = 11 So we write down 1 and carry 1

```
2 5 6
1 6 5
-----
    1
-----
  1
```

5 + 6 + the carry 1 = 12
So we write down 2 and carry 1

```
2 5 6
1 6 5
-----
  2 1
-----
1 1
```

2 + 1 + the carry 1 = 4
We write down 4

```
2 5 6
1 6 5
-----
4 2 1
-----
1 1
```

When adding in binary we follow a very similar process, but note that 1 + 1 = 10 in binary (that is 1 + 1 = 2, which is written as 10 in binary). Similarly 1 + 1 + 1 is 11 in binary.

Note

The word length of a computer is the largest single item of data that can be transferred to and from working memory in a single operation. The size of the number the processor can handle is determined by the word size and the allocation of words to variables. A variable may be allocated one or more words when it is declared. Typically a modern desktop computer will have a word length of 32 or 64 bits.

Example

An example 1111+1011 in binary is:

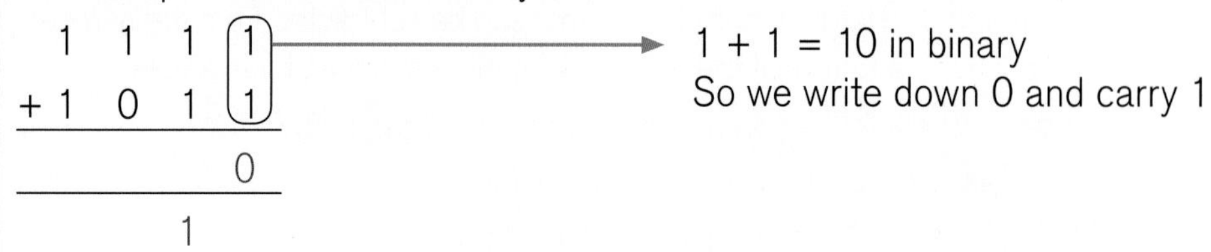

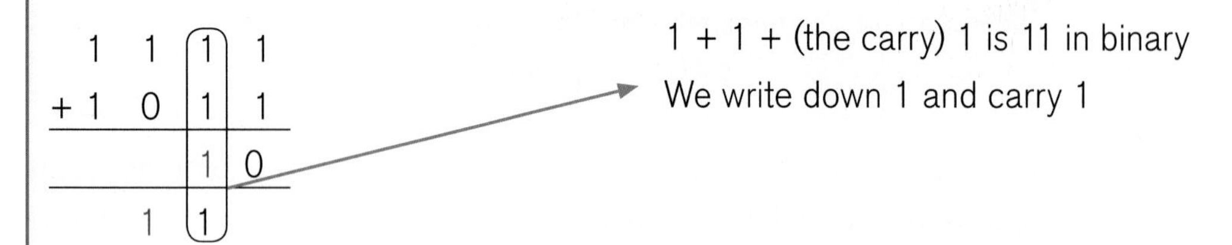

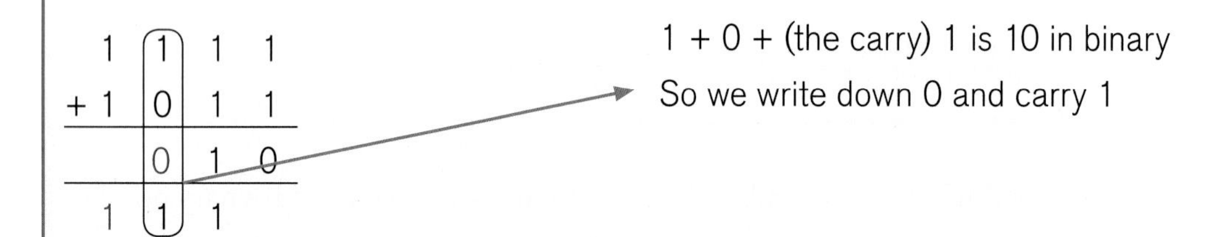

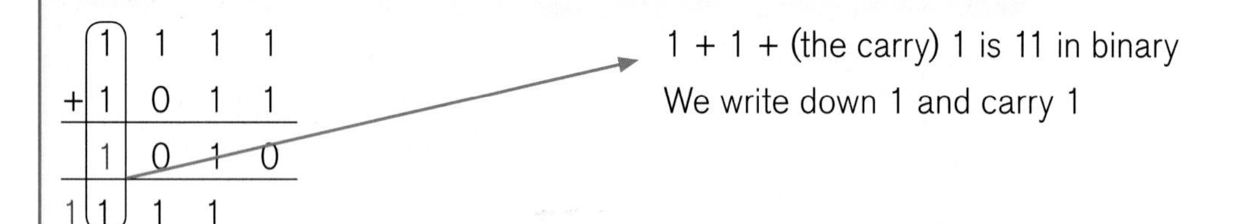


```
   1 1 1 1
 + 1 0 1 1
 ---------
 1 1 0 1 0
 ---------
 1 1 1 1
```

The final carry is the final digit in the sum, giving the answer 11010

In this example, when we added together two 4-bit binary numbers the answer was a 5-bit binary number.

If, for example, we used a computer that only stored 8 digits and added 11000011 to 10000111 we would get:

```
   1 1 0 0 0 0 1 1
 + 1 0 0 0 0 1 1 1
 -----------------
   0 1 0 0 1 0 1 0
 -----------------
 1         1 1 1
```

In this case, the last carry will be lost and we have an **overflow** error

Key Term

Overflow When a number becomes too large to store in the number of bits allocated, it is said to 'overflow' and some bits are 'lost', leaving an incorrect value.

If using just 8 bits, we will have added 195 to 135 and got the result 74. In 8 bits, the largest number we can represent is 1111111, which is 255. 195 + 135 is 330, which is larger than 255 so the result is too large to store in the 8 bits.

Binary shifts

If we convert the denary value 5 to its binary equivalent we get:

128	64	32	16	8	4	2	1
					1	0	1

Now converting 10 to binary we get:

128	64	32	16	8	4	2	1
				1	0	1	0

And 20:

128	64	32	16	8	4	2	1
			1	0	1	0	0

As we multiply by 2 the binary equivalent has simply moved one place to the left, padding with 0s in the right hand columns.

The column headings we have been using are all powers of 2:

128	64	32	16	8	4	2	1
2^7	2^6	2^5	2^4	2^3	2^2	2^1	2^0

So shifting the binary number to the left one place is equivalent to multiplying by 2, two places by 4, three places by 8, and so on.

Similarly, shifting right is equivalent to dividing by 2 for each place the number is moved.

Example

Divide the binary number 1011000 by 4.

Shifting the number two places to the right we get 00101100.

Check: 1011000 = 176, 101100 = 44

176/4 = 44 ✓

Hexadecimal

Large binary numbers are quite difficult to remember and when programmers work with these values they need something that is easier to recognise and appreciate. Converting between base 10 and base 2 constantly would be time consuming and likely to lead to errors. We need something that still uses the base 2 but is simpler to appreciate. A byte has 8 bits and splitting this into two nibbles, each with 4 bits provides an answer.

In 4 bits, we can store numbers between 0000 and 1111, that is 0 to 15.

Key Term

Hexadecimal A number system based on 16 that uses the symbols 0–9 and A–F (to represent the denary values 10–15).

If you recall in base 2, we have just two symbols, 0 and 1 and in base 10, we have 10 symbols, 0–9. A system based on having 16 symbols for the numbers between 0 and 15 would be base 16 or **hexadecimal** (or *hex* for short).

We do, however, need to find symbols for the hexadecimal numbers representing 10–15 and we use A to E for this.

Base 10 (denary)	Base 2 (binary)	Base 16 (hexadecimal, hex)
0	0	0
1	1	1
2	10	2
3	11	3
4	100	4
5	101	5
6	110	6
7	111	7
8	1000	8
9	1001	9
10	1010	A
11	1011	B
12	1100	C
13	1101	D
14	1110	E
15	1111	F

The column values for base 16 are:

256	16	1
16^2	16^1	16^0

This gives us a simple way to convert from hexadecimal to denary using the column values.

Examples

2B in hexadecimal is:

256	16	1
	2	B

That is, two lots of 16 plus eleven 1s, so 32 + 11 = 43.

Here is another example. AC in hexadecimal is:

256	16	1
	A	C

10 × 16 + 12 × 1 = 160 + 12 = 172

Converting from denary to hexadecimal is similar to the process for binary; we divide by 16 repeatedly and record the remainders.

Examples

60 in denary converted to hexadecimal:

60	÷	16	=	3	Rem	12	This is the number of 1s (C)
3	÷	16	=	0	Rem	3	This is the number of 16s (3)

60 in denary is represented by 3C in hexadecimal.

Another example: convert 191 denary into hexadecimal.

191	÷	16	=	11	Rem	15	This is the number of 1s (F)
11	÷	16	=	0	Rem	11	This is the number of 16s (B)

191 in denary is represented by BF in hexadecimal.

Hexadecimal is used by programmers as a simple way of dealing with binary numbers. It is based on using a nibble for each hexadecimal digit.

Using the examples above, 43 is 32 + 8 + 2 + 1

Using this to show 43 in binary we get:

128	64	32	16	8	4	2	1
0	0	1	0	1	0	1	1

Split this into two nibbles:

16s					1s			
8	4	2	1		8	4	2	1
0	0	1	0		1	0	1	1

Now looking up the hexadecimal values for each of these nibbles we get 2B, so the equivalent of 43 in denary is 2B in hexadecimal.

We can convert binary values to hexadecimal values by splitting the binary number into nibbles and converting each nibble to the equivalent hexadecimal symbol.

Example

Converting 10011100 in binary into hexadecimal:

16s					1s			
8	4	2	1		8	4	2	1
1	0	0	1		1	1	0	0
= 9					= 12 or C in hex			

10011100 is 9C in hexadecimal.

Similarly, converting from hexadecimal to binary is very straightforward.

Convert each digit to its binary equivalent and combine the nibbles to make the binary number.

Example

Converting the hexadecimal number AE to its binary equivalent:

A = 10					E = 14			
1	0	1	0		1	1	1	0

So AE in hexadecimal is 10101110 in binary.

Questions

1 Convert 18, 41, 135 and 221 in denary to binary.

2 Convert 1101, 11101, 10101010 and 11111101 from binary into denary.

3 How many kilobytes are there in 3 terabytes?

4 How many megabytes are there in 2 petabytes?

5 Add the following binary numbers, showing your workings:

(a) 1101 + 10001

(b) 10011 + 11111

(c) 11000111 + 11101

6 Convert the following binary numbers to hexadecimal:

(a) 10000011

(b) 10101100

(c) 00111110

(d) 11111111

7 Convert the following hexadecimal numbers to binary and to denary:

(a) 3B (b) AE (c) 23 (d) 5C

Check digits

When data is transferred, it is possible for this data to be corrupted. Data copied by a user, for example a credit card number, may also be entered incorrectly. To avoid such problems, extra data is transferred with the number as a check digit or checksum.

The check digit is calculated from the original number using a suitable algorithm or method and appended to the value before being transmitted or used. European Article Numbers (EAN) are used on products. There are various forms for the EAN, but one, EAN8 uses a seven-digit number plus a checksum digit. These are the type of codes used for barcodes on products.

Example

To calculate the EAN8 for a number:

1 Starting at the first digit on the left, multiply by 3 then 1 alternately.
2 Add these values together.
3 Subtract from the next highest multiple of 10 to get the check digit.
4 Append the check digit to the right of the number to form the EAN8.

Figure 16.1 *This is the barcode for this EAN8 number.*

If an item is allocated the seven-digit number 5234131 we can calculate its EAN8 number using this method:

Item number	5	2	3	4	1	3	1	
Multiply by 3, 1, etc.	*3	*1	*3	*1	*3	*1	*3	
Add these values	15	2	9	4	3	3	3	=39
Subtract from next highest multiple of 10 to get check digit	40–39=1, so check digit is 1							
EAN8	5	2	4	3	1	3	1	1

The EAN8 is 52341311.

If we apply the same method to this new number it will be a multiple of 10 and that is how the system checks that the number is valid.

Another example is basic parity checking on binary numbers. The number of 1s in the data is counted and the check digit is set at 1 or 0 so that the number contains an even number of 1s; this is even parity. We could also choose to use odd parity where the number of 1s should be odd. Provided the systems communicating agree on this protocol, a simple check on receipt will identify corruption to a single bit in the number.

Example

We wish to transmit the seven binary digits 1100100 using even parity.

Counting the number of ones in this binary we get 3.

We are using even parity so we append a 1 to the original number to get 11001001. This now has four 1s, an even number.

If the second bit of the value is corrupted, we would transmit 10001001, which has an odd number of 1s (that is three 1s) and the system would request that the data be resent.

Characters

Key Terms

ASCII (American Standard Code for Information Interchange) A 7-bit code to represent a set of characters available to a computer.

Character set The complete set of characters available to a computer.

When you press the key on a computer keyboard, a code is generated that the computer can convert into a symbol for display or printing. It is clearly very important for systems to agree on these codes and their meanings if the data is to make sense. In 1960, the American Standards Association agreed a standard set of codes to represent the main characters used by telegraph systems. This is called **ASCII (American Standard Code for Information Interchange)**. This system was designed to deal with basic textual messages and included codes for:

All the main alphabetic characters, upper and lower case	52 characters
All the numeric symbols 0–9	10 characters
32 punctuation and other symbols plus 'space'	33 characters
32 non-printable control codes	32 characters

So, in total 127 characters.

In binary 127 is 1111111 so this system required 7 bits. Initially the ASCII **character set** used a 7-bit binary number plus a parity bit to give an 8-bit binary code.

Some ASCII codes are:

Binary	Hex	Decimal	Character
0100000	20	32	'space'
1000001	41	65	A
1000010	42	66	B
1011010	5A	90	Z

Binary	Hex	Decimal	Character
1100001	61	97	a
1111001	79	121	y
1111010	7A	122	z
1111111	7F	127	'delete'

If you look at a complete table of ASCII values on the internet you will see that the character values increase from 'A' to 'Z' then from 'a' to 'z'. When sorting these values their numeric value is used and consequently 'Z' comes before 'a' when sorting characters, for example 'Zebra' will be sorted to come before 'apple'.

ASCII was excellent for sending textual messages in English but it failed to deal with a range of other characters we often need. It did not include any non-English symbols or many mathematical symbols. As 8-bit computers became the norm and errors in transmission were reduced or even eliminated by the technology, the ASCII character set was extended to use the full 8 bits to represent characters. This increased the number of characters that could be represented by 128 and conveniently used just one byte to store each character.

Key Term 

Unicode A character set that uses code pages to provide a range of language symbols. There are several billion possible character codes available to Unicode.

The **Unicode** system for encoding characters was originally a 16-bit system that enabled over 65 000 characters and symbols to be represented. This was quickly updated to overcome the 16-bit restriction by using a series of code pages to represent the chosen language symbols. There are several billion possible character codes available to Unicode. Unicode has largely replaced the ASCII system, though the Unicode system still allocates the same numeric values to the original ASCII character set. ASCII could now be considered a subset of the Unicode system for coding characters.

Questions 

8 What is meant by the *character set* of a computer?

9 Explain how ASCII represents the character set of a computer.

10 What happens if you sort the list 'Apple, grape, cherry, Damson' in a program using ASCII or Unicode to represent the character set?

11 Explain the difference between using an ASCII character set and a Unicode character set.

Images

This simple image, typical of those found in early space invader games, can be represented in just eight bytes. Using 0 for white and 1 for black and one row for each row of the image.

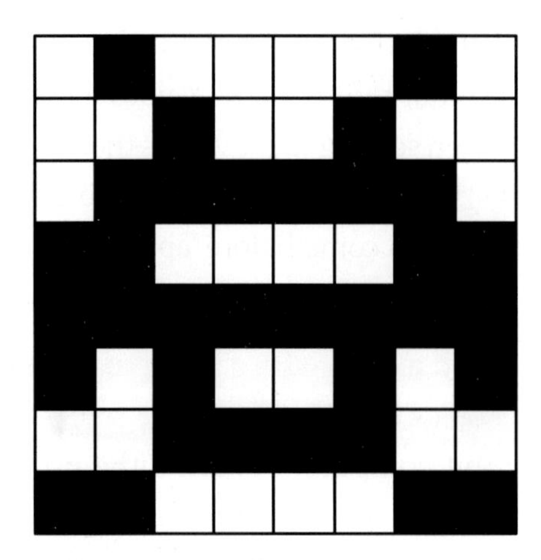

0	1	0	0	0	0	1	0
0	0	1	0	0	1	0	0
0	1	1	1	1	1	1	0
1	1	0	0	0	0	1	1
1	1	1	1	1	1	1	1
1	0	1	0	0	1	0	1
0	0	1	1	1	1	0	0
1	1	0	0	0	0	1	1

In reality images are far more complex than this and this simple drawing of a cat has 100 × 123 pixels. That is just under 2 kilobytes.

This image is made up of dots and, when enlarged, we can see that the image becomes less defined and these dots or pixels can clearly be seen.

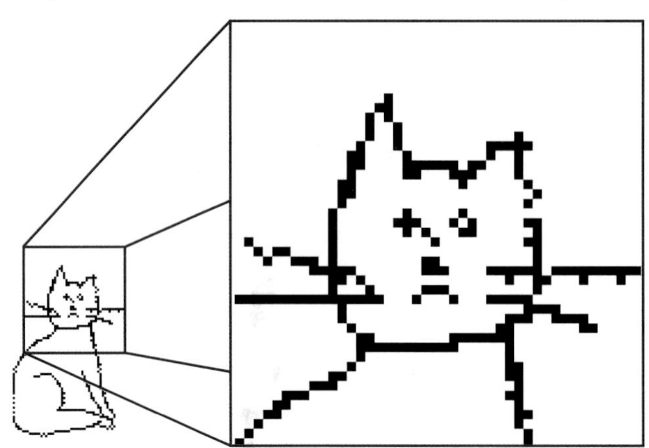

The following screenshot shows what the computer has stored for just a small section of this image:

00000000	00	01	02	03	04	05	06	07	08	09	0a	0b	0c
00000000	01000111	01001001	01000110	00111000	00111001	01100001	01111011	00000000	01100100	00000000	11110111	00000000	00000
00000010	00000000	00000000	00110011	00000000	00000000	01100110	00000000	00000000	10011001	00000000	00000000	11001100	00000
00000020	00110011	00000000	00000000	00110011	00110011	00000000	00110011	01100110	00000000	00110011	10011001	00000000	00110
00000030	11111111	00000000	01100110	00000000	00000000	01100110	00110011	00000000	01100110	01100110	00000000	01100110	10011
00000040	00000000	01100110	11111111	00000000	10011001	00000000	00000000	10011001	00110011	00000000	10011001	01100110	00000
00000050	10011001	11001100	00000000	10011001	11111111	00000000	11001100	00000000	00000000	11001100	00110011	00000000	11001
00000060	10011001	00000000	11001100	11001100	00000000	11001100	11111111	00000000	11111111	00000000	00000000	11111111	00110
00000070	00000000	11111111	10011001	00000000	11111111	11001100	00000000	11111111	11111111	00110011	00000000	00000000	00110
00000080	00000000	01100110	00110011	00000000	10011001	00110011	00000000	11001100	00110011	00000000	11111111	00110011	00110
00000090	00110011	00110011	00110011	01100110	00110011	00110011	10011001	00110011	00110011	11001100	00110011	00110011	11111
000000a0	00110011	01100110	00110011	00110011	01100110	01100110	00110011	01100110	10011001	00110011	01100110	11001100	00110
000000b0	10011001	00000000	00110011	10011001	00110011	00110011	10011001	01100110	00110011	10011001	10011001	00110011	10011
000000c0	11111111	00110011	11001100	00000000	00110011	11001100	00110011	00110011	11001100	01100110	00110011	11001100	10011
000000d0	00110011	11001100	11111111	00110011	11111111	00000000	00110011	11111111	00110011	00110011	11111111	01100110	00110
000000e0	11111111	11001100	00110011	11111111	11111111	01100110	00000000	00000000	01100110	00000000	00110011	01100110	00000
000000f0	10011001	01100110	00000000	11001100	01100110	00000000	11111111	01100110	00110011	00000000	01100110	00110011	00110
00000100	01100110	00110011	10011001	01100110	00110011	11001100	01100110	00110011	11111111	01100110	01100110	00000000	01100
00000110	01100110	01100110	01100110	01100110	10011001	01100110	01100110	11001100	01100110	01100110	11111111	01100110	10011
00000120	00110011	01100110	10011001	01100110	01100110	10011001	10011001	01100110	10011001	11001100	01100110	10011001	11111
00000130	01100110	11001100	00110011	01100110	11001100	01100110	01100110	11001100	10011001	01100110	11001100	11001100	01100
00000140	11111111	00000000	01100110	11111111	00110011	01100110	11111111	01100110	01100110	11111111	10011001	01100110	11111
00000150	11111111	10011001	00000000	00000000	10011001	00000000	00110011	10011001	00000000	01100110	10011001	00000000	10011
00000160	10011001	00000000	11111111	10011001	00110011	00000000	10011001	00110011	00110011	10011001	00110011	01100110	10011
00000170	00110011	11001100	10011001	00110011	11111111	10011001	01100110	00000000	10011001	01100110	00110011	10011001	01100

http://hhdsoftware.com/free-hex-editor

Even for this simple image the data being stored by the computer is very complex. This image of a shop sign in Portmeirion in Figure 16.2 is far more complex. We can still see the same sort of data, but this time it is displayed in hexadecimal for convenience.

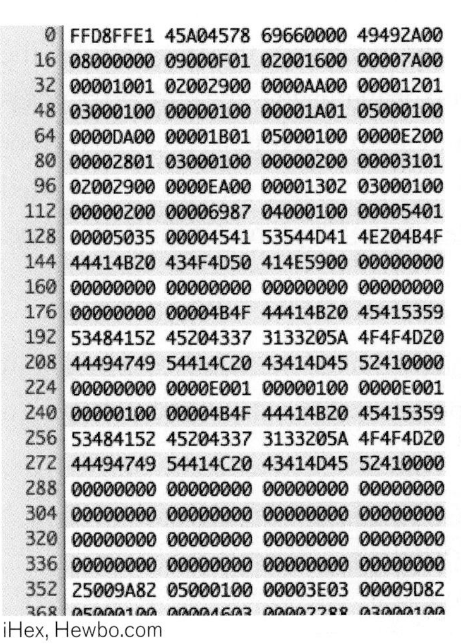

0 FFD8FFE1 45A04578 69660000 49492A00
16 08000000 09000F01 02001600 00007A00
32 00001001 02002900 0000AA00 00001201
48 03000100 00000100 00001A01 05000100
64 0000DA00 00001B01 05000100 0000E200
80 00002801 03000100 00000200 00003101
96 02002900 0000EA00 00001302 03000100
112 00000200 00006987 04000100 00005401
128 00005035 00004541 53544D41 4E204B4F
144 44414B20 434F4D50 414E5900 00000000
160 00000000 00000000 00000000 00000000
176 00000000 00004B4F 44414B20 45415359
192 53484152 45204337 3133205A 4F4F4D20
208 44494749 54414C20 43414D45 52410000
224 00000000 0000E001 00000100 0000E001
240 00000100 00004B4F 44414B20 45415359
256 53484152 45204337 3133205A 4F4F4D20
272 44494749 54414C20 43414D45 52410000
288 00000000 00000000 00000000 00000000
304 00000000 00000000 00000000 00000000
320 00000000 00000000 00000000 00000000
336 00000000 00000000 00000000 00000000
352 25009A82 05000100 00003E03 00009D82

iHex, Hewbo.com

Figure 16.2

Key Term

Pixel A pixel is the smallest element of an image. Pixels are the dots that make the image on the screen.

The cat drawing was in black and white and uses two colours; the shop sign is far more complex with many more colours. If a **pixel** is to be able to represent more than one colour, we need to use more bits to make a range of colours available.

- With 1 bit we can have two colours, for example black and white.
- With 2 bits we can have 2^2 colours, or four colours.
- With 3 bits we can have 2^3 colours, or eight colours.
- With 8 bits we can have 2^8 colours, or 256 colours.
- With 16 bits we can have 2^{16} colours, or 65,536 colours.

Figure 16.3 *The same image with eight colours and with just four colours*

Key Terms

Colour depth (bit depth) The number of bits used for each pixel.

Resolution The number of pixels or dots per unit, for example ppi (pixels per inch) or dpi (dots per inch).

Metadata Data about data. In the case of an image, information about the image data that allows the computer to recreate the image from the binary data in the file.

The number of bits used per pixel is called the **colour depth** (or **bit depth**), and the greater the colour depth the greater the number of colours we can achieve. 16 bpp (bits per pixel) is often regarded as high colour, 24 bpp as true colour and 32 bpp or more as deep colour.

The greater the colour depth, the more data we need to store for the image file and consequently, the larger the image file size.

Another factor that affects the size and quality of the image file is the **resolution** of the image. The resolution of an image is the number of pixels per unit, for example pixels per inch (often referred to as dots per inch or dpi – strictly speaking dpi refers to the density of dot placement in printed output). The more dots per inch, the larger the file storing the image will be.

Estimating the size of an image file

We need to know the size of the image; that is, the width and height in pixels and the colour depth in bits per pixel. The image of the shop sign on page 159 (Figure 16.2) is:

Height	3056 pixels
Width	2092 pixels
Colour depth	8 bits

We multiply these together to get the number of bits:

3056 × 2092 × 8	51 145 216 b
÷ 8 for the number of bytes	6 393 152 B
÷ 1 000 000 for megabytes	6.393 MB

There will be some overheads but these will be relatively small, and rounding up will provide a suitable estimate.

Approximate size as a RAW data file: 7 MB

Saving as jpg images significantly reduces the size, though some detail is lost in the process. The amount it will be compressed depends upon the nature of the image. Images with large areas of the same colour will compress more than those with lots of small detail.

As a jpg file, this takes just 1.1 MB of disk space.

How does the computer know what to do with these numbers in order to display the image? Since the data is all stored in binary for the computer to be able to make sense of it and display the image, it needs to know something about the data. It needs to know the size of the image in terms of height and width. It also needs to know the colour depth and various other bits of information about the image. This is called **metadata** (data about data).

Figure 16.4 shows some of the metadata stored for the photo in Figure 16.2. You can see that the resolution is 480 dpi by 480 dpi, the image size is 2292 × 3056 pixels and the colour depth is 8; that is, 2^8 or 256 colours.

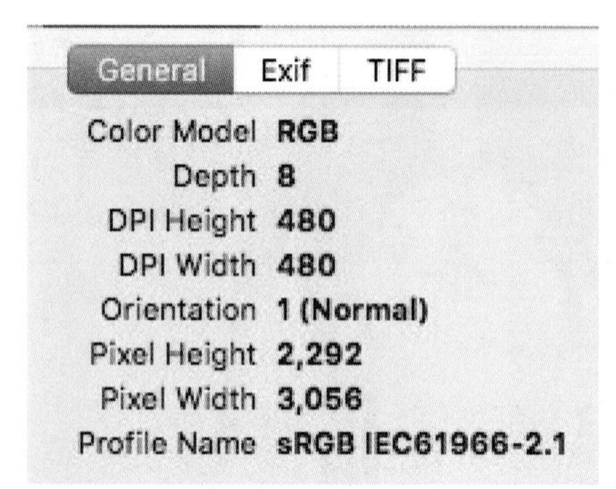

Figure 16.4 Metadata stored for Figure 16.2

Note

When images are taken using a mobile phone with GPS location, the image file is saved with metadata that identifies the location where the image was taken as well as the time it was taken. This means that the image file can be used to locate exactly where and when the image was created. This raises some concerns about privacy and, while it is possible, most people do not turn off this extra information.

Extension Activity

Using a program such as Photoshop or Gimp, modify the colour depth and resolution of an image to see at what point it becomes just acceptable for a large print, as a medium-size image on screen and as a small image on a website.

Note

Image files are stored in a variety of formats, essentially as a set of pixels either in a bitmap form or as a vector form.

In vector graphics formats, images are made up from a set of primitive components such as lines, arcs, circles, ellipses – in fact, a whole range of geometric shapes. Vector graphics are stored as a shape with further information including a set of control points that the shape must pass through.

When enlarged, bitmapped images become pixelated; that is, we can see the blocks that make up the image. Vector graphics do not become pixelated since the primitive shapes, control points and other information simply need to be recalculated to create the new shape. Therefore vector images do not suffer from loss of resolution when enlarged and they also do not suffer from the file-size issues that affect large, high-resolution bitmapped images. Since the definitions for the shapes and control points remain unchanged, the file size is not affected by the size of the image. Ultimately, though, displays and printers are raster devices that use pixels to display or print the image, regardless of the graphic type, and in order to display or print vector images they must be converted to bitmapped ones anyway.

Questions

12 How does the resolution of an image affect the size of the file?

13 What do we mean by *image size*?

14 What metadata is stored with an image file?

15 If an image has its colour depth decreased, what is the effect?

16 How many colours can be represented using a 4-bit colour depth?

Sound

Like all other data, sound is stored by a computer in binary. There is metadata stored along with the binary numbers to tell the computer what type of file it is so that it does not attempt to display it as an image or use it in some other way.

Key Term

Analogue Continuously changing values.

Sound is continuously varying data (**analogue**) but the computer needs to have this as discrete digital values if it is to be able to deal with it. To convert the original sound to a form the computer can use, the data is sampled at set intervals and the values are recorded. It is this set of saved values that is replayed by the computer.

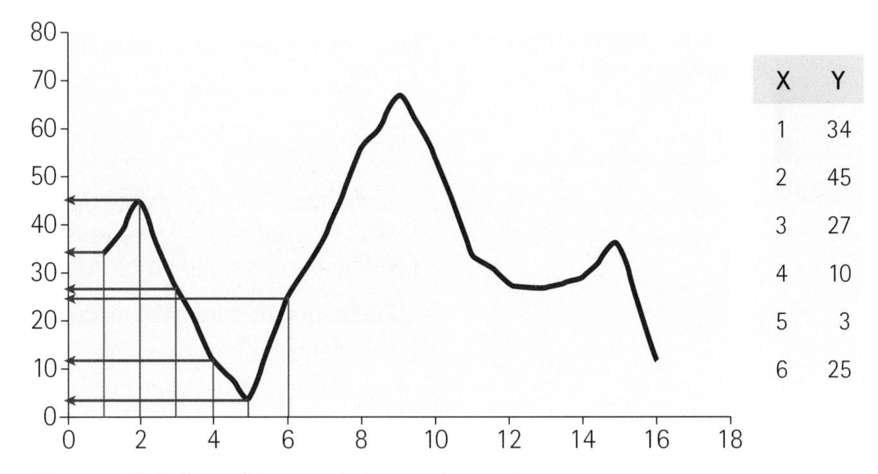

X	Y
1	34
2	45
3	27
4	10
5	3
6	25

Figure 16.5 *Sound is sampled at set intervals*

In this case (see Figure 16.5) we are sampling every one unit on the x-axis (time). From the graph we can read the corresponding values for the curve at each of these points on the y-axis. The first few are shown in the table beside the graph.

When the computer uses these values to recreate the sound we get something similar to this:

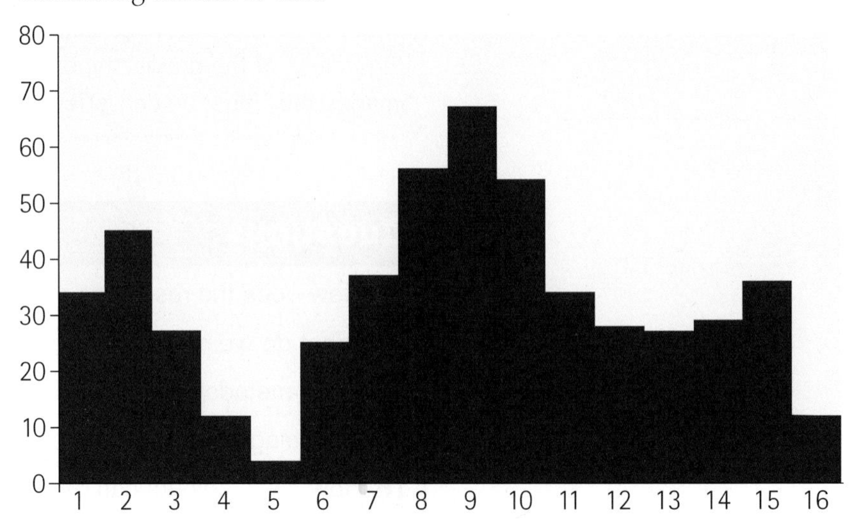

Figure 16.6 *Digital sound replayed by computer*

This is approximately the same shape as our original sound curve but not as smooth. The sound reproduced will be very similar, but not the same. The quality of the sampled sound will not be as good as the original.

The number of times the sound is sampled in one second is called the *sample rate*. If the sample rate is increased, then more samples will be taken over the same amount of time and we get a much closer approximation to the original sound. The sample rate is usually expressed in kHz (thousands of samples per second). CD quality sound is sampled at 44 kHz.

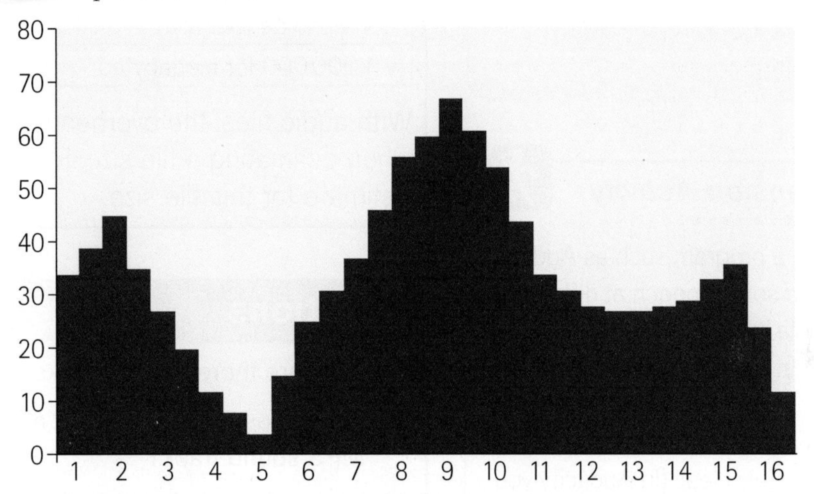

Figure 16.7 *Higher sample rates produce better quality results*

Key Terms

Bit depth The number of bits used to store each sound sample.

Bit rate The number of bits used to store a second of sampled sound.

Sample rate The number of times the sound is sampled per second, measured in kHz.

Another factor affecting the quality of the sound is the number of bits used to store each sample, that is the **bit depth**. If more bits are used for each sample then the accuracy of the sampling will be improved. Typical values are 16 or 24 bits per sample.

The **bit rate** is the number of bits of data stored for each second of sound and is simply the **sample rate** multiplied by the bit depth:

bit rate = sample rate × bit depth

Bit rates are given in kilobits per second (kbps). Bit rates for reasonable music audio quality should be 128 kbps or better; lower rates are often used on websites to reduce the download time. An audio CD will use a bit rate of 1411.2 kbps, hence why the quality of the audio on a CD is far superior to music downloaded from the internet.

The quality of digital audio depends on two things, the sample rate and bit depth. The larger these values, the larger the bit rate and the larger the file that stores the data will be.

Estimating the size of a sound file

The size of a sound file depends upon the number of channels and the bit rate.

Example

For a 1 minute stereo sound sample using two channels sampled at 44 100 samples per second with a bit depth of 8 bits

The bit rate is the number of channels × the sample rate × the bit depth:

bits per second = 2 × 44 100 × 8	705 600 bits per second
for 60 seconds this is 60 × 705 600	42 336 000 b
÷ 8 for bytes	5 292 000 B
÷ 1 000 000 for megabytes	5.3 MB

With audio files, the overheads are quite small and can be ignored when estimating a file size. Rounding to 5.5 MB provides a good estimate for this file size.

Extension Activity

Using a program such as Audacity, record some speech at different sample rates and bit rates to see at what rates the speech becomes clear enough to just make out, then at what rate it becomes completely clear. (In Audacity you can set these using 'Set sample rate' and 'Set sample format'.)

Questions

17 Why are there so few tracks on a typical audio CD?

18 How does the sample rate affect the quality of the playback for an MP3 sound track?

19 What effect does a high bit rate have on the number of sound files that can be stored on a CD?

Compression

Key Term

Compression Reduction in file size to lessen download times and storage requirements.

In order for data to be displayed in browsers, transferred across the internet or stored on portable media, various file standards for documents, visual and audio files have been adopted. Some of these file standards include **compression** to reduce the size of the file. In order to be clear, an image for a computer display needs to be around 1 MB. For video using 25 frames per second it is easy to see how the files will become very large and have prohibitive download times, even with fast broadband connections.

There are two principle approaches to compressing files that vary in how much data is lost in order to reduce the file size.

Lossy compression

Lossy compression involves removing some of the data from a file in order to reduce its size. For photographs, it is the only method that can achieve significant file reductions because the sequence of pixels is unpredictable. Lossy compression relies on the removal of data, which is the least likely to be noticed by the human sense, in the case of an image the eye. A file that has been compressed using lossy compression cannot be restored to its original condition.

The image here was originally 1.2 MB, it has been compressed to 364 KB, then to 166 KB, you can see the loss of detail in the images:

Figure 16.8 *Lossy compression; the same image compressed to 364 KB then 166 KB*

Lossless compression

Sometimes it is important not to lose any of the information in a file, for example if anything were removed from a computer program then it would not run correctly. Likewise, a text file must have all the letters transmitted accurately or else it might not be understood.

Sometimes it is possible to compress a file without losing any information. This involves storing enough information about a file so that it can be recreated later, exactly as it was before, for example consider the sentence:

Ask not what your country can do for you; ask what you can do for your country.

The words in this can be stored as follows:

Index	Word
1	ask
2	not
3	what
4	your
5	country
6	can
7	do
8	for
9	you

Then, the sentence can be recreated using the sequence:

1 2 3 4 5 6 7 8 9 1 3 9 6 7 8 4 5

We are using a table where each word is added in the order that it occurs and is given a code number. The text is then represented by a code number. If a word is repeated, there is an opportunity to make savings, by giving the code number instead of the word. There is enough information here to recreate the original sentence exactly.

Other common standards include:

- **JPG or JPEG (Joint Photographic Experts Group)**
  This is a compressed bitmap image file format commonly used for photographs. You can usually choose how much compression you want, so for a small image on a web page it is often acceptable to choose a large compression factor.

Extension Activity

1 Take a paragraph from a children's book or all the text in an early reading book and list every word used in a dictionary.
2 Create the sequence that will recreate the book using the dictionary.
3 Count how many bytes this would need to store it at one byte per character in every word and two bytes per number in the sequence.
4 Count how many bytes are needed to store the original text (remember each space counts as a character).
5 Is the 'compressed' version smaller or larger than the original? When will the compressed version of some text be larger than the uncompressed version?

- **GIF (Graphics Interchange Format)**
  This is a lossless bitmap image compression standard but it is only suitable for small images such as logos with a limited number of colours. A sequence of GIF images can be displayed so as to produce animations.
- **PDF (Portable Document Format)**
  This is an open standard for exchanging documents. Text and graphics are displayed exactly as in the original, with no need to have the software that created the original document. Many applications are capable of reading or creating PDF documents.
- **MPEG (Moving Pictures Expert Group)**
  This is a set of standards designed to encode audio-visual information. It uses lossy compression for both the sound and visual components. Various versions of MPEG are used for digital transmissions via cable and satellite as well as for terrestrial digital channels. It is used to encode DVD movies too and can be decoded by most domestic audio-visual equipment.
- **MP3 (Moving Pictures Expert Group Audio Layer 3)**
  This has become the standard format for distributing digital music files on the internet. It uses lossy compression to reduce file sizes to about a tenth of the original. The compression algorithm is intended to remove sounds that are generally beyond the limits of most people's hearing, although some people claim that the loss in quality is noticeable.

Questions

20 What is *file compression*?
21 Describe the difference between lossy and lossless compression.
22 Explain why compression must be lossless when sending a computer program as an email attachment.
23 Describe one advantage and one disadvantage of storing music as MP3 files.
24 Explain the importance of compressing image and video files when transmitting them over the internet.

17 Logic

Key Terms

Logic gate A circuit that produces an output based on the inputs.

NOT A logic gate that outputs the opposite value to the input.

AND A logic gate that outputs 1 if both inputs are 1.

OR A logic gate that outputs 1 if either, or both, of the two inputs is 1.

We have already mentioned John von Neumann and the principle that all modern computers, data and instructions are based on the binary system. This follows from the ease with which we can decide between two states – off or on, true or false, 0 or 1 – using simple transistors and capacitors.

The memory in a computer uses many small transistors and capacitors to store data and it is possible to wire these transistors together so that they can make simple logical calculations, such as: Are both inputs 1? Or is only one of the inputs 1?

These simple circuits are called **logic gates** and there are three fundamental ones we need to know about: **NOT**, **AND** and **OR**.

NOT gate

Key Term

Truth table A method for recording all the possible input combinations and determining the output for each.

The NOT gate is a very simple gate: if 0 is input then it outputs 1 and if 1 is input it outputs 0.

We express this relationship between input and output as a **truth table**.

It is usual to use algebraic variables such as A, B, C and so on for inputs, and P, Q, R and so on as outputs.

A	P
0	1
1	0

We also have a diagram to represent the NOT gate:

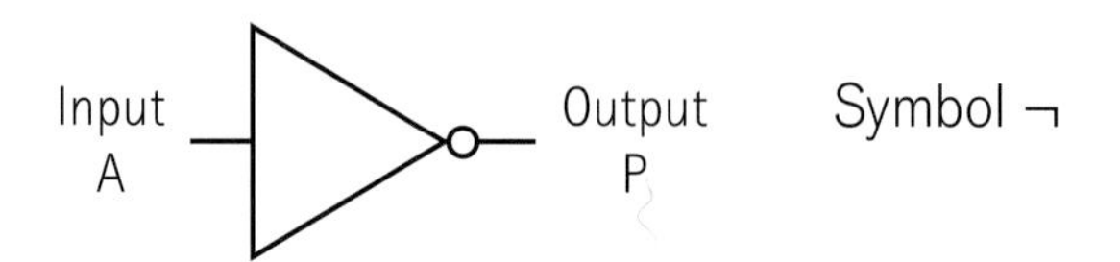

Figure 17.1 *NOT gate*

AND gate

The AND gate tells us whether both of the inputs are 1, by outputting 1, otherwise it outputs 0.

The truth table shows two inputs, A and B, and all the possible combinations of values for A and B.

A	B	P
0	0	0
0	1	0
1	0	0
1	1	1

Notice that output P is only 1 when both inputs A and B are 1.

The diagram for this gate is:

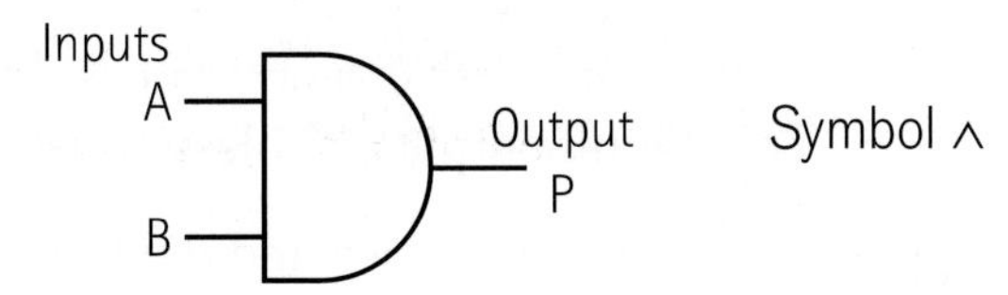

Figure 17.2 *AND gate*

OR gate

The OR gate tells whether one or both of the two inputs are 1 by outputting 1, otherwise it outputs 0.

The truth table shows two inputs, A and B, and all the possible combinations of values for A and B.

A	B	P
0	0	0
0	1	1
1	0	1
1	1	1

Notice that output P is 1 when either input A or B, or both inputs A and B, are 1.

The diagram for the OR gate is:

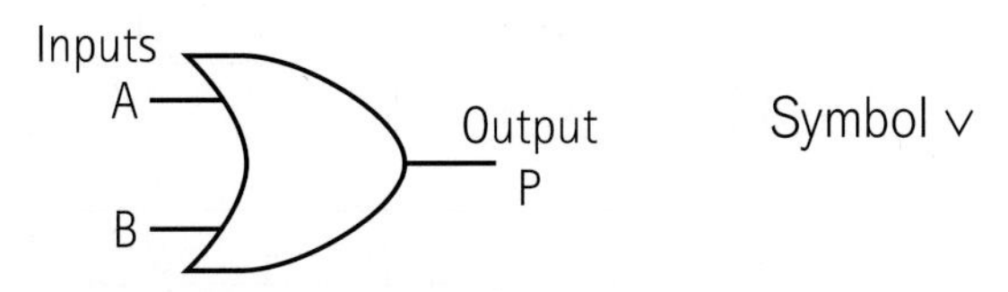

Figure 17.3 *OR gate*

Key Term

Logic circuit A circuit made by combining a sequence of logic gates.

We can combine these three gates to make more complex **logic circuits**, for example the NAND gate. This is made up of an AND gate followed by a NOT gate:

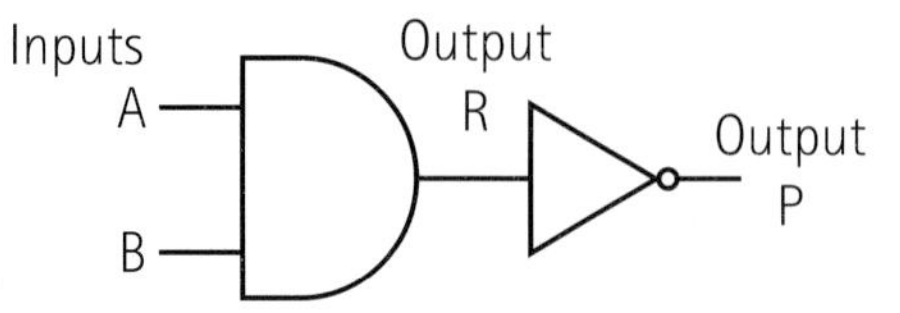

Figure 17.4 *AND and NOT gates forming a NAND gate*

The logic for this gate can be worked out using a truth table too. Listing all the possible input combinations for A and B, then taking the output from these, R as the input to the NOT gate.

A	B	R = A AND B	P = NOT R
0	0	0	1
0	1	0	1
1	0	0	1
1	1	1	0

This circuit outputs 1 unless both inputs are 1.

By using truth tables and working out the output at each stage in the circuit to use as inputs into the next stage, we can work out the output from some more complex circuits.

Example

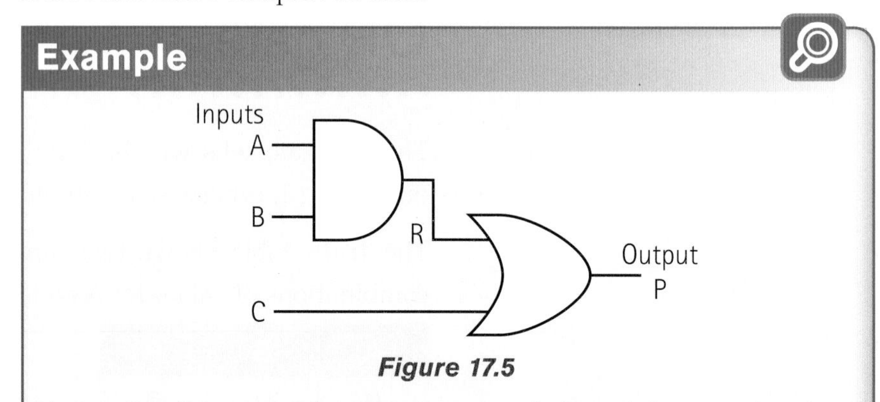

Figure 17.5

Notice that this circuit has three inputs, A, B and C, so we have more possible input combinations than in the previous examples.

The truth table looks like this:

A	B	C	R = A AND B	P = R OR C
0	0	0	0	0
0	0	1	0	1
0	1	0	0	0
0	1	1	0	1
1	0	0	0	0
1	0	1	0	1
1	1	0	1	1
1	1	1	1	1

Key Term

Boolean algebra A method for expressing mathematically a logic circuit.

We use a form of algebra to write down these circuits, called **Boolean algebra**. This form of algebra is named after the English mathematician, George Boole. In the 1840s, he derived the notation to express, in a mathematical form, the logical concepts that the early Greek mathematicians and philosophers had identified.

The circuit in Figure 17.5, P = (A AND B) OR C, would be written as: $P = (A \wedge B) \vee C$

Example

Let us look at another Boolean expression: $P = (A \vee B) \wedge C$

The diagram is:

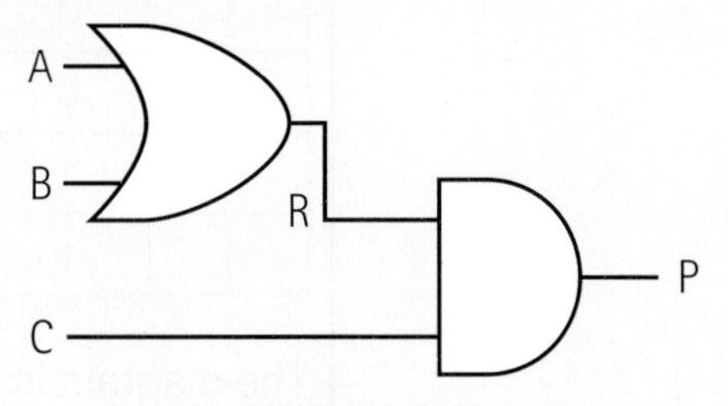

Figure 17.6

The truth table for this is:

A	B	C	R = A ∨ B	P = R ∧ C
0	0	0	0	0
0	0	1	0	0
0	1	0	1	0
0	1	1	1	1
1	0	0	1	0
1	0	1	1	1
1	1	0	1	0
1	1	1	1	1

Example

If we draw the truth table and the logic circuit diagram for the expression $P = \neg(A \wedge B) \wedge C$

The truth table is:

A	B	C	$A \wedge B$	$R = \neg(A \wedge B)$	$P = \neg(A \wedge B) \wedge C$
0	0	0	0	1	0
0	0	1	0	1	1
0	1	0	0	1	0
0	1	1	0	1	1
1	0	0	0	1	0
1	0	1	0	1	1
1	1	0	1	0	0
1	1	1	1	0	0

The diagram is:

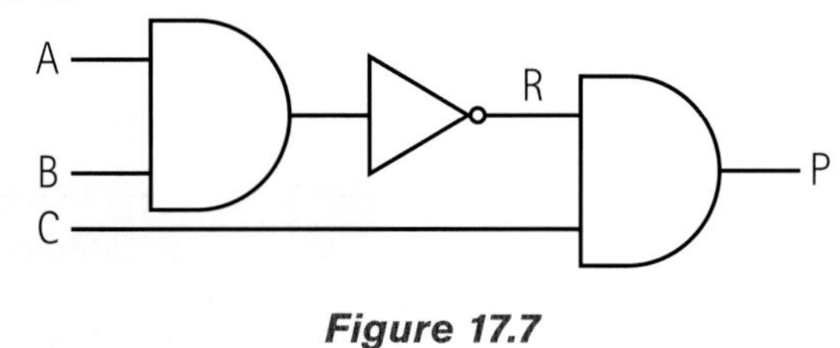

Figure 17.7

Logic in programming

We need to understand Boolean algebra in order to use many facilities within programming languages. Writing a program requires us to identify a logical process that the computer can follow and we need to be able to provide suitable Boolean expressions for the computer to use when making decisions about what to do next. For example we might want our program to stop if one of two things happens, perhaps we find a matching item in some data or we reach the end of a data file.

The computer might be given an instruction that says:

```
repeat

...

until data match found OR end of file reached
```

The computer's CPU will evaluate this expression using the logic:

Is there a data match?	End of file reached?	STOP
NO	NO	NO
NO	YES	YES
YES	NO	YES
YES	YES	YES

This is, of course, simply using the truth table for an OR gate.

We will often require the computer to evaluate a logical expression in order to make a decision, for example:

```
if x > 10 AND y > 12 then…
```

This tells the computer to check the values of *x* and *y* in the program and to do 'something' if both *x* is bigger than 10 and *y* is bigger than 12.

x > 10 ?	y > 12 ?	Then execute the following code
NO	NO	NO
NO	YES	NO
YES	NO	NO
YES	YES	YES

```
while x < 10 AND NOT(end of file)
```

x < 10 ?	eof	NOT (eof)	Execute the following code
NO	NO	YES	NO
NO	YES	NO	NO
YES	NO	YES	YES
YES	YES	NO	NO

This tells the computer to check if *x* is less than 10 and that it has not reached the end of a data file. If both things are true it carries on and does what it is asked, but if they are not both true it will stop and move on to the next instruction in the program after the 'endwhile' command.

Questions

1 Draw a truth table for the following Boolean expressions:
   (a) $\neg(A \vee B)$
   (b) $\neg A \wedge \neg B$
   (c) $(A \wedge B) \wedge \neg C$
   (d) $\neg(A \wedge B) \vee C$
   (e) $A \wedge \neg(B \vee C)$

2 Draw the logic circuits for each of the expressions in question 1.

3 Draw the truth tables for $A \wedge (B \vee C)$ and $(A \wedge B) \vee (B \wedge C)$.
   (a) Calculate $3 \times (4 + 5)$ and $(3 \times 4) + (3 \times 5)$
   (b) What do you notice?

18 Translators and programming tools

Translators

We have seen that the processor runs programs that are fed to it as a series of instructions. These instructions are in the form of binary bit patterns. Processors cannot handle instructions in any other form. For example, an instruction can look like this:

10110000	01100001
opcode	operand

Key Terms

Opcode This is the part of the instruction that tells the CPU what operation is to be done.

Operand This is the part of the instruction that tells the CPU what to apply the operation to.

This instruction consists of two component parts. These parts are: the operation code, often abbreviated to **opcode**, and the **operand**.

The opcode is the part that tells the processor what to do, such as add a number or move a byte of data. The operand supplies the processor with the data that is to be worked on by the opcode. The operand might be an actual number, or more commonly it will be an address where the required data can be found or where it must be sent.

In the example above, the opcode is telling the processor to copy a value into the accumulator. We will look at this in more detail later.

Some opcodes, but not many, do not have an operand, for example an opcode that simply tells a program to stop.

Instructions in pure binary are called machine code. This is an example of a low-level language. It is called low level because it works deep down, directly on the computer hardware and not high up at the user level.

It is perfectly possible to write programs by setting out all the binary encoded instructions. In the early days of computers, this was the only way it could be done.

The bits could be entered by setting switches and plugging in cables, as in the case of ENIAC in Figure 18.1. Data could be input by using paper tape as in the case of Colossus or punched cards.

Figure 18.1 *The early computer ENIAC (Electronic Numerical Integrator And Computer)*

Key Points

- Computers run programs given to them as a set of instructions.
- These instructions must be in binary-coded format.
- Binary-coded instructions are called machine code.

Giving instructions in this way is obviously very tedious and it was very easy to make errors. Humans are not conditioned to think in terms of 0s and 1s.

There had to be better ways to give instructions to the processor and over the years more and more convenient ways were developed. This process continues to this day, where ever more easy ways are still being produced to pass instructions to a computer.

Questions 

1 Describe two ways that you have given program instructions to a computer.

Assembly language and translators

Key Terms

Translation The conversion of human-friendly program writing back to pure machine code.

Translator A program to convert high-level or assembly-level commands into machine code.

The evolution of programming techniques beyond pure machine code has led to writing programs in a more human-friendly way and then converting what is written back to pure machine code. This conversion is called **translation**. The translation is achieved using special software, unsurprisingly called a **translator**.

We have seen that it is possible, although not sensible, to write a computer program in pure machine code. There is one advantage of doing that however. It enables the programmer to have complete control of what the program does, instruction by instruction.

There is an easier way to have this level of control though. Every machine instruction can be given an easy-to-remember code such as ADD or MOV. This easy-to-remember code is called a mnemonic, which means a way to remember something more easily.

Here's how it works. A table is set up in memory where each machine instruction is stored alongside the more human-readable mnemonic. This means that the programmer can still write programs that control each step of the process but doesn't have to remember or look up what the machine-code instruction is. A translator takes care of the substitution later.

Earlier we looked at the machine-code instruction:

10110000	01100001

Note

This is just one of many reasons why you will often see hexadecimal numbers used in computers.

This is an instruction that is recognised by Intel processors. If you gave this instruction to a different processor, it would not mean the same thing. That is another reason why writing programs in machine code can cause problems.

This instruction is hard to remember, so a programmer might change it into hexadecimal so that there is less to recall.

It could then be written:

```
B0 61
```

You should be able to see that this is the same.

Question

2 What would the instruction FD E2 look like in binary?

The opcode `B0` means move data into the register called `AL`. `AL` is the code for part of one of the accumulators in a typical PC. (Think 'Accumulator Low' – it's the lower part of an accumulator.)

61 is the operand, which you will realise is the same as decimal 97.

The assembly language programmer would write:

```
MOV AL, 61h
```

which reads 'move into the register AL, the value 61 hexadecimal.'

Usually you wouldn't specify a number like this. It is far more useful to get the value from another memory location. This is how variables are accessed.

The instruction could be modified to get a value from a memory address by using square brackets. The instruction would be something like:

```
MOV AL, [1E]
```

Key Term

Instruction set The complete set of instructions that a processor can handle.

The processor of most modern computers is able to handle typically well over 100 different opcodes. The complete set of instructions that a processor can handle is called its **instruction set**.

Learning these is a difficult job and most programmers don't need to know them. However, having an understanding of what is going on is important for any programmer, computer engineer, or GCSE Computer Science student!

Example

Assembly language

A program written using mnemonics is said to be written in assembly language. The assembly language program cannot be executed by the processor. It must be translated into machine code by an assembler.

An easy way to understand how to program using assembly language is by looking at a simulation called the Little Man Computer (LMC). It won't let you write real assembly language programs to run directly from a computer's operating system but it will show you very clearly how it all works.

The program in Table 18.1 is an example of a program written in assembly language for the Little Man Computer. That is, it is written using mnemonics. Each operation of the processor is specified. Each instruction does just one thing. Just like pure machine code, this is a one-to-one language. Just like pure machine code, it is a low-level language.

Note

The Little Man Computer is a simulation of how a processor and memory work. It is much simplified but that makes it a lot easier to see what goes on in a real computer. Various versions are available online for free download. You should practise writing a few programs using it.

Table 18.1

Assembly language instruction	What it means
`INP`	Input a number and store it in the accumulator
`LOOP SUB NUM`	Start of a section of code, labelled `LOOP` and immediately subtract the value labelled `NUM` from what is in the accumulator
`OUT`	Output whatever is in the accumulator
`BRZ QUIT`	If the content of the accumulator is zero, jump to the code labelled `QUIT`
`BRA LOOP`	Branch to the code labelled `LOOP`
`QUIT HLT`	This is a label `QUIT`. It refers to the instruction `HLT`, which halts the program
`NUM DAT 2`	This is a data store labelled `NUM`. It is set up to hold the value 2

So, to summarise, this is a countdown program. It takes a number from the user and keeps taking 2 away from it, outputting the current value until the accumulator contains the value 0.

Questions

3 Rewrite the program on page 177 as an algorithm, a flowchart or in pseudocode.

4 Identify a logical error that might cause a problem when running this program.

5 Write and test a program for LMC that multiplies two numbers together.

Assemblers

Key Term

Assembler Software that translates an assembly language program into machine code.

Now of course the processor cannot understand instructions written in assembly language. It needs instructions such as `10110000 01100001` and cannot deal with mnemonics like `ADD`. So, the assembly language program must be translated into machine code. This requires translation software called an **assembler**.

Assemblers can do more than just substitute machine code for mnemonics. They usually have extra features to make life easier for the programmer, such as allowing the use of labels. A label is an easy-to-remember word that stands for a memory address.

The program on page 177 has three labels: `LOOP`, `QUIT` and `NUM`.

So instead of writing `BRA 1` (branch to address 1), the address can be written using a label such as `LOOP`. The assembler assigns an address for the label `LOOP` and the programmer doesn't have to worry about where the instruction is.

Writing programs in assembly language is easier than using machine code but it is still hard work. This is because every single step of the way has to be set out by the programmer. If you want a loop, you have to spell out exactly how the loop is to be set up and executed.

Low-level languages are one-to-one languages. Each action by the processor has to be specified by an instruction written by the programmer. This gives the programmer full control but it's not easy.

High-level languages

High-level languages are more like human language, normally English. They make programming a lot easier because the programmer can concentrate on the logic of the program and not worry too much about how the hardware is going to handle it. Because of this, they are referred to as problem-oriented in contrast to low-level languages which are machine-oriented.

Each high-level instruction gets translated into a number of machine instructions, so high-level languages are often called one-to-many.

For example, a program to count down written in the Python programming language could be like this:

```
num=int(input('Enter a number '))
for i in range(num,0,-2):
print (i)
```

This is a lot shorter and easier to understand than the assembly language program in Table 18.1.

Because high-level languages are so useful and improve productivity so much, there are huge numbers of them, each one designed to cope with a different type of problem or approach.

Here are some examples:

Language	Use
JavaScript®	Making web pages interactive.
Visual Basic	An easy way to write programs for Windows® computers.
C++	Useful for many large-scale projects.
Python	Good for learning to program and a wide variety of development uses.

Key Term

Source code The program written by the programmer in a high-level language before it is converted to machine code.

The code that is written by the programmer is called the **source code**. It cannot be run by the processor.

Just as with assembly language, it is necessary to translate programs written in high-level languages into pure machine code. There are two main approaches to this, compilation and interpretation. They each have their advantages and disadvantages.

Compilers

Key Term

Object code The machine code produced by a compiler.

Compiles work through the source code, spot certain errors and translate all the code into a machine code file, which is called **object code**. Object code is in fact machine code. The compiled code is sometimes called an executable file if it is now ready to be run direct from a computer's operating system.

Advantages of compiling code

- The executable file is more or less unreadable to a casual observer. This means that valuable trade secrets are less likely to be passed on to customers.
- Compiled code runs faster than the same code that has not been compiled.
- There is no need for the customer, or whoever is using the program, to have a copy of the translating software. This can have economic as well as storage benefits.
- Compilers often optimise code. That means they analyse it to find more effective or economical ways to achieve the same result.

Disadvantages of compiling code

- When you are developing the code, it has to be compiled in full, over and over again every time a mistake is discovered or an improvement made.
- You cannot try out individual commands to see their effects.
- A compiled program is specific to a particular processor. It won't run on a different one. It may not be possible simply to recompile it. A different processor may require a different programming approach.

Interpreters

Interpreters work through the source code and translate it one command at a time, then immediately execute it. If an error is found, the process stops there and then, allowing it to be corrected or debugged.

No object code file is produced. The program has to be interpreted again every time that it is run. This means that whoever is using the program needs to have a copy of the interpreter.

Advantages of interpretation

- It is easier to debug.
- Errors are picked up at the time of translation, line by line. There is no need to read through a lengthy error report at the end of translation.
- It is easy to experiment and try different approaches. You don't need to recompile to try each change.

Disadvantages of interpretation

- The code runs more slowly than compiled code, because translation and execution take place for each line of code.
- The code does not get optimised.
- The source code must be made available to the customer so it could be adapted or copied.

- The user must have a copy of the interpreter resident in memory. This occupies extra memory and may require financial outlay.
- One approach that is often used is to develop a program using an interpreter and then when it is completed and tested, compile it at that stage.

Key Points

- High-level languages are one to many, i.e. one high-level instruction corresponds to many machine instructions.
- High-level languages are more like human languages.
- High-level languages are problem-oriented, not machine-oriented.
- High-level languages are translated into machine code by either a compiler or an interpreter.

Editors

An editor is software that is used to write source code. It can be really simple and just allow code to be written, edited and saved, like Windows Notepad® or Unix vi or nano (see Figure 18.2).

```
num=int(input('Enter a number '))
for i in range(num,0,-2):
    print(i)
```

Figure 18.2 *A program written using the plain text editor nano*

Editors are different from word processors in that they do not support any formatting like bold, italic, tables or images. This is important because you want your source code file to be uncontaminated with any of the embedded codes that all word processors add. You can, if you want, write source code with an ordinary word processor but if you do, you must make sure to save your work as a text-only file.

There are many specialised editors that make programming a bit easier.

Pretty printing

Lots of editors examine your source code as you work. They can make your code more readable without changing what is saved. Some are designed to work with specific programming languages. Others try to be smarter and work with many.

They will do things like:

- identify loops and indent for easy reading
- identify variables and present them in a different colour.

```
num=int(input('Enter a number '))
for i in range(num,0,-2):
    print(i)
```

Figure 18.3 *The same program written using a specialised programming editor with pretty printing*

Figure 18.4 *A coder at work*

The IDE

An IDE is an Integrated Development Environment.

It is a software tool that provides many of the utilities required to develop a program – all in one place.

Common features of an IDE include:

- an editor, often optimised for a particular language
- tools for debugging such as the facility to inspect variables
- step-by-step progression through a program
- a build feature that compiles and links with other needed parts of the program.

In addition, many IDEs also include a compiler and possibly an interpreter too.

Error diagnostics

All IDEs have a repertoire of features that can be used to track down errors in code.

This is known as debugging and the tools used for this are called debuggers.

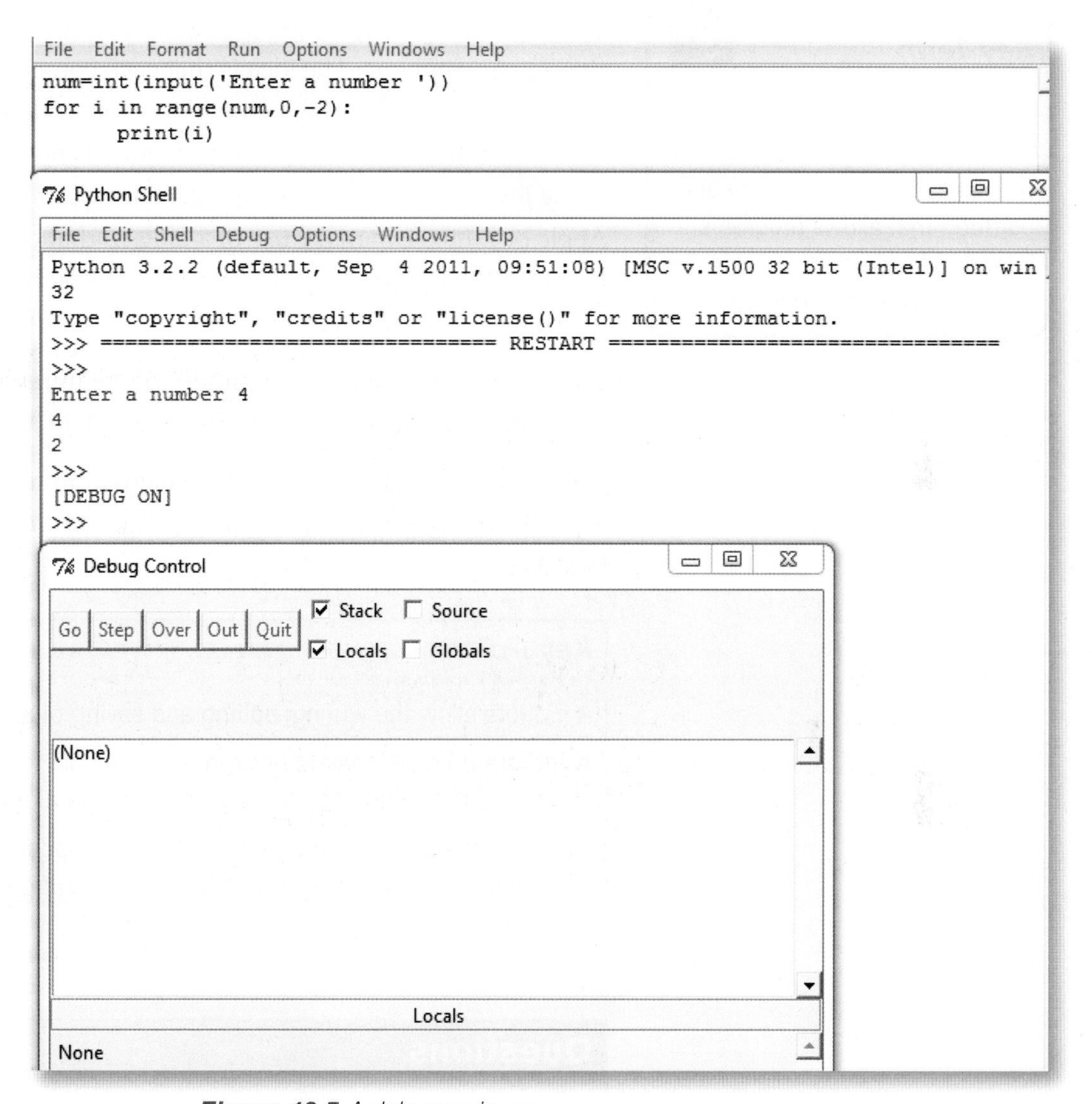

***Figure 18.5** A debugger in use*

Extension Activity

1. Examine two IDEs for any programming language that you use.
2. Make a list of the features provided at the top-level menu for each one.
3. Which of these are most likely to be useful to you in your GCSE work and why?
4. Which IDE do you prefer and why?

Run-time environment

A run-time environment contains all the necessary facilities to run a program, possibly on a different platform from that used to create it. It has no tools for changing the program.

Key Term

Virtual machine This is an emulation or simulation of a particular computer system or platform that allows programs intended to run on one computer system to run on a different one.

Some programming languages are designed to work with a wide variety of computers. The idea is that each computer type implements a standard 'environment' which will support code written in a standard way. For example, many websites include functionality that is written in the Java® programming language. Each 'platform', such as Windows, Apple or Linux, can make use of a plug-in that can work with the code. In effect, these plug-ins produce a **virtual machine** that can cope with the code in its own environment.

This allows developers to ignore the requirements of a particular platform, knowing that their code will work in all of them.

Java has for a long time been one such environment but there are always worries that such an inter-platform facility can also allow security breaches.

Key Points

- Editors allow the writing, editing and saving of source code.
- Integrated development environments bundle together all the tools needed to construct, translate and package a program.
- A run-time environment provides a virtual machine that can run compiled or semi-compiled code without having the facilities to edit the program.

Questions

6 Explain the usefulness of pretty printing.
7 List three components of a typical IDE.
8 What is a *virtual machine*?
9 What is the purpose of an editor in computer programming?
10 What is the purpose of a compiler in computer programming?
11 Distinguish between source code and object code.
12 Distinguish between high- and low-level programming languages.

19 Legal, ethical, cultural and environmental issues

Introduction

The widespread use of computer technology in all aspects of daily life has brought many benefits for the individual and society. Computer systems are involved in most human activities. The list of how computer systems affect us is endless but a few examples will show something of the extent.

Safety	guiding aircraft, controlling trains, supporting signalling systems, monitoring patient body signs
Travel	smartphone apps, GPS systems, train and bus timetables, flight bookings
Business	orders, stock control, payroll
Retail	online ordering of more or less anything, logistics systems that control delivery of goods
Entertainment	DVDs, Blu-ray Disc™, online film and television services for home and mobile
Communication	email, chat, social networks, business transactions, mobile phones
Education	virtual learning environments (VLEs), exam marking, unlimited sources of information on the web
Politics and government	campaigns, voting (in some countries), payment of taxes, passport and visa applications
Science	number crunching, simulations, visualisations, distributed processing to process data for research (e.g. DNA)

But alongside these benefits, the widespread use of computer technology has also generated several problems, from computer crime to issues with the freedom of the individual. The fact that we depend upon computer technology in so many aspects of our daily lives brings a reliance on technology that makes us all more vulnerable to these problems.

Legal issues

Computer crime consists of a wide range of existing and new criminal activities including unauthorised access to data and computer systems for the purpose of theft or damage, identity theft, software piracy, fraud and harassment such as trolling. Many of these activities are criminalised by acts of parliament.

Computer Misuse Act (1990)

Under the provisions of the Computer Misuse Act it is a criminal offence to:

- make any unauthorised access to computer material
  - with the intent to commit further offences (for example blackmail)
  - with the intent to modify the computer material (for example distributing viruses).

The first provision refers to unauthorised access (commonly called *hacking*). The second provision refers to anything that impairs the performance of a computer system including the distribution of viruses.

Features used to minimise these threats include:

- digital signatures or certificates that use encrypted messages to confirm the identity of the sender
- SSL (Secure Socket Layer), a protocol that enables encrypted links between computers to ensure the security of a transaction
- user IDs, passwords and access rights used for basic identification of users and their legitimate rights to access specific data
- anti-malware software such as anti-virus and anti-spyware applications used to identify and remove suspicious software on a computer system
- firewalls that sit between the system and external access to protect the system from external threats.

Freedom of Information Act (2000)

The purpose of this act is to provide the public with access to information held by public authorities.

- Public authorities are obliged by the act to publish certain data about what they do.
- Members of the public can request information about the activities of public bodies.

This act covers any recorded information held by public bodies, for example government departments, local authorities, state schools and the police. Journalists often use this act to scrutinise the activities of public authorities.

Communications Act (2003)

The Act is in place to deal with communications that contain credible threats of violence, such as trolling or stalking, or communications that contain material grossly offensive to identified individuals and intended to cause harm.

The Communications Act (2003) has several provisions that have an impact on the use of computer technology. Among the provisions in the Act are that it is illegal to:

- access an internet connection with no intention of paying for the service, making it a crime to piggyback onto other people's WiFi without their permission
- send offensive communications using any communications system, including social media.

Those who repeat the messages are also subject to the provisions of this Act, and re-tweeting an offensive message may be illegal.

Data Protection Act (1998)

The Data Protection Act (1998) sets out the requirements for the control of stored data about an individual, and the rights of the individual to access, check and correct this data.

There are eight provisions in the Data Protection Act:

1. Data should be processed fairly and lawfully (that is the data must not be obtained by deception and the purpose for the data being collected should be revealed to the data subject).
2. Data should only be used for the purpose specified to the data protection agency and should not be disclosed to other parties without the necessary permission.
3. Data should be relevant and not excessive.
4. Data should be accurate and up to date.
5. Data should only be kept for as long as necessary.
6. Individuals have the right to access data kept about them and should be able to check and update the data if necessary.
7. Security must be in place to prevent unauthorised access to the data.
8. Data may not be transferred outside the EU unless the country has adequate data protection legislation.

The data controller in an organisation is responsible for the accuracy and security of data kept about the data subject.

There are some exemptions to the data protection act principles:

- national security: any data processed in relation to national security is exempt from the act
- crime and taxation: any data used to detect or prevent crime or to assist with the collection of taxes is exempt from the act
- domestic purposes: any data used solely for individual, family or household use is exempt from the act.

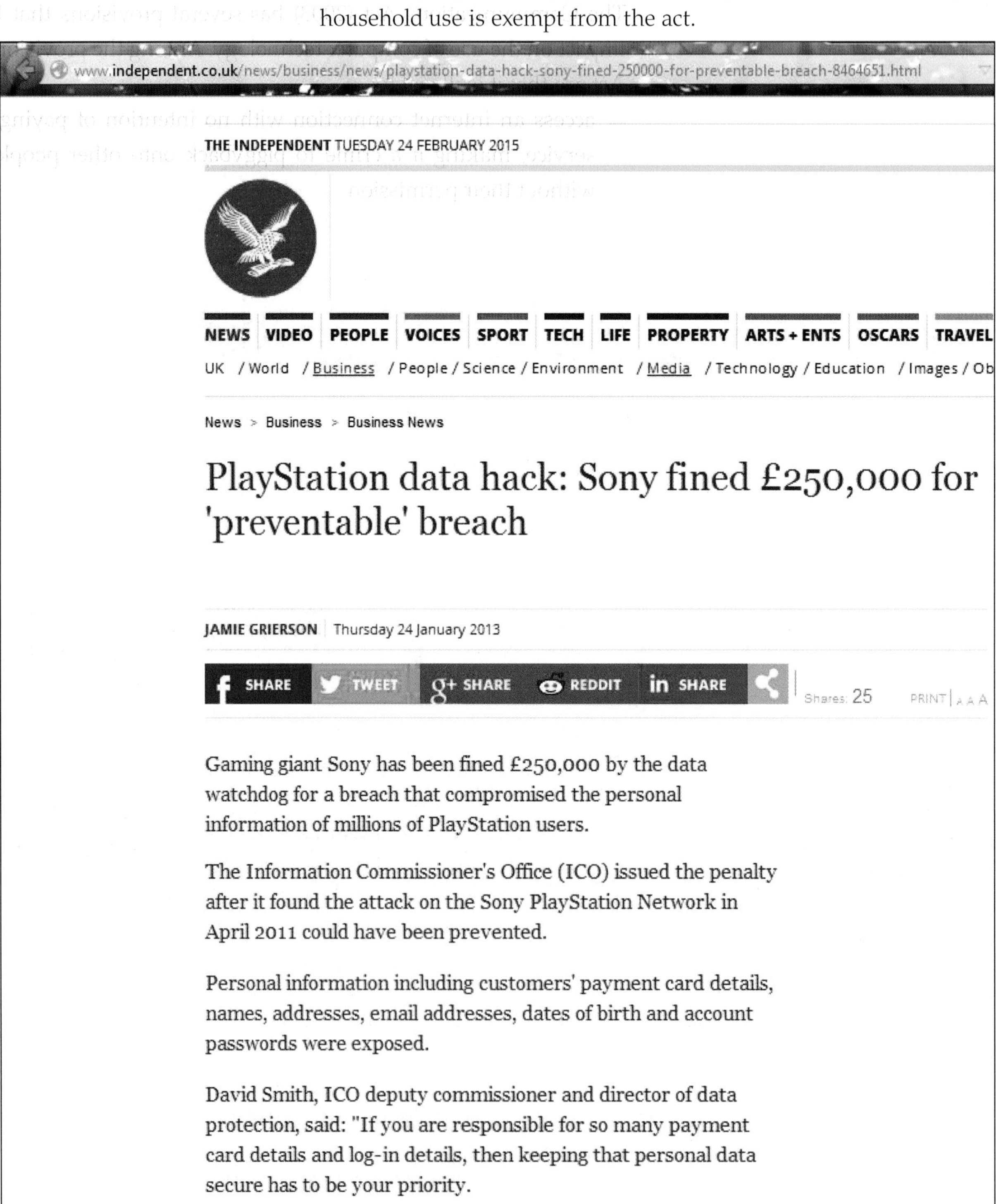

www.independent.co.uk/news/business/news/playstation-data-hack-sony-fined-250000-for-preventable-breach-8464651.html

THE INDEPENDENT TUESDAY 24 FEBRUARY 2015

NEWS VIDEO PEOPLE VOICES SPORT TECH LIFE PROPERTY ARTS + ENTS OSCARS TRAVEL

UK / World / Business / People / Science / Environment / Media / Technology / Education / Images / Ob

News > Business > Business News

PlayStation data hack: Sony fined £250,000 for 'preventable' breach

JAMIE GRIERSON Thursday 24 January 2013

SHARE TWEET SHARE REDDIT SHARE Shares: 25 PRINT | A A A

Gaming giant Sony has been fined £250,000 by the data watchdog for a breach that compromised the personal information of millions of PlayStation users.

The Information Commissioner's Office (ICO) issued the penalty after it found the attack on the Sony PlayStation Network in April 2011 could have been prevented.

Personal information including customers' payment card details, names, addresses, email addresses, dates of birth and account passwords were exposed.

David Smith, ICO deputy commissioner and director of data protection, said: "If you are responsible for so many payment card details and log-in details, then keeping that personal data secure has to be your priority.

In this case that just didn't happen, and when the database was targeted - albeit in a determined criminal attack - the security ...es in place were simply not good enough.

www.independent.co.uk/news/media/

Figure 19.1 *Organisations can be prosecuted under the DPA for breaches of data security*

Copyright, Designs and Patents Act, CPDA (1988)

The CDPA protects the intellectual property of an individual or organisation. Under the Act, it is illegal to copy, modify or distribute software or other intellectual property without the relevant permission. This act also covers video and audio where peer-to-peer streaming has had a significant impact on the income of the copyright owners.

Most commercial software will come with a license agreement specifying how the purchaser may use the product. In most cases a licence key will be required to access the software to prevent unauthorised copying and distribution.

May 26, 2015 11:24 am

Publishers win landmark case against ebook pirates

Henry Mance, Media Correspondent

Share Author alerts Print Clip Comments

British publishers have won their first ever blocking order against pirate ebook sites, as the battle over online copyright spreads beyond music and film.

A ruling by the High Court in London means that internet service providers, such as BT, Virgin Media and Sky, have 10 days to block access to the sites, which are hosted in Russia and the US.

Figure 19.2 *Publishers win copyright case against ebook pirates*

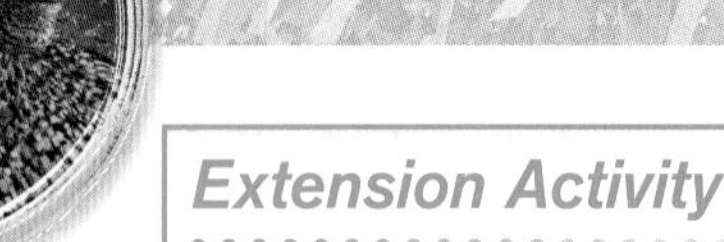

Extension Activity

1. Research news stories related to each of the Acts discussed in this chapter and choose one that you find interesting.
2. Write a brief discussion, looking at both sides of the story.

Creative Commons

Creative Commons (CC) is an organisation that issues licences whereby the holder of the licence can reserve copyright to parts of the work, whilst allowing parts to be copyright free for others to modify as they choose. Under such licences the author may choose to allow complete access for non-commercial use only, allowing redistribution of the work providing the user abides by certain conditions.

This form of licence is often referred to as 'some rights reserved', as opposed to the CPDA's 'all rights reserved'.

Key Points

- The Computer Misuse Act makes unauthorised access to computer material illegal.
- The Freedom of Information Act allows the public to see data related to the activities of public authorities.
- The Communications Act makes it illegal to access WiFi networks without permission and to send offensive communications.
- The Data Protection Act sets out the requirements for the control of stored data about individuals.
- The Copyright, Designs and Patents Act protects the intellectual rights of individuals and organisations.
- The Creative Commons licence allows the author to give up some of the rights to allow others to modify and redistribute their work under certain conditions.

Open-source and proprietary software

Much of the software we buy is written by organisations trying to make a profit. This is called *proprietary software*. The source code is kept securely and versions of the software are distributed as executable programs. The user is not able to access the source code and cannot modify it. Copyright laws also forbid this modification. In return for the money paid, these organisations fully test the product and regularly provide upgrades to fix bugs or improve features of the program. If the product has faults in it, then the user can contact the organisation for an upgrade or fix. These products usually have a significant amount of online support available for them. Microsoft® is perhaps the most well-known producer of proprietary software worldwide.

Software developed under open standards has its source code freely available so that others can access it and make changes to it to develop their own version of the product. Open-source software is often regularly updated by a community of developers. These updated versions are then made available to anyone for little or no cost. Despite being free, this software is often of very high quality because of the community of highly skilled developers who regularly test, fix and improve the product. On the downside, there is no one to blame if it goes wrong. Examples of open-source software include Libre Office, Mozilla Firefox, the Android™ platform, Linux and the Python programming language.

Open-source software	Proprietary software
Access to the source code	No access to source code
May be free of charge	Always some cost involved
Users can modify the software	User cannot modify the software
Can be installed on as many computers as necessary	Extra licences must be obtained before installing it on other computers
No one is responsible for any problems with the software	Full support from the software developer
Usually only community support	Commercial and community support available

Extension Activity

Identify some common proprietary applications and then try to find an open source and/or free alternative to them.

Figure 19.3 *Libre Office is a suite of office programs available for free download*

Ethical and cultural issues

Ethics refer to what is right and wrong. People may argue about individual cases, but on the whole most people agree about most things that constitute ethical behaviour. Ethics are not the same as legalities, although a good legal system will be based on a society's ethical outlook on life.

Ethics are to some extent a personal thing, but there are codes of ethics laid down by various organisations including associations of computing professionals. The BCS (British Computer Society) has some fairly typical ethical standards that it thinks computing professionals should adhere to. They include not undertaking work that is beyond your capability, not bringing your profession into disrepute, avoiding injuring others and not taking bribes.

Generally, most people think that they have a right to a degree of privacy concerning much of their own lives. The internet has changed this right even if many disagree with it. The use of social networking and other sites has made it harder to keep one's details private.

However, it is still generally agreed by most people that privacy should not be deliberately compromised by the widespread publishing of personal details. Journalists have invaded many people's privacy in the search for stories but some would argue that this may sometimes have been in the public interest, for example when exposing criminal or dishonest behaviour. It is probably impossible to maintain as much privacy as one would like and it is unlikely that people will ever agree completely on what is acceptable.

Censorship and the internet

Internet censorship is the deliberate suppression of what can be accessed or published on the internet. Governments or organisations may impose these restrictions for various reasons, including to limit access to:

- socially unacceptable material
- what they regard as dangerous information.

The extent to which the internet is censored varies from country to country, depending upon the political and social situations in those countries. (See Figure 19.4.)

Access to websites is filtered by reference to blacklists that are set up with unacceptable sites and through dynamic examination of the website content for unacceptable content. The main categories being blocked by internet service providers (ISPs) in the UK include extremist politics, extreme pornography and sites that infringe copyright.

Total control of information through censorship is very difficult to apply unless there is a single central censor. Some individuals will still share information through underlying data transfer networks, for example the deep web that cannot be found by the internet.

There is some debate about the use of internet censorship, but most see the need to censor extreme content. The real debate is about where to draw the line between protecting the public and infringing their rights to free speech and access to information.

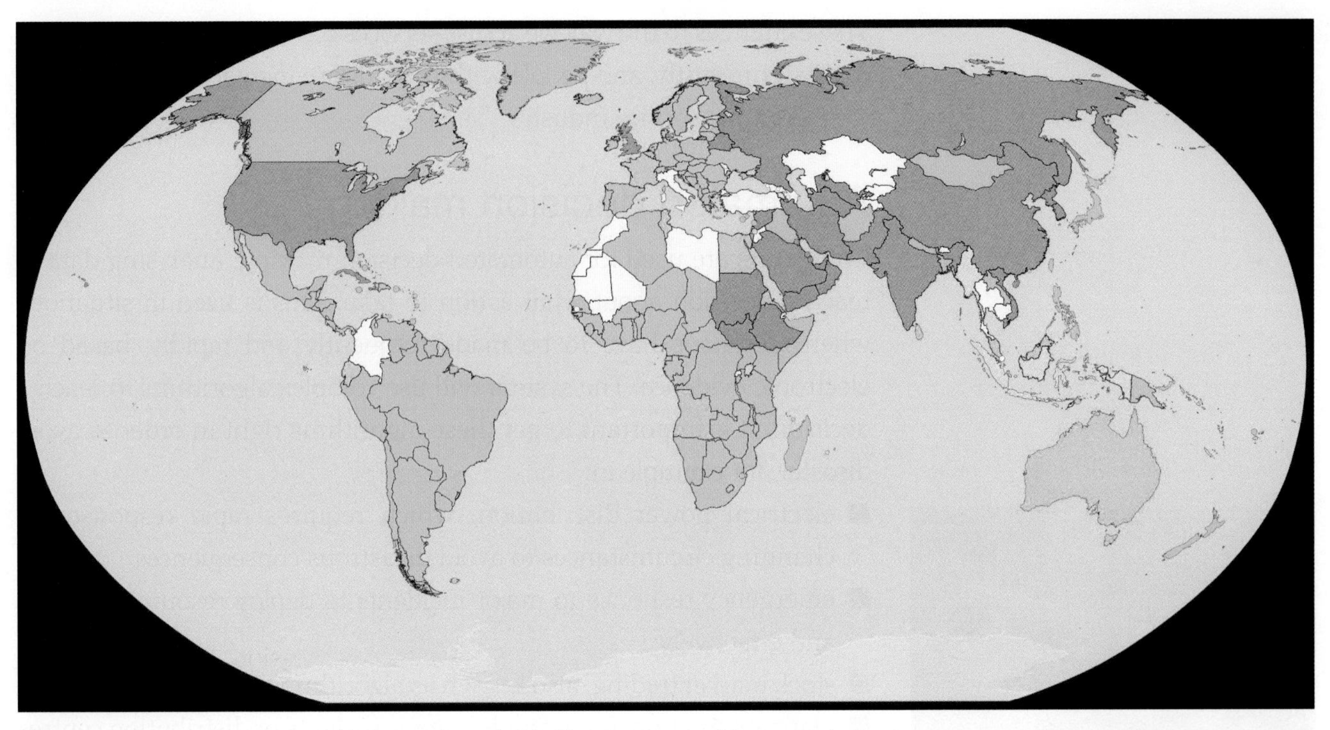

Figure 19.4 *Internet censorship by region: pink indicates censorship, green indicates no censorship and orange represents a changing situation*

Computers in the workforce

Computer technology in various forms is a major part of the workforce. The widespread use of computer technology has changed the skill set required by the modern workforce.

- Instead of requiring a welder to make a car, the manufacture now requires a technician to maintain the robot that welds the car.
- Traditional high street roles, such as shop assistant are now performed by online systems.
- Online banking allows customers to access their accounts 24 hours a day, seven days a week, move money instantly and pay for goods and services electronically without the need for bank branch workers.

Figure 19.5 *Robots building a car*

These changes to the way we access services have altered the job market quite significantly, and people with IT skills are increasingly in demand for the online service industry.

Automated decision making

Computers are used for automated decision making, analysing data to reach a decision about what action to take. This is used in situations where decisions have to be made frequently and rapidly, based on electronic evidence. The system will use complex algorithms to reach a decision. It is important to get these algorithms right in order to avoid disaster, for example in:

- electrical power distribution, which requires rapid responses to changing circumstances to avoid disastrous consequences
- emergency response to major incidents to deploy resources quickly and effectively
- stock market trading, also known as algorithmic or automated trading
- plant automation, for example chemical plants or distribution centres
- airborne collision avoidance systems
- the driverless car
- banks when dealing with credit assessment.

Figure 19.6 *Pilot or computer error?*

Privacy issues

Computer technology used to monitor behaviour

CCTV cameras around our towns and cities are used to monitor behaviour.	While this, to some, represents a big-brother approach to society, many feel the added security and ability to use the captured images to solve crime is worth the intrusion.
Electronic tags on those who have committed a criminal offence.	These tags can identify when the criminal is not in the agreed location at the agreed time or, with GPS, identify their location at any time.
Black boxes in cars, which monitor how and when people drive.	These boxes can reduce insurance premiums by rewarding safe driving.
Mobile phone signals	These can be tracked to provide evidence that can be used by the police and in court.
Workplace logging systems	Used to monitor activity at work such as any online activity, phone calls, work patterns, work quality, social media activity, etc.

Figure 19.7 *Offenders' movements can be monitored through tagging devices attached to their ankles.*

Computing in context

Data mining is an automated process that searches for patterns in large data sets in order to predict events.

- In the fight against crime and terrorism, data about individuals' activities including use of social media, financial transactions, travel, internet histories and shared contact details have provided valuable information.
- In business, data can be used to predict future sales and hence stock requirements, and effective and targeted marketing strategies.
- In medicine, it has been used to analyse DNA sequences. Matching this to medical information has led to the development of effective treatments for various conditions.

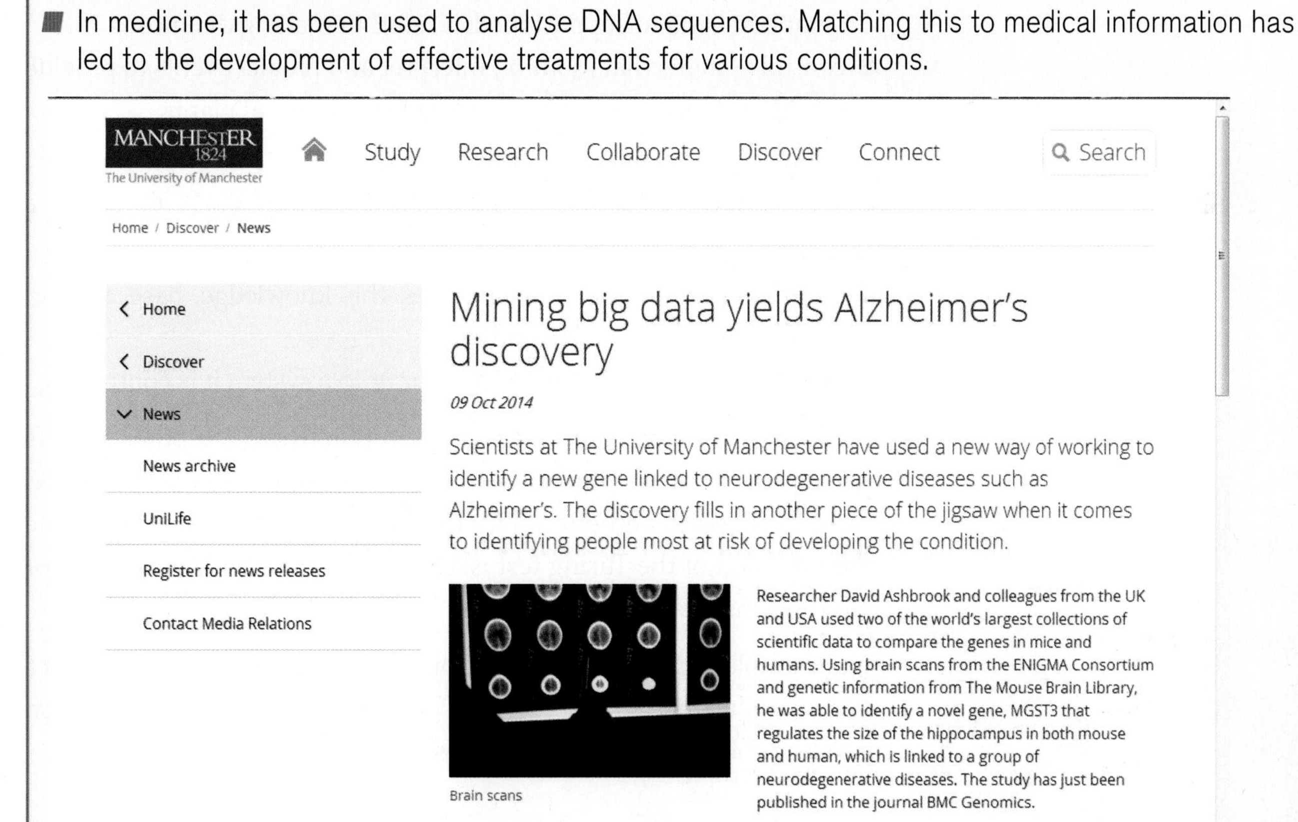

MANCHESTER 1824
The University of Manchester

Study Research Collaborate Discover Connect Search

Home / Discover / News

- Home
- Discover
- News
  - News archive
  - UniLife
  - Register for news releases
  - Contact Media Relations

Mining big data yields Alzheimer's discovery

09 Oct 2014

Scientists at The University of Manchester have used a new way of working to identify a new gene linked to neurodegenerative diseases such as Alzheimer's. The discovery fills in another piece of the jigsaw when it comes to identifying people most at risk of developing the condition.

Brain scans

Researcher David Ashbrook and colleagues from the UK and USA used two of the world's largest collections of scientific data to compare the genes in mice and humans. Using brain scans from the ENIGMA Consortium and genetic information from The Mouse Brain Library, he was able to identify a novel gene, MGST3 that regulates the size of the hippocampus in both mouse and human, which is linked to a group of neurodegenerative diseases. The study has just been published in the journal BMC Genomics.

David, who works in Dr Reinmar Hager's lab at the Faculty of Life Sciences, says: "There is already the 'reserve hypothesis' that a person with a bigger hippocampus will have more of it to lose before the symptoms of Alzheimer's are spotted. By using ENIGMA to look at hippocampus size in humans and the corresponding genes and then matching those with genes in mice from the BXD system held in the Mouse Brain Library database we could identify this specific gene that influences neurological diseases."

There is certainly a case for monitoring what is posted from an organisation's computer systems since unacceptable posts, such as trolling, or racist or sexist comments can be traced back to the organisation and reflect upon them. Is it reasonable for organisations to demand access to and monitor social network pages where the content is posted from private computers?

Computer technology used to analyse personal information

Many organisations collect data about individuals and this is often shared with partner organisations.

- Whenever we check in on social media, the location and time is logged.
- Whenever we take a picture with our phone's camera (and GPS is on), the location and time are logged.

Data is a valuable commodity and there are analysts sifting through our personal information looking for patterns and opportunities.

Artificial intelligence

Examples of artificial intelligence (AI) have been around for some time now. Early examples include chess-playing programs able to analyse millions of possible alternative scenarios in order to make a move.

Many tasks we find straightforward to do require significant processing power. For example, relatively simple things like recognising people and objects require complex algorithms for a computer program to complete.

Expert systems or intelligent knowledge-based systems are examples of artificial intelligence and can perform at a level similar to human experts in certain areas.

There are numerous examples where AI is used on a daily basis including:

- credit card checking that looks for unusual patterns in credit card use to identify potential fraudulent use
- speech recognition systems that identify key words and patterns in the spoken word to interpret the meaning
- medical diagnosis systems used to self-diagnose illness from the symptoms and to support medical staff in making diagnoses
- control systems that monitor, interpret and predict events to provide real-time process control, for example in chemical plants.

All of these systems have a similar structure:

- a knowledge base, which holds the collected expert knowledge, usually as 'IF THEN' rules
- an inference engine that searches the knowledge base to find potential responses to questions
- an interface to connect with the user or to a system it is controlling.

Intelligence is more than pattern recognition; there are other aspects that define what we know as intelligence, including creativity and social intelligence and our ability to interact with other humans. One interpretation of the Turing test is: can a computer fool an interrogator into thinking it is a human being?

One example of this is the chatbot. Sophisticated chatbots are sometimes used as malware to fool people into parting with personal information or to lead them to malicious websites.

Computing in context

The Loebner prize is a prize of $100 000 to be awarded to the first computer whose responses are indistinguishable from those of a human being. This is based on the Turing test for intelligence described by Alan Turing in 1950. There is an annual contest for this prize but, at the time of writing, this prize has not been won by any of the entrants.

Rose Wins Loebner Bronze

Written by Sue Gee

Saturday, 26 September 2015

A chatbot called Rose outperformed three other finalists in the 2015 Lobener Prize contest, but was only awarded the annual prize for being the best conversationalist as Rose was clearly not a human.

The annual Loebner Circus was held at Bletchley Park last weekend and the outcome was unsurprising.

None of the chatbots fooled the judges sufficiently to pass as a real human, which would be rewarded with a silver medal and $25,000. Instead the annual prize of a bronze medal and $4000, awarded for the most human-seeming chatbot in the competition went to Bruce Wlicox who had already won the contest three times, in 2014, 2011 and 2010.

The Loebner Prize competition has lowered its sights over the years. When Hugh Loenber first proposed it in 1990 he offered $100,000 and a Gold medal for the first computer program to pass the Turing Test.

Alan Turing depicted on the Loebner Prize Gold Medal

Figure 19.8 *Rose wins bronze medal in Loebner prize competition*

Environmental effects of computer technology

Computers are made from some pretty toxic material that needs to be handled with great care when disposing of old equipment including airborne dioxins, polychlorinated biphenyls (PCBs), cadmium, chromium, radioactive isotopes and mercury. In many parts of the world computers are considered hazardous waste, but they are often shipped off to countries with lower environmental standards for disposal. In some cases people, often children, pick over the waste to extract metals that can be recycled and sold, thus exposing them to significant danger.

Figure 19.9 *Picking over discarded computer equipment to extract metals*

Most modern computers consume low levels of electricity but are often left running permanently with data centres accounting for around 2 per cent of all energy used on the planet, the same as air travel.

Extension Activity

Discarded computer equipment contains many toxic chemicals. Find out what these chemicals are and each one's toxic effects.

Questions

1. What is the difference between proprietary and open-source software?
2. Karen decides to use open-source software to run her business. What are the implications for Karen in this decision?
3. A distribution warehouse uses computer technology to monitor its workforce. Describe two ways the distribution centre management might monitor the workforce.
4. What issues may result from unwise posts on a social media site?
5. An ambulance service uses automated decision making to decide in which order to respond to calls. Describe the advantages of using a computer program rather than a person to do this.
6. Discuss the problems with and benefits of large-scale data capture for the individual.
7. Discuss the environmental impact of computer use.

20 Non-Examined Assessment – hints and approaches

An important part of the assessment for OCR GCSE Computer Science is the programming project. This part is also called the *Non-Examined Assessment* (*NEA*).

Whereas most of the assessment is carried out by examination, the programming project is designed to give candidates the opportunity to demonstrate their ability to produce practical solutions to problems in a longer time frame.

In this part of the assessment, there will be a choice of programming problems to tackle. Dealing with the problems involves applying computational thinking and programming skills to come up with working solutions.

Most of the scenarios that you will face in the NEA will include some 'messy' problems that do not always have complete and obvious solutions. The point of the assessment is often to sort through a problem and pick out those parts that are suitable for a computer solution and leave out those that are not. There will be opportunities to suggest alternatives and additions to the closed tasks in the questions.

This assessment always involves writing program code. The programs must be written in a high-level language. Various programming languages can be used for this work. Usually it is the choice of the candidate or the teacher.

The programming code forms part of a report. The structure of the report is not laid down by the exam board. Making it communicate what you know and can do is part of the assessment.

Remember, templates are not allowed, you must structure the report yourself.

Notes

- You should have plenty of programming experience before embarking on the NEA.
- Ideally, throughout your work so far, you will have had plenty of experience writing program code in at least one high-level language in order to back up the theoretical work that you have covered.
- To get the best results in the NEA, you will need to show a wide variety of programming skills. It is not a good idea to leave it until this point to gain basic experience.
- You should also have had experience in writing programs that are, at least to some extent, modular. Make sure that you have written at least some functions or procedures.
- Look on your NEA as an opportunity to 'show off', not as a burden to be dealt with as quickly and briefly as possible.

It will not always be the case that the problems can be totally solved by computer programs. Your report should ideally show awareness of this.

In general, your work for the NEA should show that you can:

- analyse problems in computational terms
- design programmed solutions to problems; this involves producing the necessary algorithms, then writing program code to implement them
- debug program code.

Look for opportunities to show that you can think creatively and come up with new ideas.

The scenarios for the NEA will be varied but there will be a general approach that applies to them all.

In each exam session there will be a choice of three scenarios from which you choose one.

General form of the NEAs

There will be a progression through the tasks that starts with a clearly defined, closed problem requiring a fairly simple piece of coding.

This will normally be followed by more complex tasks based on the same scenario that require more ambitious programs to be written.

The assessment will also require some creative development to incorporate new ideas.

Example

Here is an example scenario, together with comments on each task.

An online vendor wants to organise an automated system to take and fulfil orders.

The vendor will need to store details of customers and goods and have a means of allowing the customers to order goods. Any system of this sort will also require various reports to the vendor management.

1. Design, write and test a program that takes personal details from a prospective customer such as first name, last name, telephone number, street address, postcode and email address.
   - The program should only accept valid data and should store it in a suitable data structure.
   - This is a straightforward task that could make use of various built-in data structures available in most high-level languages, for example the Python programming language has dictionaries that might come in handy later on to make searches easier.
   - This question insists on some validation.
   - There is no requirement at this stage to store data permanently.
2. Design, write and test a program to store the details input by a customer in a file saved on secondary storage.
   - This section requires file handling, but not much more. To test it, you will need to retrieve the data that is stored. The easiest way to do this is to use a text editor although you could, if you wanted, write extra code to retrieve the data from file. This is not really necessary because there are further opportunities for reading back data in later stages.
3. Design, write and test a program that accepts order details from a customer, such as stock number, name of item, cost and quantity for each of ten items then stores them to a file.
   - This is similar to question 2 but you might need to think of ways to make this data set link to the customer data. This might influence what you choose to do in question 5. You might also be making decisions about choice of programming language. Some of the solutions might be more easily produced using SQL, which can be accessed from your other programming language.
4. Extend the program in question 3 to produce a list of all the order details for each customer.
   - This is where the planning mentioned in question 3 might pay off and make life easier. There is no one way to do this. A lot will depend on the capabilities of the programming language(s) you choose.
5. Add an extra feature for the online vendor that might encourage greater sales to their customers.
   - This is where your creativity can come in. The extra feature might be fairly simple. A lot will depend on your programming skills and the time that you have available. A simple addition could be to incorporate automatic discounts for loyal customers. Ways of determining this could be considered. Totals could be produced of money spent or number of items ordered.
   - Another more complex and ambitious possibility would be to suggest similar products to customers. This would involve producing another file that has other products stored.

Skills needed

The NEA is designed to allow you to 'show off' your technical skills. Throughout, you should look for opportunities to demonstrate not only programming skills but also the other associated skills such as analysis, design, communication of the solution and testing and evaluation.

You should be looking for chances to show that you have thought beyond the bare essentials of the tasks. It will probably be necessary to look things up in order to get ideas and see how similar problems have been solved by others.

Being original

Credit is given for coming up with original and creative solutions but this does not mean reinventing the wheel. You will probably need to use or adapt well-known algorithms. No one would expect you to produce a brand new algorithm to do some common operation such as sorting a list, although you can if you want to!

What is important is that any material that you 'borrow' or adapt is fully acknowledged. You must provide references for ideas and material. If they have come from a website, you need to give the URL of that website and also the date when you last accessed it.

The NEA requires the demonstration of certain broad areas of skills. These are assessed under the following headings:

- Programming techniques
- Analysis
- Design
- Development
- Testing, evaluation and conclusions

These skills can be demonstrated at any point in the submitted work. It is not necessary to separate the work into sections named according to this list although you might find it easier to do so.

Bear in mind that organising your work in a logical manner is useful in helping you to think the whole problem through and also to whoever is marking your work. In fact, organising your approach to the tasks and how your work is submitted is another criteria on which your work will be assessed.

Programming techniques

The specification itemises certain skills that you need to show in your programming techniques. There are also certain programmatic elements that you should normally include.

It is not always essential that the work should include all of these features if they are not naturally needed by the work, but most of them should be there in order to get the higher marks.

Extension Activity

Suppose you are asked to write a program that inputs a text file and creates a dictionary from it. The dictionary could be used to decide if a lossless compression function would be efficient. The program records each word and the number of times each word occurs.

1 Look at the list of techniques and programming elements itemised in this chapter.
2 Make a table of which techniques you would need and for what aspects of the program.

You also need to realise that if other techniques are useful, then there is no reason not to use them even if they are not on the list, for example sometimes a program can be made more elegant if functions are used. There is no mention of functions in this list, but the use of suitable techniques above and beyond those mentioned here is recommended in order to demonstrate higher skills. Indeed, without using functions or procedures, it is hard to demonstrate a modular approach.

The official list of techniques and programming elements is:

(a) variables, operators, inputs, outputs and assignments
(b) the three basic programming constructs used to control the flow of a program: sequence, conditionals and iteration
(c) suitable loop structures
(d) a range of different data types including Boolean, string, integer and real
(e) basic string manipulation
(f) basic file-handling operations: open, read, write and close
(g) arrays or equivalent, as appropriate.

Choice of programming language

The exam board does not tell you exactly which programming language to use, but it does say:

The non-exam assessment should be done using a suitable high-level language such as:

- Python
- C family of languages (for example, C#, C++, and so on)
- Java
- JavaScript
- Visual Basic/.Net
- PHP
- Delphi
- SQL
- BASH

Your choice will depend on:

- what you are used to or feel confident about
- the computer platform(s) available to you
- what your teacher recommends
- your ambitions (for example, you may want to develop skills in web-oriented languages such as JavaScript, SQL or PHP).

Block-based 'languages' are generally not suitable.

Efficient programming techniques

It is not enough simply to make a program that 'works'. A good program is written economically with no excess baggage. Often this is best achieved by being careful with dividing the work into modules.

You should look at your work after you have written some code and ask yourself 'is there a more economical way of doing this?'

```
INPUT MenuChoice
IF MenuChoice = 1 THEN
  Option1
  ELSE
  IF MenuChoice = 2 THEN
    Option2
    ELSE
    IF MenuChoice = 3 THEN
      Option3
      ELSE
      IF MenuChoice = 4 THEN
        Option4
        ELSE
        Option5
      ENDIF
    ENDIF
  ENDIF
ENDIF
```

While this works, a more efficient approach, if the feature is available, might be the use of CASE – ENDCASE.

```
INPUT MenuChoice
CASE MenuChoice OF
  WHEN 1: DO Option1
  WHEN 2: DO Option2
  WHEN 3: DO Option3
  WHEN 4: DO Option4
  OTHERWISE DO Option5
ENDCASE
```

The efficiency of the final coding will be improved by careful design and through developing efficient and effective algorithms to describe the solutions.

Analysis

Analysis is about looking at the problem as a whole and breaking it down into its component parts. It is where you can show that you understand the computational thinking skill of decomposition.

It should be clear what the component parts are, for example a program for ordering items from a website would probably break down the process into stages such as these:

- Get the customer details.
- Store the customer details.
- Get the items required.
- Search for items required.
- Store the items required.
- Calculate the bill total.
- Arrange payment.
- Send acknowledgement to customer.

Each of these steps should be justified. To get the highest marks in any part of the NEA the report should contain as much detail as possible with explanations for any decisions made.

The analysis of a problem should end with a program specification that clearly sets out what the program must achieve.

This specification should be used later in the final testing and evaluation as a means of judging the success of the product.

Design

The design section is very important. You do not normally start coding a solution until you know where you are going with it. The sections of the program need to be clearly identified. Most programs are, or should be, modular, that is designed and written in clearly demarcated sections.

For each section there should be an algorithm.

Algorithms

Algorithms are important not only to help you plan your work but also to demonstrate to whoever is marking the work that you have thought it through and understand the steps needed to solve the problem.

Algorithms can be expressed in various ways, most often either by using pseudocode (see page 105) or flowcharts (see page 106). You can also sometimes express them adequately in a simple series of concise statements.

It is important to realise that just providing program code is not the same as providing an algorithm. The algorithm leads to the program code and should be produced before it.

Work that lacks good algorithms will not get the higher marks.

Testing can be planned in the design stage, although plenty of testing will happen that is not pre-planned.

Ideally, the design work should be in sufficient detail so that if it were handed to a competent programmer, the same solution, more or less, would be produced.

Robustness

Programs should not 'fall over' too easily. In use, people are likely to enter bad data or otherwise misuse the program. If they do, this should not cause the program to crash.

The design of the program should anticipate at least some possible 'exceptions' and guard against them with at least basic validation tests.

To trap every possible error is not realistic when you have limited time to produce your work, but you should at least make some efforts in that direction.

Development

Development is where the student presents the work to the reader.

The work that you do has to be reported to the reader; in this case, the reader will be the teacher (and the moderator). It is your responsibility to communicate what you did. It is definitely NOT the responsibility of the reader to go hunting for things that should be clearly presented. Clarity is essential.

A good approach to the development section is to look on it as telling the story of how the work was done and how it developed.

At some stage, all the program code you write must be included in the report. A good way to do this is to present it section by section along with any commentary about it or output from it.

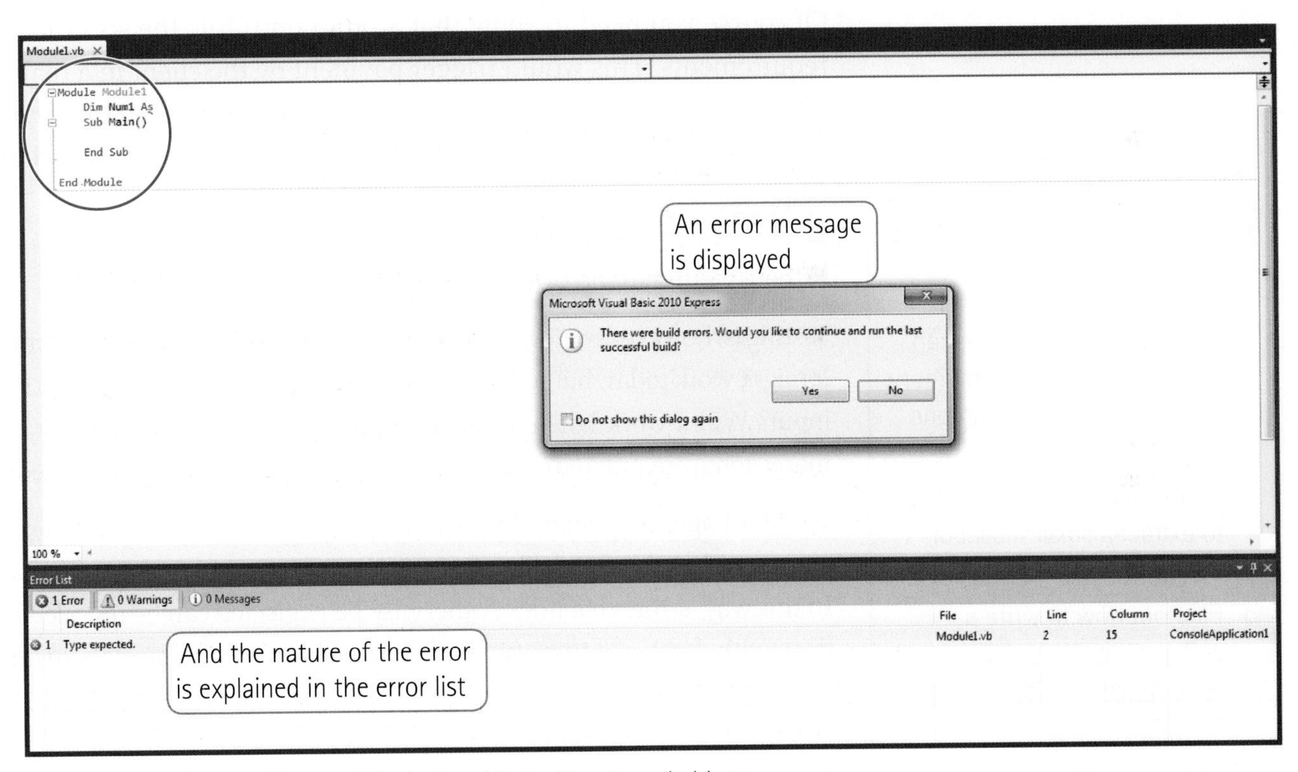

Figure 20.1 *The variable num1 is declared but without a suitable type*

A good development section will include details of the variables used as well as a description of each module.

Program code should always include its own embedded comments.

Some testing will be part of the development process. It is natural to try sections of code as you go and, if necessary, make adjustments. Some of this trial and error approach should be included in the development narrative, illustrated with screenshots.

```
y = 100
x = 10
REPEAT
x = x - 1
t = y/x
OUTPUT t
UNTIL x = 0
```

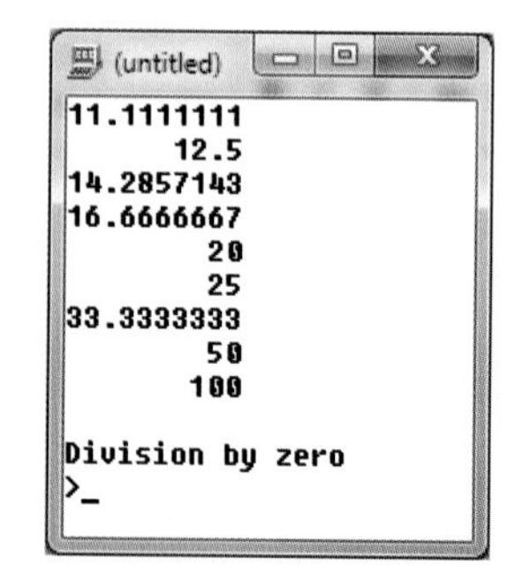

Testing, evaluation and conclusions

Testing and demonstrating

There is a difference between testing and demonstrating that a program does what is intended.

Of course you need to show that a program fulfils the specification requirements. This would trigger payment by the client in a real-life situation. Some testing is necessary to demonstrate this. In fact, this testing at the end should be planned in the design stages and also could usefully be subdivided into sections such as:

- alpha testing (done by the developers)
- beta testing (done by selected users).

Testing is, however, more than just a demonstration that a program 'works'. It might work today, but will it work next week, when lots of data has been input? Will it work when a careless user inputs 'B' when asked for how many items are ordered? Will errors cause data to be lost or corrupted?

To guard against potential problems, programs need to be tested quite aggressively, with the deliberate intention of trying to make them crash. In this way, errors that might otherwise be neglected can be revealed and dealt with. Look at it this way, a successful test is one that reveals an error.

Iterative testing

This is the testing that you do as you go along. All the while you will be testing chunks of code and making changes if necessary. Iterative means repeating, so you will often be going back to earlier code to make changes in the light of things that you discover further along in the process.

Final testing

This is where you test the finished product(s) against the program specifications.

You need to produce a set of test data that tests the reaction of the program to normal and abnormal circumstances.

Extension Activity 

1. Find out how your chosen programming language can store lists of items in memory. Does it offer more than one way?
2. Write some simple SQL code to extract a small subset of data from a stored list of items.
3. Find out how to write a self-contained module in your chosen programming language.
4. Find out whether your programming language is able to generate an executable file. What are the benefits and drawbacks of having this facility?
5. Suppose you have written a program for question 3 in the example on page 201. Devise a set of test data that could uncover some possible errors in the code.

Example

Suppose the program must accept the price and the item code of ordered goods. All items in stock are between £1 and £100 and have to be entered as whole numbers. They have item codes in the format of a letter followed by five numerals such as A45344.

You should test that the program accepts valid data but rejects inputs such as A or 5%, or amounts that are out of range, preferably without crashing.

You can set out test data in a table such as this one:

Test	Data	Reason	Expected result
Item code	B67566	Normal format	Accepted
Item code	AB65877	Incorrect format (too many letters)	Rejected
Price	50	Normal data in range	Accepted
Price	5000	Normal data out of range	Rejected
Price	46 pounds	Abnormal data: not numeric	Rejected

Task

Describe the purpose of a simple program that you have written and devise a simple table of test data.

Evaluation

You should make a summary of how well the program or group of programs fulfils its original intentions. This should clearly refer back to the requirements specification or success criteria. If there are shortcomings, it is best to point these out, even if time does not permit reworking the code. Suggestions for an imagined 'next version' can be included, but they should be sensible and realistic.

It is useful to get someone else to try out your programs. Your evaluation could include some feedback from them.

Make sure that throughout your report, you use proper computing technical terms. The correct use of these is taken into account in the assessment process.

The evaluation is focused on the software product(s) you have produced, not on your learning processes. There is no need to say how much you did or did not enjoy doing the work or how difficult you found it.

Glossary

Accumulator (ACC) Stores the results of any arithmetic or logical operations carried out by the ALU.

Adware Software that automatically displays advertising when a user is online.

Algorithm A series of steps designed to solve a mathematical or other problem.

Arithmetic and logic unit (ALU) Performs all the arithmetic and logical operations within the CPU.

Analogue Continuously changing values.

AND A logic gate that outputs 1 if both inputs are 1.

Application Software designed to carry out a useful real-world task.

ASCII (American Standard Code for Information Interchange) A 7-bit code to represent a set of characters available to a computer.

Assembler Software that translates an assembly language program into machine code.

Assignment Setting the value of a variable or constant.

Binary A number system based on 2, using just two symbols: 0 and 1.

Bit Binary digit 0 or 1; symbol *b*.

Bit depth The number of bits used to store each sound sample.

Bit rate The number of bits used to store a second of sampled sound.

Boolean algebra A method for expressing mathematically a logic circuit.

Bus A part of the computer architecture that transfers data and signals between the components of the computer.

Byte eight bits; symbol *B*.

Cache memory Special high-speed memory used by a computer.

Central processing unit (CPU) Contains the control unit, ALU and cache memory.

Channel A communication link carried on any suitable medium such as a wire conductor, fibre-optic cable or wireless signal; for example a bit-stream can be sent between devices on a WLAN along a channel formed by a particular sub-frequency in a WiFi frequency band.

Character set The complete set of characters available to a computer.

Clock chip The electronic device in a computer that controls the timing of signals.

Colour depth (bit depth) The number of bits used for each pixel.

Command line The place where commands can be given to the operating system.

Compression Reduction in file size to lessen download times and storage requirements.

Computational thinking Applying the methods of computer scientists to problem solving.

Computer architecture The internal, logical structure and organisation of the computer hardware.

Constant A label referring to a location in memory containing a value that can be accessed but not changed by a program.

Control unit Works with the CPU to control the flow of data within the system and to decode instructions.

Current instruction register (CIR) Stores the next instruction ready to be decoded.

De-encapsulation Removing the data from inside an encapsulated item.

Declaration Identifying a variable, constant or array to a program so that memory can be allocated for it.

Defragmenter Software that brings together fragments of files on a disk and collects all the free space in one area.

Denary A number system based on 10, using ten digits: 0–9.

Dual-core / Quad-core processor A CPU with multiple processors: a dual-core has two; a quad-core has four.

Embedded system A computer system that forms part of an electronic device.

Encapsulation Enclosing the data inside another data structure to form a single component.

Ethernet A set of standards used to connect devices in a LAN. Nowadays, it tends to use mainly UTP and fibre-optic links or WiFi standards. Ethernet networks split messages into units called *frames*. Ethernet is still very widely used and provides reliable and high-speed links.

Fetch–decode–execute cycle The process of fetching the instructions from memory, decoding them and then executing them that the CPU performs continuously.

File Stored data saved on a suitable medium.

Firewall Software that limits access to and from a computer system.

Firmware Software that is stored permanently in a device.

Hexadecimal A number system based on 16 that uses the symbols 0–9 and A–F (to represent the denary values 10–15).

Instruction set The complete set of instructions that a processor can handle.

Instructions A set of commands that a processor can recognise and act upon.

Interoperable The ability of different systems and software applications to communicate and exchange data, and to use the information that has been exchanged.

Iteration (repetition) Where a group of instructions is executed repeatedly until a condition is met, or while a condition is true (a loop).

Keylogger A program that records every keystroke of the computer user; often used to gain confidential information in order to commit fraud.

Kilobyte 1024 bytes.

Layering Rules organised into a distinct order in which they need to be applied.

Logic circuit A circuit made by combining a sequence of logic gates.

Logic error When the logical structure of a program produces unexpected results.

Logic gate A circuit that produces an output based on the inputs.

Memory address register (MAR) Stores the location for data to be fetched from or sent to memory.

Memory data register (MDR) Stores data that has been fetched from or is waiting to be sent to memory.

Metadata Data about data. In the case of an image, information about the image data that allows the computer to recreate the image from the binary data in the file.

Non-volatile memory Retains data even when the power is turned off.

NOT A logic gate that outputs the opposite value to the input.

Object code The machine code produced by a compiler.

Opcode The part of the instruction that tells the CPU what operation is to be done.

Operand The part of the instruction that tells the CPU what to apply the operation to.

OR A logic gate that outputs 1 if either, or both, of the two inputs is 1.

Overflow When a number becomes too large to store in the number of bits allocated, it is said to 'overflow' and some bits are 'lost', leaving an incorrect value.

Pixel A pixel is the smallest element of an image. Pixels are the dots that make the image on the screen.

Platform A combination of hardware and operating system that supports the running of particular applications.

Program A self-contained set of instructions that can be stored and used by the processor.

Program counter (PC) Stores the location of the next instruction in a program to be executed.

Programming language A means of writing programs in a form that can be passed to a computer to process.

Protocol Set of rules and standards governing how networks should function and communicate.

Random access memory (RAM) The main memory of a computer that stores data, applications and the operating system while in use. When the power is turned off, RAM loses its data.

Resolution The number of pixels or dots per unit, for example ppi (pixels per inch) or dpi (dots per inch).

Sample rate The number of times sound is sampled per second, measured in kHz.

Scheduling The process of arranging, controlling and optimising work and workloads.

Selection A condition to decide the path through the program and which set of instructions to execute next.

Sequence When a list of instructions is carried out in order, one after the other.

Software The general term for computer programs.

Source code The program written by the end user in a high-level language before it is converted to machine code.

Spyware Malicious software that detects what the user is doing and sends details back to the originator of the spyware.

Syntax error When the rules of a language are broken by a program.

TCP/IP (Transfer Control Protocol/Internet Protocol) A set of protocols that governs the transfer of data over a network.

Translation The conversion of human-friendly program writing back to pure machine code.

Translator A program that converts high-level or assembly-level commands into machine code.

Trojan horse Harmful software disguised as something useful.

Truth table A method for recording all possible input combinations and determining the output for each.

Typecast Casting a variable using str, int or float.

Unicode A character set that uses code pages to provide a range of language symbols. There are several billion possible character codes available to Unicode.

Utility A small program designed to carry out a limited maintenance task.

UTP (unshielded twisted pair) A common connecting cable made from copper wiring; two wires are twisted around each other to minimise induction and cross-talk between the cables.

Variable A label that refers to a location in memory containing a value that can be accessed or changed by a program.

Virtual machine An emulation or simulation of a particular computer system or platform that allows programs intended to run on one computer system to run on a different one.

Virtual memory A section of the hard disc used as if it were RAM to supplement the amount of main memory available to the computer.

Virus A piece of code capable of copying itself, which may damage a system by corrupting it or destroying data.

Volatile memory Loses data when there is no power.

WiFi A common standard for wireless connectivity based on a standard known as IEEE 802.11. This is a good example of how widely accepted standards have led to practical solutions for connecting devices.

Worm Self-replicating, malicious software that can spread through a system or network.

Index

Acknowledgements

Photo credits

p.v © Bettmann/Corbis; **p.vi** © Alfred Eisenstaedt/Time Life Pictures/Getty Images; **p.1** © Rick Friedman/Corbis, **p.2** © Photograph provided courtesy of Carnegie Mellon University; **p.4** *top* © Heritage Image Partnership Ltd/Alamy Stock Photo; *middle* ©UPP / TopFoto; *bottom* © Andreas Rentz/Getty Images News; **p.6** © Science & Society Picture Library/SSPL/Getty images; **p.7** © LOS ALAMOS NATIONAL LABORATORY/SCIENCE PHOTO LIBRARY; **p.13** © PNWL/Alamy Stock Photo; **p.14** *top left* © Sergey Jarochkin/123RF; *bottom left* © Leslie Wilk/Alamy Stock Photo; *right* © Dmitrii Bachtub/Alamy Stock Photo; **p.16** *top right* © RGB Ventures/SuperStock/Alamy Stock Photo; *bottom left* © Science & Society Picture Library/SSPL/Getty images; **p.17** © Nancy Nehring/Getty images; **p.18** © Oatfeelgood/istock/thinkstock; **p.23** *top* © Science & Society Picture Library/SSPL/Getty images; *bottom right* © Andrew Lloyd/Alamy Stock Photo; *bottom left* © mingis/istock/thinkstock; **p.24** © Gianni Furlan/Hemera/thinkstock; **p.25** © Vladimir Caplinskis/123RF; **p.26** © PC Gamer Magazine/Future/gettyimages; **p.32** *top* © Editorial Image, LLC/Alamy; *bottom* © inga spence/Alamy; **p.36** © Gewoldi/istock/thinkstock; **p.50** *left* © Opka/iStockphoto/Thinkstock; *right* ©scanrail/iStockphoto/Thinkstock; **p.70** © Hodder & Stoughton Ltd; **p.71** © vasabii/Thinkstock/iStockphoto/Getty Images; **p.78** © SSPL/Hulton Archive/gettyimages; **p.84** *top* © Rob Bartee/Alamy; *bottom* © B Christopher/Alamy Stock Photo; **p.85** © Prisma Bildagentur AG/Alamy Stock Photo; **p.87** © bagiuiani/Thinkstock/iStockphoto/Getty Images; **p.88** *top* © MrIncredible/Thinkstock/iStockphoto/Getty Images; *bottom* © Xfce Development Team; **p.102** *both* © TfL from the London Transport Museum Collection; **p.158** © Vasiliy Vasilyev, HHD Software Ltd; **p.159** *all* © George Rouse; **p.165** *both* © George Rouse; **p.175** © Bettmann/Corbis; **p.182** © AndreyPopov/iStockphoto/Thinkstock/Getty Images; **p.188** © The Independent; **p.189** © The Financial Times Limited 2016. All Rights Reserved; **p.191** © Daniel Armando Rodriguez/Document Foundation; **p.193** *top* © Jeffrey Ogden; *bottom* © Bloomberg/gettyimages; **p.194** *top* © AKSARAN/Getty Images; *bottom* © stocksolutions/Fotolia; **p.195** © The University of Manchester; **p.197** © Sue Gee www.i-programmer.info/Hugh Lobener; **p.198** © Peter Essick/Aurora Photos/Corbis

© Microsoft product screenshots reprinted with permission from Microsoft Corporation.

Linux® is the registered trademark of Linus Torvalds in the U.S. and other countries.

Blu-ray Disc™ is a trademark owned by Blu-ray Disc Association (BDA).

Microsoft and Windows are either registered trademarks or trademarks of Microsoft Corporation in the United States and/or other countries.

UNIX is a registered trademark of The Open Group.

Mac and OS X are trademarks of Apple Inc., registered in the U.S. and other countries.

Python is a trademark or registered trademark of the Python Software Foundation, used by Hodder & Stoughton with permission from the Foundation.

Every effort has been made to trace all copyright holders, but if any have been inadvertently overlooked the Publishers will be pleased to make the necessary arrangements at the first opportunity.